Why Social Media is Ruining Your Life

Why Social Media is Ruining Your Life

Katherine Ormerod

ʿC

To Beth, Lauren, Ashley, Chloe and Nikki for inspiring this book

An Hachette UK Company
www.hachette.co.uk

First published in Great Britain in 2018 by Cassell,
an imprint of Octopus Publishing Group Ltd, Carmelite House,
50 Victoria Embankment, London EC4Y 0DZ
www.octopusbooks.co.uk
www.octopusbooksusa.com

Text copyright © Katherine Ormerod 2018
Design and layout copyright © Octopus Publishing Group 2018

Distributed in the US by Hachette Book Group,
1290 Avenue of the Americas, 4th and 5th Floors, New York, NY 10104

Distributed in Canada by Canadian Manda Group,
664 Annette St, Toronto, Ontario, Canada M6S 2C8

ISBN 978-1-78840-062-6

A CIP catalogue record for this book is available from the
British Library.

Printed and bound by CPI Group (UK) Ltd, Croydon, CR0 4YY

10 9 8 7 6 5 4 3 2

Senior Commissioning Editor: Romilly Morgan
Creative Director: Jonathan Christie
Senior Editor: Leanne Bryan
Senior Production Manager: Peter Hunt

Contents

Introduction

You shall not covet your neighbour's house. You shall not covet your neighbour's wife, or his male or female servant, his ox or donkey, or anything that belongs to your neighbour.

— EXODUS 20:17

Do you ever obsess about your body? Lament your belly size and lack of thigh – or even leg – gap? Do you sometimes lie awake at night, spinning about the state of your career? Is it perhaps a feeling that everyone else seems to go on endless holidays and live in perfect houses that you could never afford, filled with perfect décor and perfect, perfect children? Doesn't it just seem like everyone is living a life that's better than yours? Have you ever felt something like that? Because I definitely have, and the truth is that there's a major cause of this *holistic* life dissatisfaction.

Mention social media to any group of women – mums on the school run, girls in the common room or professionals at after-work drinks – and you'll hear the same thing: "I wish I could stop scrolling." Since its early infancy in the 1990s, social media has become part of the furniture, spanning all generations and all walks of life. It's estimated that *2.77 billion* of us will be using social media by the end of 2019. As with radio and TV before, we've welcomed these platforms into our homes, our workplaces and public spaces, ushering in a new era of community and social structures without much thought. As new social media applications have boomed hand in hand with the mobile phone explosion – 95 per cent of Americans own a phone and 77 per cent carry a smartphone – we have seen a complete and utter revolution in the way we consume news, products and, most importantly, each other. We did not wait or even pause momentarily to survey the fallout from such a significant shift; there's been no clear post-mortem on the long-term impacts of social media exposure from either the medical or academic professions. It's all too recent, too fresh and too pervasive. Yet, we're already at a point where unplugging from the system seems unthinkable for most. One thing's for sure: what has been done cannot be undone – the proverbial milk has been spilt and social media is now part of the fabric of modern life.

Offering opportunity, discovery and the chance to forge new relationships in one hand, and self-criticism, alienation and potential mental-health crises in the other, social media is a double-edged sword which cuts deeply both ways. And, while there's been plenty of cultural anxiety around the use of social media, research has been too mixed and limited to convincingly persuade the majority of us to actually alter our patterns of behaviour.

Humans have always struggled with too much technological change in too short a time, and we're currently stuck between a rock of headlines screaming loudly to predict digital doomsday and a hard place of inconclusive research which divides expert opinion. After all, there are countless studies which have established that social media has changed our lives as much for the better as for the worse.

It's worth remembering that, before social media, it was the internet that was considered the scourge of modern life. This new technology was supposed to herald the end of life as we knew it, causing isolation, alienation and the withdrawal of the next generation from the community and themselves. While it has certainly made an indelible impact, the internet has not, thus far, marked the death knell for the human race. Over time, government legislation has started to curb some of its worst (though by no means all) excesses, and school protocols and internet safety awareness have gone some way to protect the youngest from the world wide web's deepest cesspools. Simply put, we have come to understand that the internet offers both good and bad. Before the internet came along, it was television that was rotting children's brains, while computer games were desensitizing them to violence... No matter what the technology, change always comes with fear, and advancement with pitfalls. There is no such thing as perfect technology because it is *us*, fallible humans, who use it. But we mustn't forget that we're also the ones at the controls.

Like most forms of media or technology, it's easy to argue that the new social media platforms are more a mirror to a complex human psyche than fundamentally destructive. However, the idea that the new technology is entirely neutral is slowly being undermined, often by whistle-blowers from within the now multi-billion-dollar social media companies. Tech insiders have revealed the way programmers have exploited our brain's natural reward system to hook us to our feeds – what some call "brain hacking". And our compulsive need to stay engaged has so penetrated our lives that billions of us around the world are suffering from "nomophobia" – a dread of being separated from our phones and accounts, even for a few hours. Consequently, our lives have changed entirely, with far-reaching implications in how we build relationships, value ourselves and map out our life expectations. Whether the new technology has been engineered to manipulate human psychology or not, the ways in which we use it deserve more scrutiny.

It's a Woman's World

Tellingly, many of the adverse effects of social media use appear to be inherently gendered. Women make up the majority of audiences across all the visual platforms, notably Instagram and Pinterest, as well as Facebook and Twitter. They also post the most selfies, share more personal issues, log on more frequently and spend more time on social media overall. In the US, women use social media more than men – by a gap of 73 to 65 per cent. As Dr James A Roberts, a professor of marketing and an expert on consumer and technology behaviours, explains: "Women form deeper attachments to their devices than men. They score higher on the behavioural addiction scale, and we've found that's down to the reasons that women use smartphones – unlike men who are still in the main using their phones for traditional purposes like communication, information and entertainment – women often focus their use of technology on maintaining social relationships through social media".

If we can be certain of anything, it's that we haven't properly come to terms with the new world order. Many of us are grappling with the more challenging impacts of social media without any real idea of how to navigate the new waters. Instead, we're coping alone, consuming social media content from the moment we wake to the instant before we sleep and allowing the worst sides of it to slowly eat away at our self-esteem, sense of identity and happiness.

While privately and among friends, we women may discuss how social media makes us feel, or has changed our perspectives and the way we interact with each other, on a cultural level we're not openly acknowledging a fistful of issues. We don't want to sound like Luddites. We don't want to admit that looking at pictures of other people makes us feel bad about ourselves. We don't really want anyone else to know how much time we spend scrolling through our feeds. And, of course, underlying this is the desire to avoid anything which might, just might, mean we have to stop scrolling.

The Social Media Rap Sheet

So what proof do we have of the downsides of our collective social media habit? The facts are crystal clear: there's a barrage of cold and hard research pointing to correlations between social media use and mental health issues spanning anxiety and depression, which will be explored in depth throughout this book. A study in 2016 found that spending just one hour a day on social networks reduces the probability of a teenager being happy by around 14 per cent and that girls are more adversely affected than boys. At its worst, the UK charity NSPCC has gone so far as to blame social media for the dramatic increase in the number of children admitted to hospital for self-harm. There is no wriggle room here – social media is clearly linked to an increase in mental health problems and is depleting our children's happiness at a deeply worrying rate. Is it any wonder that French schools are planning a total ban of phones from all primary and secondary schools by the end of 2018?

And the concern is not just reserved for girls and young women. This is an undeniable cross-generational crisis, created in the main by the new "norms" presented by social networks. In 2017 more than 80 per cent of women in a UK survey said that Instagram and Facebook "added pressure to be the perfect mum", while Terri Smith, CEO of Australian perinatal depression helpline PANDA, has spoken about the damage caused by "social media representations of ideal families". Even when we've reached a level of maturity to know that these images *can't* be entirely reflective of real life, they can still get to us and undermine our happiness. A recent study reported that mothers who more frequently compared themselves on social media sites had a higher incidence than average of depression, were more likely to feel overloaded in their parental role and less competent as parents – the very last things that any mum juggling responsibilities needs. Women can feel just as inadequate viewing fantasy images of the "mommy glow" with kid-mess-free interiors in the backdrop as teenagers may feel when they see Kim Kardashian's plumped-up lips.

A 2017 Harvard Business Review report surveyed the academic literature to argue that social media may "detract from face-to-face relationships, reduce investment in meaningful activities, increase sedentary behaviour...and erode self-esteem". For mums, add in sleep deprivation, increased levels of anxiety, a massive reduction in attention span and, ironically, social isolation, and you've got a cocktail of crappy side effects. And those are just for starters.

Even Facebook has begrudgingly accepted that "passive" social media use (more on that later) has a negative impact on both mood and mental health. Citing both academic and internal enquiries, researchers for the social network admitted that, "in general, when people spend a lot of time passively consuming information – reading but not interacting with people – they report feeling worse afterward." When the world's biggest social media platform has conceded there's a problem and tech leaders have admitted they've barred their own children from logging on, it's time to have a calm look at the impact of our edited worlds.

Technology Addicts Anonymous

One of the biggest causes of concern among the parents, educators and care-givers across the world that I interviewed for this book is the amount of time we spend per day on our devices. Today we *live* on our screens, jumping from laptops to tablets to smartphones, seamlessly switching from games to social media platforms to smartphone apps to webpages. While it's not only social media that we're consuming, a 2016 Global Web Index survey of more than fifty thousand global internet users found that the average person has eight social media accounts and spends one hour and fifty-eight minutes a day – or a third of their entire internet time – browsing them. Smartphone and social media use are not synonymous but they are deeply linked, and a compulsion to check one often means a compulsion to check the other.

Drawing from his work on social media and smartphone addiction, Dr Roberts explains: "Generally people are reluctant to think of behaviours as addictions. We're programmed to believe that we could be addicted to alcohol or drugs, but when it comes to behaviours, we're certainly resistant to accepting that addiction could apply. With social media and smartphone use, what we're seeing in many cases certainly fits the definition of behavioural addiction – engaging in behaviour which you know will have negative consequences for both you and the people around you. It doesn't make logical sense for people to do things that harm them – unless they are addicted. Why else would so many Americans check their social media accounts while driving? Putting themselves and others at risk isn't in their self-interest, but the truth is they just can't stop themselves."

Highlighting the six core components of addiction, Dr Roberts presents a convincing description of the way many of us feel about our phones. "There's salience (how deeply ingrained is your smartphone in your life), tolerance (are you using your phone more and more? Checking your accounts endlessly?), euphoria (the excitement or anticipation you get just before or after you use your cell phone), conflict (is your phone causing trouble in your life with work or relationships?), withdrawal symptoms (do you panic when you're separated from your phone?) and relapse (have you tried to cut back and failed?). Relapse is one of the issues that a psychiatrist will go to first – because when you attempt to cut back you have made a clear decision that something is harmful, but if you are unable to stop, you can be pretty sure you're in an addictive situation." If you recognize any or all of the above, it's certainly worth starting to analyse your behaviour.

According to a report released by research firm Dscout in 2016, the typical mobile phone user touches his or her phone 2,617 times a day. For the top 10 per cent of users in the study, increase that to 5,427 touches a day. Data confirmed by Apple themselves indicates that the average user with Touch ID unlocks their phone every 11 minutes, 15 seconds. Most of us will spend a staggering *seven years* of our lives on our phones. For anyone who might suggest that smartphones' overuse has been blown out of proportion, I'll give you just over ten minutes to try to rationalize these mind-blowing figures. If you had to honestly count how often you reach for your device, where do you think you would rate on the scale? Does work get in the way of your phone time? What about your commute? Can you identify with the 75 per cent of other smartphone owners who admit to using their phones on the toilet? Perhaps 11 minutes and 15 seconds actually feels like a pretty long time?

Not only are we conspicuously and compulsively handling our phones, but we also believe them to be of utmost importance to our lives. In 2011, a McCann WorldGroup analysis of the youth market found that 53 per cent of millennials aged 16–22 (at the time) would rather lose their sense of *smell* than lose access to an item of technology (a phone or a computer). And that was seven years ago. Ask yourself, what would you be prepared to sacrifice in return for your connectivity? Imagine you couldn't log on to the web, or ever access your phone. What would you give up to get it back?

Forget life; choose your phone
The encroachment that phones have made into our rest time, and the resulting global decline in sleep quality and quantity, is one of the biggest charges against phone use. A 2017 survey by Accel and Qualtics revealed that 79 per cent of millennials keep their phones by or in their bed and over half check their phone in the middle of the night. Elsewhere, 55 per cent of British respondents in a 2015 Deloitte report said they look at their phone within 15 minutes of waking and 28 per cent checked within five minutes before going to sleep *every* night. The inability to actually switch off isn't a niche issue. When it starts intruding into your rest time, being connected 24/7 can be incredibly bad for your health. It's been conclusively proven that the longer your screen time during the day, the worse you sleep at night. And as well as having a massive impact on your quality of life, sleep deprivation has been associated with everything from weight gain to high blood pressure and lower life expectancy. If we're talking about self-care, no rational person would ever have their phone in their bedroom.

Social media can also erode our ability to be, well, social. Sherry Turkle, a leading professor in the field of the impact of technology on society, has warned of an "empathy gap", in which young people are unable to develop the social skill of empathy due to their need for constant stimulus and their increasingly distracted family interaction. "These days we find ways around conversation," she explains in *Reclaiming Conversation: The Power of Talk in a Digital Age*. "We hide from each other even, as we're constantly connected to each other."

A 2015 poll found that 89 per cent of Americans admitted they took out a phone at their last social encounter and 82 per cent said that they felt the conversation deteriorated after they did so. Research has proven that even a silent phone sitting innocently on the table inhibits conversation. Turkle also relates use of digital technologies to "simulation", saying that they offer "the illusion of friendship without the demands of intimacy".

Denial is a powerful force when it comes to social media use, but who hasn't been guilty of the occasional Saturday night binge on their favourite platform? The issue is how often you personally access your social media accounts and how that usage makes you feel. Even though I'm very conscious of my own use and try to spread the message about the dangers of social media at any opportunity, I'm certainly not immune to the pull of the scroll. More than anything, I can identify with the idea that social media use is a time drain, which takes me away from getting things done. There have been times when I've thought, "Right, I need to reduce my consumption of these pictures", but I've never been able to completely disengage, even when I know it's making me feel bad. One of the reasons we all keep coming back to social media is that we believe there will be a chance it will make us feel better, but in reality, when you're in a rut, it just makes you feel worse and traps you in a vicious cycle. Just like everyone else, I know it's time to take a break, but I just don't seem to be able to unplug.

A Social Me-Dia History

My social media story has been coloured by many factors, including my age and my job background. I remember the first time I ever heard about Facebook, back in March 2006. I was in my final year of university in Edinburgh, writing my dissertation, and suddenly there were these rumours of a new "exclusive" online club called Facebook. In its early days, the site targeted college students, choosing influential kingpins in specific social circles to spread the message – if I remember correctly, the first person who introduced it to me was a guy who put on "nights" at clubs in the city. To join, you needed a university email address, and it definitely felt like something intercollegiate rather than a platform that would soon capture the attention of every mum and her cat. There were plenty of discussions among my group of friends on the positives and negatives of signing up – at the time the cons surrounded issues of privacy and the fact that it was seen as a bit "uncool" to be showing off about what you were doing. How quaint and antiquated that all sounds now. It goes to show how much the world has changed since the advent of social media, or how much social media has changed our world.

I was an immediate convert. Whenever I needed a break from ten thousand words on the relationship between second- and third-wave feminism, I'd log on to Facebook. Soon I started to dread the days when I was in the library and I didn't have access to the internet (this was the Stone Age – aka the pre Google-on-your-phone era). Offering a brief, but effective, respite from the intense brainwork of my history degree, Facebook soon became one of my favourite pastimes. As an early adopter, I'd often meet people who had never heard of it – or didn't have an accepted university email address but really wanted to set up an account – so it definitely felt good to be part of the inner circle. In the early days, it felt as though Facebook was a diary of our after-dark escapades, and there were a host of seriously dodgy – and definitely unedited – pictures that were uploaded on to the site. Early messages were written directly on friends' walls, with invites to events with free or cheap booze seemingly a focus. It was basically "pure" and unfiltered from both a visual and a content point of view – a mix of cute messages and candid pictures taken on BlackBerry cameras. It was only later when I was building my career that I started to be conscious of the impression of myself I was projecting to the outside world and considered vetting the content.

Over time, of course, things changed and moved on. Looking through my timeline images, the shift started when I got a job at *Grazia* magazine in 2012 (five years after starting my career in fashion) and was instructed by my editor to upgrade to an iPhone and set up an Instagram account. Since then, fewer and fewer of the pictures I've posted feature friends or, indeed, any other people, and more and more are images of me on my own in exotic or exclusive places and locations. As my pictures have become more glamorous and aspirational, my interaction with my Facebook community has conversely plummeted and migrated to Instagram. Now I rarely log on to chat to people or even stalk their timelines, as I keep in touch with friends on WhatsApp and use social media as a platform not for socializing but for forming career-related contacts, building a community around causes that I'm passionate about and earning money as an influencer.

There's no doubt that starting to grow an Instagram audience has had a huge impact on the way I see myself and feel about my life. Initially I felt really reluctant to get involved and I wasn't comfortable with posting images of myself at all. My partner at the time was anti social media in general and constantly berated me for vanity and self-obsession. Even more troubling was the feeling among fashion-industry insiders that editors were "cheapening" themselves by sharing their personal lives. Again, it's now hard to believe, but anyone who was serious about a career in fashion journalism in 2012 needed to think carefully about whether or not they were going to "risk" their integrity by uploading pictures of themselves – as that was seen as something that bloggers (still a dirty word back then) did, not journalists on a reputable publication. Peers who had started to get involved were often ridiculed for their posts, and self-promotional content was equated with extreme narcissism. That feeling is still present in certain areas of the industry, but obviously the context has shifted somewhat.

My first handle was @katherine_grazia, which gives you an indication of how important my job role was to my content. The amount of people who thought the magazine title was my surname was concerning, but it provided protection from the "cringe factor": I was posting as *part of my job*, not because I thought I looked beautiful or wanted other people to see how wonderful my life was. Basically, it gave me carte blanche to build a following without feeling embarrassed about showing off. For Gen Z and younger millennials, the idea that starting a social media account is anything but a rite of passage may be difficult to grasp, but for older millennials like me, who cut their teeth in the old school yet were expected to adapt to the new technology, there was a lot of hand-wringing involved.

Since then, social media has provided me with so many #blessings. It's given me an independent income stream and enabled me to connect with thousands of other people and speak to them directly in one of the most supportive and genuine communities I've ever known. At times, I've legitimately *loved* taking pictures, felt creatively challenged and fulfilled, and experienced genuine happiness that I've finally found somewhere to express myself without anyone to tell me what I've done wrong. However, I've also dealt with the full gamut of emotion that social media can generate. It has made me worry about things like engagement and algorithms, made me question myself, and made me wonder what's wrong with me and why people don't like me. It's made me want to buy things that I can't afford, made me feel like I'm lazy in comparison to other people and, at times, made me feel very low. It's also made me feel overweight, unattractive, poor, unstylish, lonely, left out, unpopular and seriously devoid of a sense of humour.

However clued up on the "system" you are, however much you use social media for your business and however much you keep telling yourself not to be affected by what you consume online, no-one is immune. Whether it's the occasional pang of envy or jolt to your self-esteem caused by a single picture or a more sustained Saturday-night-in-on-your-own-scroll-mania, social media can make even a balanced and mentally well-adjusted person have severe moments of self-doubt and angst.

While this might all sound very doom-like, I do truly believe there are meaningful positives to take away from all of my experiences. The big questions are: what's the secret to filtering out the bad but keeping the good; and how can we make sure that we keep all this in perspective and consciously control our social media use – something which we can pass down to future generations?

Picture Perfect?

What does "perfect" look like to you? Is it about blemish-free skin and a straight smile? Or happy relationships and a beautiful home? Perhaps your idea of perfect is based on career success or a well-maintained six-pack? Or really do we mean all of the above and more? Perfection in its very definition is the state of being *or becoming* perfect, the process of refining something until it is flawless. In the age of social media, the action of perfecting is something we have quickly learned to master. If we aren't perfect to start off with, no matter... A flattering filter here, a retouch tweak there; a quick clear-up of one corner of a messy house, a smile which covers a tricky day. Each and every fault can be erased and replaced with new and increasingly homogenous upgrades to make you feel like the very best version of yourself – or, even better, more like someone else you admire. We can whiten our teeth, slim our thighs and blur our pimples to improve our genetics and supposedly our appeal to each other. We can also turn a miserable, rainy day into a summer classic and curate a schedule of images which not only show us in the best light but suggest a life of rounded perfection. And why not? That's what other people want to see, isn't it?

As a consumer journalist with a decade of experience working on women's magazines, I've been trained to see content as a mix of fantasy and reality – the fashion spreads, which inspire us to dream, but also the real-life stories, which allow us to empathize. Fashion titles have quite rightly had their fair share of criticism over the years, especially in relation to their promotion of an unrealistic body image and lack of diverse representation. These accusations are, in the main, entirely justified, and anyone who has worked in traditional magazine publishing will know that images of white – most likely blonde – thin women dominate any single magazine issue. While things are slowly shifting, there's no point pretending that the days of magazine dominance were a long-lost utopia of diversity.

What traditional magazines did have, however, was a huge focus on relatability, something which is now often painfully edited out of the social media sphere. Every issue of every title I ever worked on offered a mix of content that the reader could identify with – providing support for their struggles and challenges – as well as inspiration for their aspirational desires. We'd cover fertility, heartbreak and financial ruin, *as well as* the hottest new heels of the season. There was also often a light-heartedness and self-deprecation – the countless "test run" stories I wrote which involved me spending a week in 10-inch platforms, Google Glasses or waist-training corsets were always teed up for laughs. (Spoiler alert: they always made me look ridiculous, especially the Google Glasses. But that was the point.)

As the curated imagery of social media has become more and more prominent, the space devoted to real-life issues and collective empathy around life's challenges, both extraordinary and universal, has diminished. Scroll through Facebook or Instagram today and you'll find that lifestyles are a procession of idyllic holidays, "leaning-in" career promotions, material consumption and happy family moments, all captured in the most aesthetically attractive frame possible. Ill-health, failure, loss, sadness, struggle, hard work, setbacks – indeed anything not entirely positive – has become increasingly underrepresented in our discourse, because it doesn't fit the mould of the often image-focused world of social media. We also take ourselves *seriously* seriously, and the pressure to be immaculate has definitely come hand in hand with a new po-faced attitude, in which our personal brands can't be compromised by any lightweight or anecdotal content. Aside from the comedy-focused accounts (which are understandably hugely successful), the standard social media feed is so focused on self-promotion that we can't bear to look foolish in front of others.

According to a 2017 research paper, these days women rarely compare their appearance to women they see in billboards and magazines and only sometimes compare their appearance to others they see on TV. Instead it's social media comparisons which are making women feel unhappiest. Because these women are supposedly more accessible and "normal" – not A-list actresses or internationally famous pop stars – the standards they set feel like a bare minimum. If those in your community most like you can achieve a level of life success and perfect appearance, why can't you too?

And through these platforms we're also all looking up to new heroes. The status of these new "micro-celebrities" is key to the social media system. Super-users by nature, these "influencers" have the faces, bodies and wardrobes that we pore over as avatars of the new era. Their vast reach opens them up to the very good, very bad and everything in-between that social media has to offer. However, I've found that, whether it's a beautiful model on set or an Instagram star with a million followers, the women who seem to have everything are just like the rest of us: struggling, self-doubting and feeling under huge pressure to look and feel a certain way. For them there is often no escape from the strain of keeping up appearances. Though they're projecting a lifestyle which we're all hungrily aspiring to, the reality is that they are often addicted to their phones, deeply insecure and highly anxious about their social media profile.

However, in the new media moment, these women can also be potent agents of change. These are the women that other women listen to. Their advice, their philosophies and their styling tips guide the way that the social media community at large behaves. Through engagement with their, often unbelievably enormous, audiences, they are able to challenge cultural values, bring causes to the masses and undermine traditional structures of power. Contrary to popular opinion, influencers don't just make us buy things (though they're certainly very good at it). Instead, they have meaningfully influenced our attitudes. From providing role models for under-represented and marginal communities, busting taboos around hidden struggles like miscarriage and poor mental health, and promoting feminist and environmental issues (#FreeTheNipple, #SayNoToPlastic), they have enacted change on a global scale. Young women won't listen to their parents, teachers or researchers. But they will listen to those sitting on top of the new media pedestal. This is why this book has included the voices of female influencers across a broad array of social communities to help explore the biggest issues that we face online today. Between them they have an audience of almost 10 million followers, a particular experience with the highs and lows of the social media experience, and the capacity to help make us all wake up to the crisis we're sitting on. They are not just the new power players; they're also the experts. It is their words that will really help to burst the bubble.

Social media has inarguably set destructive standards of flawlessness and comparison, which continuously deplete millions of women's self-belief, every minute of every day. We're working so hard to live up to these new benchmarks that we're burning ourselves out, and we're striving so hard to maintain our image that we're self-perpetuating an unobtainable reality. Until girls and women alike see the social media fantasies for what they are – constructed realities – and stop comparing their lifestyles, bodies, partners and even families to those seen on their feeds and screens, they will never be able to realize their potential in the workplace, their relationships or in their quest for happiness.

I'm not attempting to be holier than thou or sanctimonious; we all like nice pictures of ourselves, and there's a reason social media is so popular. Glamour, fantasy and the creative worlds curated by social content-makers can be fun, artistic and beautiful, and there's nothing wrong with taking enjoyment and positives from social media consumption, creation and interaction. But the conversation *must* be re-framed, because if we continue projecting fantasy as reality and continue believing, or even semi-believing, in the make-believe, the dangers are both very real and very present. While my aim is to always err on the side of balance, the changes that social media have brought to our lives *are* sensational, therefore deserve to be probed and laid bare as such.

The Comparison Trap

When you look at other people's lives on social media, how does it make you feel about yours? If the answer is "a bit rubbish", rest assured you're not the only one. Social psychologist Leon Festinger's classic 1954 social comparison theory suggests that individuals evaluate their own abilities and success by gauging their position in the social pecking order. His argument is that we can only really rate our own position in life by comparing it to those of others within our communities, which means the boundaries of those communities really matter.

In times of yore, aka when we lived offline, there were two ways that social comparison could work: upward and downward. When we saw others we judged to be in a worse position than ourselves, it would often lead to an improvement in self-appraisal, however, when we saw people we deemed to be living superior lives to us, or having superior abilities and attributes, it had a tendency to create a sense of inadequacy and insecurity, and had an overall negative effect on our self-evaluation.

When all we see is the very, *very* best side of the people in our communities online, curated especially to exclusively highlight their best attributes, is it any wonder that most of us feel that we are on the back foot in relation to pretty much everyone we know? Instead of upward and downward comparisons, we are seeing exclusively those who appear to be superior to us, in every single way. Comparing ourselves to idealized versions of each other is, scroll by scroll, overexposing us to upward social comparison, which has a massive knock-on impact on body image, self-esteem, expectations and life satisfaction.

Of course, there is nothing new in the process of comparison itself, but social media puts it into hyper-drive – especially among young people. A 2017 poll of more than 1,900 girls and young women by the

UK charity Girlguiding found that 35 per cent of girls aged 11–21 said their biggest worry online was comparing themselves and their lives with others. But it's not just the kids. In a recent study by UK disability charity Scope, 60 per cent of adult Twitter and Facebook users reported feelings of jealousy when comparing themselves to other users too. As we consume more and more information about each other, we're finding it perilously easy to slip into the quicksand of comparison.

On social media, comparison breeds envy at every corner. Instead of feeling grateful for what we have, we believe we need to be more, just to come up to scratch. Our careers, our wardrobes, our lifestyles, even our children (let's not even get started on apps to make babies and children look "cuter") – none of them are enough. So, what's the solution? Aside from more honesty in our content creation, the more we accept that digital identities are simulations rather than true benchmarks from which to judge our own position in life, the kinder we can be to ourselves. The time is nigh to stop battering ourselves with comparisons to versions of others which just don't exist. We need to forget about coveting what our neighbours appear to have; the time is nigh to stop battering ourselves with comparisons to versions of others that just don't exist.

Every Voice Counts

On the positive side, during my research through the murky and addictive algorithms social media has been built from, I have heard plenty of accounts from followers as well as influencers, both micro and mega, explaining that the engagement they found online had increased their confidence hugely. Discovering that there are people out there who think and feel like you can make everyone, both old and young, feel less marginalized. One of social media's most positive contributions to modern life is that it can help you find "your people".

"Growing up I wasn't used to seeing successful women that looked like me," says Freddie Harrel, a fashion and lifestyle blogger, beauty entrepreneur, and confidence coach and speaker with 136k followers on Instagram. Born and raised in Paris to Cameroonian parents, she explains, "In France, if you open a fashion magazine you will not see a single, remotely 'tanned' face. There is no diversity. At all." One huge advancement that social media has facilitated is a democratization of the types of men and women we see in aspirational positions. Communities have been built around individuals whose stories would have been edited out of the traditional media environment, because of systemic prejudice.

On any social platform you will find groups which celebrate, inform and serve plus-size women, LGBT women, women of colour and women of faith. All shapes, all sizes, all shades and all creeds are welcome to join in. From a racial perspective, the proportion of white, black and Latino users across all social media sites is roughly the same, although more black and Latino people use Instagram in comparison to their white counterparts, while Pinterest is more popular among white users than other groups.

"Social media has really changed the landscape and I follow some incredible women of colour on Instagram – many of whom have built a huge following – who inspire me," Freddie continues. "There's now not [only] one version of what a successful woman looks like, and that is so important for younger generations coming up behind us."

Leandra Medine, founder of fashion and lifestyle platform ManRepeller.com (one of the first blogs to achieve fashion-industry recognition) explains that these relationships can make women feel both supported and empowered. "The notion of making women feel less alone and more understood is a cornerstone of Man Repeller. Social media can facilitate a community if you are open and vulnerable – and if the people you don't know come out to support you, care to listen to your story and dare to share their own. That's a really strong and impactful experience. The number of private messages I have received from strangers, and the outpour of their personal narratives that they've generously shared...it's a true connection."

Like Me So I Can Love Myself

However, what happens when no-one engages? When you don't receive any likes or comments on your posts? Or more likely "too few" likes against your own standards? We all know that adolescents are eager for peer validation. I can remember the threat of "peer pressure" being rammed down my throat through school, especially when it came to smoking (I completely caved and ended up with a 20-a-day habit – the moral of the story: listen to your parents). But a need for acceptance from our community isn't something most of us leave behind on graduation day. In today's digital age, a desire for validation has intensified for the straightforward reason that social media has made it quantifiable. Those little numbers under our captions and pictures, and the threat of eerie silence around our digital updates, give each and every one of us a clear indication of how liked we are. Instead of increasing our confidence in our own self-definition, we are becoming more and more aware of what our peers think of us, often "caving" to that pressure way into our adult lives.

Sean Parker, one of Facebook's earliest investors (Justin Timberlake in the film *The Social Network*) told news and information website Axios in an interview in 2017 that a social media site is a "social-validation feedback loop...exploiting a vulnerability in human psychology". He explained that he and other early social media pioneers built their platforms to "consume as much of your time and conscious attention as possible" with the "like" button devised to give users "a little dopamine hit", which in turn would fuel a desire to upload more content.

In a world where you can tangibly rate your popularity and see exactly who in your social circle cares, "chasing the likes" has become a collective interest which can veer into an obsession. The "like" function wasn't part of the original social media blueprint – indeed, Facebook only introduced it in 2009, five years after its initial launch. Almost a decade later, we tap out 4.5 billion likes each day on that platform alone, meaning there's a hell of a lot of validation out there to ensnare with what we share.

So how does that craving for endorsement impact our psyches? In 2014 Thailand's government psychiatrist Dr Panpimol Wipulakorn warned through the country's Department of Mental Health that young Thais were experiencing emotional problems when images they posted of themselves weren't receiving the desired level of likes. This lack of validation could, she argued, "affect their thoughts. They can lose self-confidence and have a negative attitude toward themselves, such as feeling dissatisfied with themselves or their body." In a far-reaching conclusion she finished, "This could affect the development of the country in the future as the number of new-generation leaders will fall short. It will hinder the country's creativity and innovation."

A 2016 study from UCLA (University of California, Los Angeles) used MRI scanning to examine the brains of teenagers aged 13–18 while they used social media. The results showed that viewing likes underneath a picture they had posted activated the same brain signals as eating chocolate or winning money. Another interesting finding was that teens were much more likely to click the "like" button on images that had already received lots of love from their peers, showing that endorsement from others made them more likely to offer validation to others. While the study highlighted the particularly sensitive reward circuitry in adolescents, it's not a reach for most adults to relate to. I can certainly identify with the feelings described. Anyone who says they don't feel good when an image or comment they've created clocks up lots of likes and comments is probably lying. The validation can feel like a rush, a sense of "something I've said or done matters to people". It's only natural to feel this way; after all, we are social beings at heart and we're hard-wired to feel good about approval from others. It's also not difficult to see why posts that have already gained lots of likes might inspire us to click our own little hearts. Aside from subconscious conformity, there's a sense that we must be "missing" something if we don't like it too. Did we not get the joke? Or aren't we quite up to speed with a new trend? If everyone else thinks it's so cool, why don't we?

When likes become an indicator of popularity and social standing, gaining approval from others can momentarily improve our self-esteem and release a hit of dopamine, which backs up that feel-good emotion. A *New Statesman* 2017 survey showed that for 89 per cent of social media users, getting a high level of likes makes them feel happy, but revealingly for 40 per cent of those people, the happiness only lasts as long as the likes keep coming in. For 12.5 per cent of people, they will still feel happy after an hour; for 10.2 per cent, they will feel it for the entire day; and only 3.1 per cent will be sustained for a week. Overall 62.7 per cent of respondents agreed or strongly agreed with the statement, "I feel a buzz when someone likes my post." No matter what, we all love to be liked.

Conversely, a perceived lack of engagement can create a huge dent in our self-esteem. Who hasn't posted a picture or comment on social media only to feel deflated minutes later when no-one has liked or commented on it? We don't need to be told it feels crap to be ignored, left hanging in digital time and space without that little pick-me-up that a "successful" post can offer. Is it any wonder that a whole industry exists to help individuals pay for likes, that so many of us ask friends to like our pictures to up our digital cred or that we end up deleting so many images and captions that haven't generated enough likes? But then...the allure of the dopamine high returns and you find yourself posting another image. This cycle can become a pathological obsession, and if you find yourself checking your likes every minute of the day, it's no surprise the process can have a huge impact on your mental state. A solid body of research has proven that the lower your self-esteem to start with, the more a lack of engagement on social media can impact you negatively, meaning those who feel the most need for validation are also the least able to cope with the effects of receiving low engagement.

Worryingly it was suggested in a 2018 article by the Canadian *Globe & Mail* that social media platforms are capitalizing on our hunger for validation by holding back likes to keep us checking our accounts. Quoting Matt Mayberry, who works at a California startup called Dopamine Labs, the article claims: "It's common knowledge in the industry that Instagram exploits this craving by strategically withholding 'likes' from certain users. If the photo-sharing app decides you need to use the service more often, it'll show only a fraction of the likes you've received on a given post at first, hoping you'll be disappointed with your haul and check back again in a minute or two."

In response, Mike Krieger, the CTO of Instagram, used Twitter to deny that there was any intention to withhold likes, but he did admit that there might be a replication lag and that the platform tries to "strike a balance of being timely + [and] not over-sending notifs [notifications]". The idea that our social media apps could be so calculatingly taking advantage of our human weaknesses is obviously abhorrent – but we have to remember that this is business and the more we connect, the more they profit. Ultimately it is in the interest of every social media platform to make us feel this way.

Disentangling our sense of worth from the numbers is one of the most important steps in moderating the impact that social media can have on our lives, but it's far trickier than it sounds. Sure, you can go cold turkey, delete your accounts or take a break (something which a 2015 study proved will increase your life satisfaction), but for many of us that's not always a practical solution. Social media can sometimes be part of our job, or we may need to stay connected or maintain a digital presence to be relevant for other professional reasons, such as networking. Unless your social media use is causing you relentless anxiety, depression or unhappiness, there is definitely a time and place for it and there are many positives to be taken away. It's just about knowing how to control that time and ensuring you're in the right frame of mind – two things we are often entirely unconscious of as we click on our apps and get ready to scroll.

Real or Fake? And Why It Matters

In the early days of the internet there was a utopian belief that anyone could be anyone they wanted to be online. It was suggested that the space would be non-gendered, without racial bias, and would offer individuals the chance to present themselves exactly as they wished, without prompting the assumptions people make, from our accents to body shapes, that colour all of our identities in real life. "On the internet no-one knows you're a dog", is an adage taken from a 1993 *New Yorker* cartoon by Paul Steiner featuring two computer-savvy canines. The point being made was that the internet was a plane of anonymity where individuals were liberated to redefine who they were to the world. Of course, now the biggest social media stars have their own accounts and the @DogsOfInstagram feed has over four million followers. Despite this, our understanding of identity in the digital space has certainly been transformed.

As time has gone on, internet obscurity has instead become associated with illegal activity. And research has proven that real-life preconceptions immediately bled over to the internet. Doctors are instantly presumed to be white men, for example, and judgements are made based on people's names, even without images, to determine either race, class or social status. While the internet has helped connect communities of all stripes, it certainly hasn't eradicated prejudice against those of non-white ethnicities or non-heterosexual sexualities, nor stopped those of differing religions judging each other – in fact there's little doubt that the internet has enabled and intensified hate speech against both mainstream and marginalized communities as well as given a platform for extremists.

However, a kernel of that concept of self-invention has continued to shape our understanding of the online world. Stretching the truth is part and parcel of the digital experience. Consider profile pictures or given ages on internet dating sites. A 2008 study found that 81 per cent of matchmaking site participants lied or misrepresented themselves in some, albeit often small, way. Not everyone online is catfishing (creating a fake identity online to impersonate someone entirely different), but then again, very few of us are always entirely honest. Without the non-verbal cues which we rely on to see if someone is telling the truth in real life, it can be all too easy to be fooled.

And being duped we are. Escapism is an entirely understandable drive, and social media can offer a platform to express and explore fantasy identities. However, we've failed to develop a collective understanding that many of the images and captions which make up many profiles are, at best, misrepresentations of the truth and, at worst, outright lies. Somehow our scepticism has been put on the backburner; we all seem happy to suspend disbelief. Only posting the beautiful side of our lives without mentioning the less photogenic parts, or even the daily grind, isn't "living in truth". None of these things are unlawful and they are entirely reasonable in the context of the games of micro-deception that everyone else is playing online. But even the little tweaks we're making to our realities are distorting our understanding of normality and making hundreds and thousands of people feel disappointed with the reality of their lives. In the era of fake news, the fact that so many people are living "fake" lives, photographing fake designer shoes and posting #IWokeUpLikeThis selfies with a full face of slap on, is perhaps no shocker. It is, however, having a massive influence on our perceptions of the world and ourselves.

For one thing, it's important to acknowledge that how we represent ourselves online can have a dramatic impact on our success in life. According to a 2017 CareerBuilder survey, 70 per cent of employers use social media to screen candidates before hiring, and three in ten HR departments have a member of staff dedicated solely to social recruiting. The study showed that a positive online persona was not only advantageous for job recruitment, but also that *more than half of all employers wouldn't hire a candidate that didn't have a social media account*. From excessive posting to provocative or inappropriate pictures, there are a range of obvious turn-offs for employers. But the fact it's also now almost a requirement to cultivate a certain image in the digital realm as part of your résumé is most significant.

What's more, the process doesn't finish after you've signed your contract – more than half of all bosses say they monitor the digital accounts of their current staff, so opening up about mental health issues, home-life struggles and relationship challenges online comes with definite risks. Basically, your future or current boss will probably read it, so you'd better think twice before you post anything. Judgements on what a "positive persona" is, of course, are subjective, but from a professional perspective it's obviously far "safer" to keep things upbeat, iron out the wrinkles of life and make everything seem fabulous. The sad truth is that you don't have a "personal" life on social media – even if your posts are private, things can slip through the net. Everything you publish in the online realm could potentially have a bearing on your professional success and reputation.

On the flipside, there is a vocal "authenticity police" force out there ready to jump on perceived fakery in an instant. Digitally naming and shaming others on social media has become a hot new pursuit, with followers calling out individuals with audiences both big and small. The New Statesman chronicled the case of a beauty blogger who was accused of Photoshopping her images to edit out crowds from iconic tourist destinations by creating a composite between two images and passing them off as authentic. Since the blogger made money from these constructed images through sponsored posts, many of her followers felt that she had lost her integrity. As the author of the article, Amelia Tait, says, "Though a Photoshopped sunset is not as damaging as the 'fake news' spread during and since the United States Presidential Election, it is still a worrying aspect of the erosion of authenticity online." While, in my personal opinion, much of the disgruntlement from the digital community was not much more than trolling – singling out one blogger when there are literally hundreds of thousands of people doing the same kind of thing seems patently unjust – Tait has a solid point. Social media's ability to stretch the truth in a way that we have accepted and internalized has permeated all areas of life, including our thoughts, our decisions and our votes. It's not a private or personal thing: it's a political attitude which can have a bearing on how we view both the superficial and essential organized structures of our society. To be anti-Trump and complain about governmental gaslighting seems somewhat disingenuous if you're publicly misrepresenting the truths of your life too.

Aren't we all complicit?
So what do I edit out of my life online? Well I definitely make my pictures look "prettier" by adjusting the light balance of the vast majority of my social media images – when you're shooting in London, for six months of the year you're basically in low- to no-light situations. I've definitely added saturation to colours in images and filters to make them look more jolly (bleak, rainy days are another London perk). I'm not a massive selfie-taker, but if I were I wouldn't flinch at taking out a massive zit, though personally I wouldn't touch my wrinkles (that poreless, smoothed plastic skin just looks freaky to me), my crooked teeth or any of my features because I would be embarrassed not to look like myself when people meet me in real life. Elsewhere I am a witch with removing things from the background of my images – cables, cigarette butts and green wheelie bins are my pet peeves and I have Photoshopped them out of lots of my pictures. I also really know how to take a flattering shot and generally choose the image that makes me look tallest and slimmest (I'm 5ft 3in/160cm). I don't obsess about the way my face looks (that doesn't mean I don't notice the flaws) but I wouldn't post a picture that I thought made me look squat.

The sum of all of this is that my pictures are probably about 90 per cent real and about 10 per cent "fake", but certainly 100 per cent the best that I can look. As an educated woman, a feminist and someone who considers the impact of my actions on others, it's worth questioning why I always want to project "acceptable" images of myself. Aside from the obvious answer of vanity – I wouldn't frame an unflattering photo and put it on my mantelpiece at home, so why should I do it online? – it's a mixture of different reasons. Firstly, if I posted entirely unfiltered, un-lightened, images, which were taken in one shot rather than the 50 or so I usually pick from, I probably wouldn't have built the same following on social media. The images would have looked grey, depressing and entirely uninspiring. Since I run a business which values the numbers of my audience, it's important to me that my images have appeal. Secondly, I don't think we have to rehash the argument that a feminist can wear lipstick and expensive shoes and still believe in equal pay, treatment and opportunity. I've worked as a fashion editor; I know the power and confidence that distinctive clothing can give you, and I'm entirely unashamed of showcasing that. Making an effort with my presentation is largely for me a question of self-respect and investment in myself. Images where I look put together and well dressed make me feel a sense of pride, whereas a picture of me in a sloppy tracksuit and unwashed hair would make me feel the reverse. It feels good to look good and I enjoy the theatre of putting a killer outfit together, even if I'm just at home on my own. And, finally, there is the right to artistic licence. The creativity in making a beautiful image with interesting clothes and considered make-up is arguably a case of self-expression.

The one area which I still tussle with is the way I choose to project my own body image. My desire to pick only images in which I look slimmest is definitely a product of social conditioning and deeply ingrained beliefs around what makes something or someone beautiful. Trying to leave these fixations behind is an uphill struggle – a challenge I wonder if I'll ever overcome. Perhaps not, but it's definitely a work in progress.

Of course, it could easily be claimed that what I'm doing, even at this low level of image manipulation, is helping fan those deceitful flames. If the tools are available on our chosen platforms (the in-app Snapchat filters have the power to make this 34-year-old woman look *literally* 12), by using them are we contributing to the problem?

Ultimately if the pictures look better than we do in real life, then we can't say we're not complicit in creating these unrealistic standards that are damaging the way women feel about themselves.

Walking the social media tightrope

So, how do you find the happy medium between representing yourself in a way that doesn't harm your prospects and ensuring you keep away from the darkest sides of digital deception? Where is that line? If a filter or enhanced lighting is fine, why isn't the injection of a pretty sunset in the window? Should doctored images come with a warning disclaimer? Or instead, is it about educating ourselves to doubt *everything* we see? Everyone can agree that wholesale misrepresentations of who you are, how you live and how you look don't do anyone favours. Although it is possible to fake your home, your job, your social life and your friends on social media, doing so not only raises the bar for everyone else but also makes you believe that your true life isn't good enough.

However, let's be real: most people aren't going to voluntarily start posting pictures they hate of themselves. While there is an increasingly vocal "real beauty" movement on social media, with women rebelling every day against aesthetic conformity, and burgeoning communities of posters who either for political or artistic reasons adamantly refuse to tweak any of their visuals, it isn't even close to the majority. Recommending total social media honesty is largely going to fall on deaf ears because our capitalist societies still lionize youth, slimness and financial success, and it's hugely difficult to escape that conditioning. However, surely there has to be a midway point that we can all sign up to – somewhere between still recognizing yourself and your life and endless pictures of grey skies, massive zits and green wheelie bins? And don't the social media companies who created the filters in the first place have to be part of finding that solution, rather than feeding young, impressionable minds more and more tools of mass fakery, mass perfection and identikit idealism?

How to Scroll to a Better Future

In this book I'll be exploring these difficult questions and more, and will look to carve out a new path for a healthy and beneficial relationship with social media. One where we are in the driving seat, controlling our intake and uptake of these digital platforms so they work for us, rather than being taken along for the bumpy ride. Over the course of the book I will examine several key areas of modern womanhood – identity, body image, health, relationships, motherhood, career and money, and politics – and will look at exactly how social media has impacted and penetrated each. There will be common themes throughout, but each topic will have its own specific approach, and I will provide useful takeaways at the end of each chapter to help you manage your own social media diet within that context. It's definitely not about absolutes or extremes. Social media is here to stay, as are our phones, and while "off-gridding" for a certain amount of time is gaining popularity, for most of us it's really a matter of conscious, mindful consumption rather than the unthinking binges many of us have become prone to.

The digital age has been the architect of a distinct crisis in self-worth among women. Everything looks so rosy through a social media lens, and the platforms which we're glued to have been fine-tuned to appeal to our natural desire to be accepted, admired and loved. But these worlds we're creating and consuming aren't ones which always serve our best interests – and through our addiction to them we've lost the ability to recognize that. The apps are just too entertaining, too exciting and too compelling for us to realize what they're doing to us. The tendency to compare and despair, the acceptance of inauthenticity, and the way our content can shape our real-life existence are just some of the ways that social media is redefining what it means to be a woman in the 21st century. But really, that's just the tip of the iceberg.

Chapter 1:
Why Social Media is
Ruining Your **Identity**

Who are you? What is it that defines you? Is it where you come from, or where you're going? Your parents or your music taste? Are you still trying to figure it out?

If so, don't sweat it, because social media is changing the landscape and nearly *everyone* is going through an identity crisis. Guiding how we see ourselves, and to an extent how others view us too, our identity can be shaped by nationality, social class, ethnicity, age, sexuality, wealth and gender, as well as differences ranging from political alignment to taste in books to breakfast food preference. Like a map of your experiences, these are the markers which make you "you".

Whether you're an emo avocado-toast lover or plus-size rainbow-hair aficionado, "who you are" truly matters in the digital context. Not only do we actively carve our identity, through finding communities of like-minded people and choosing to project a "personal brand" for others to judge us on, but we are also being surreptitiously categorized, as nearly every online action we take leaves a trail of "identity markers". Due to the way that the internet and social media sites are monetized, these markers or cookies inform Google, Facebook et al., what kind of content you might be interested in. From what you buy on Amazon, to the *New Yorker* article you commented on last night, to that puppy picture you sent to your sister, your on-screen actions help define your digital identity and therefore dictate the images, ads, entertainment and news which then stalk you around the internet. So the identity you formulate online actually becomes your personal key into this matrix.

To put it simply, in real life you walk down the street and consume a breadth of information geared to all kinds of people. Online, your identity is reduced by a combination of clicks and you only see things aimed at "people like you". Don't think you have a digital identity? Think again.

The Whole World's a Stage

Your digital self is your 21st-century calling card. In an age when more people own a mobile phone than a toothbrush, managing your online identity – and thus reputation – is hardly a niche activity. Whether you're updating your CV on LinkedIn or un-tagging unflattering pictures posted on Facebook, we're all making – often daily – decisions about how we want to project ourselves. In the same way we worry about looking "good on paper", we want to look good on screen too. On the whole, we emphasize our abilities, downplay anything which could cast aspersions on our character, and try at all costs to project an image of success. For example, my LinkedIn page doesn't mention that my last magazine job contract was reduced from full time to three days a week and my dating profiles definitely keep schtum about my divorce. It's all about selective disclosure.

Inspired by Erving Goffman's *The Presentation of Self in Everyday Life*, the idea that the internet is a stage and we are all in a sense performing on it has become a popular analogy. Goffman originally argued back in 1959 that our public life represents the "front stage" – a world where everyone is watching and impressions matter – but that there's also a "backstage" sanctuary where "the performer can relax; he can drop his front and step out of character." The all-seeing, all-knowing, 24/7 world of social media has ramped up the sheer volume of public information that we're all sharing, and the culture of Periscope, Instagram Stories and Snapchat, which encourage a near-live streamed existence, have significantly upped our "on stage" time. Messages and comments that are shared online are often public by default and are in a sense "on the record" – so even as we build relationships online we can never let our guard down. Today our "front stage", idealized personas are becoming more and more how we define ourselves. As our ability to maintain this supercharged good impression layer is fast-evolving, we have less and less time with the off-duty "backstage" side of ourselves.

Aside from being exhausting, keeping the show constantly on the road has proven to have a huge impact not only on *our* minds, but on our friends' as well. A 2013 paper coined a process known as the *self-promotion–envy spiral*. Triggered by a range of positive content uploaded by our friends, we end up using "even greater self-promotion and impression management" in reaction, to help cope with our feelings of envy. Basically, rampant sharing of positive information about our own lives and identities causes our friends to up the ante with their own posts, until we all feel under pressure to project a more and more impressive version of "who we are". "Of the seven deadly sins, only envy is no fun at all," said American writer Joseph Epstein, and anyone who spends their time scrolling through their friends' and acquaintances' happiness highlight reels will certainly, at some point, concur. Yes, you can feel happy for other people's success, but that doesn't mean you can't also feel slightly (and even sometimes deeply) bitter too.

Over the past eight years, Andrew Oswald, a professor of economics and behaviour at the University of Warwick, has been studying the power that envy has over our happiness, curious to find out if the new institutions of social media ("that make people feel inadequate and envious of others") are having an impact on our overall wellbeing. His findings: higher levels of envy lead to greater mental-health problems and have no power to motivate or lead to greater levels of financial success in the future. In summary, our increasingly impressive online identities equal bad news for our friends.

The process of presenting ever more admirable information online in turn leads to a temptation to misrepresent our lives. Tweaking the truth to present a slightly better version of who we are is something we consciously and subconsciously do offline too – who hasn't slightly exaggerated their job role at a party or glossed over the finer details of their relationship status when put on the spot by their family over the holidays? In the digital realm, however, the lines between harmless hyperbole and self-delusion are far easier to cross. IRL (in real life), there are limits to what we can make of ourselves, but online you can go waaaay further with self-invention: hello, catfish; hello, Facetune. Even if we don't go the whole hog, we're probably embellishing.

Camille Charrière, a French fashion blogger and podcast host, describes how she reinvented herself when she constructed her digital identity. "My fashion taste was not something I was raised or born with. Fashion wasn't a part of my upbringing at all. I read a comment on Reddit the other day which said, 'I just found out that someone I used to go to school with now has 600k followers on Instagram – just goes to show you shouldn't make fun of awkward, ginger weirdos.' The post was about me. Growing up I was a long way from being an it-kid. I really was not that girl in secondary school or even in university. When I set up my blog I basically decided to invent a new digital persona which was very different from the geeky real-life version."

There's little doubt that we are buying into these newly created digital selves, whether they're grounded in real life or not, and often embracing them wholesale. Chronic comparison anxieties generated by the ubiquity of social media imagery have come to define the lives of many women across all generations. Decisions we make about the ways in which we project our identities on social media are at the nub of this process, so the relationship between who we are online and who we are at home is in a sense political as well as personal. We all contribute to the community, and as such everyone has at least a small responsibility to define the rules of the game. As Professor Nicole Ellison, of the School of Information at the University of Michigan, explains, "When you're thinking of your own messy identity and you're comparing it to this very curated and to some extent fabricated version of what someone else's life is like, it's not a like-for-like measure." If half of us are exaggerating our wealth, success, happiness and achievements, the other half are left floundering and wondering what's gone wrong in their lives. Obviously, the answer is nothing; it's all just a question of presentation.

The Happiness Homogeneity

One of the biggest issues is that we aren't being open enough about the fact that social media is indeed a game – one where we play with ideas about our sense of self. While most people are aware, at least conceptually, that our digital identities aren't identical to our everyday realities, there is a disconnect. Many people have suggested this is down to the visual nature of many social media sites. Instagram and Snapchat have been found to be the most damaging platforms among 14–25 year olds, in terms of their impact on health and wellbeing issues such as anxiety, depression and self-identity, and this is said to be due to their image-focus. We all know the phrase "a picture speaks a thousand words", but there's rigorous scientific backup to prove that our brains process information gleaned from visuals in a different way to that from words. Back in the 1960s and 1970s, Allan Paivio developed "dual coding theory", which suggests we have two distinct cognitive processes – verbal and visual. He claimed that images have an advantage over text as they generate both verbal *and* image codes in our brains, meaning we are more likely to remember them and form more meaningful associations. By the 1980s, influential market researchers Terry Childers and Michael Houston had discovered that image-based advertisements required less exposure than verbal ads to resonate with the public, proving once again that we're more likely to take on board messages which we've consumed visually.

Even though we can write and talk about how much these images are embroidered, our minds still find it easy to recognize, and then internalize, what we see. Familiarity with certain visual cues also stimulates faster recognition, meaning the emotions that these images can generate have an increased potency.

This might go some way to explaining why social media "clichés" and trends like sliced avocado on toast or identical tourist shots continue to receive such high engagement – we like them, because we already know them. Whereas once avocado was just a fruit, now it automatically symbolizes status, relevance and consumerism, things that many of us aspire to. We've become so used to viewing images that we recognize and desire – identikit smiling shots of time-worn moments which overwhelmingly project the most positive sides of our identities. The more we see them, the more we believe them.

Our depictions of travel on social media have become an area in which homogeneity – or a relentless sameness – has started to be seriously discussed. Travel in the digital context is an important identity marker, especially for young people. Keen to display their worldly and curious characters, prove that they are wealthy enough to globetrot and affiliate themselves to the aspirational lifestyles they see their social media heroes living (some of whom appear to be in a constant state of motion around the globe), for millennials especially, travel has become about much more than a two-week summer break. When many won't be able to afford to buy their own home until they're in their sixties, travel becomes a far more tangible life goal to invest their savings in.

Importantly, where you choose to tour in a sense defines the kind of person you are. Whether it's a five-day circuit of Santorini's swanky infinity pools, a road trip to hipster-looking lake houses in upstate New York or a pilgrimage to the waterfalls of Bali, your spot on the social media trail reveals your tastes and says a lot about what you're trying to project from a personal brand point of view. Indeed, in 2017 a UK home insurance survey found that the "Instagrammability" of a destination was the primary booking motivator for 18–33 year olds – well ahead of cost and personal development.

The problem is that all the pictures have become identical: iconic tourist destination in the background, woman with her back to the camera wearing a cute dress from Réalisation or Reformation, clutching at a straw hat. When you travel to any picturesque spot in the world today you encounter lines of young women trying to recreate the same images. Even if you've never been to Italy, you've seen that picture before; *you know it, so you'd probably like it.*

"I often find myself feeling sick to my stomach when I have to post a new picture," Sara Melotti, an Italian travel photographer and blogger with over 40k followers on Instagram, explained to me. "In my field, you quickly realize that everyone's content is basically exactly the same. What people do is research which images have generated the most likes in the past and then they'll recreate a duplicate shot for their own feed. They don't care about travelling as an experience, they just want the picture to show everyone where they've been and make sure they get enough likes to feed the social media algorithms. Every time I post a picture of something a bit more unusual – but still beautiful – it doesn't get anywhere near the same engagement. It's depressing that it's only the images that people recognize that get the likes, and if you want to build your numbers, that's what you have to post. Creating this kind of soulless content doesn't just make you feel bad – it can completely destroy your self-esteem and sense of who you are."

Instead of diversity and originality, what the majority of people on social media appear to want is more of the same. Conformity is rewarded by both the community and the system – what we "like" most drives the algorithms, which in turn feed us more indistinguishable content which we happily consume. The general, appeal-to-all, lowest-common-denominator visuals are making our world view increasingly bland, and while there are other vantage points to be found – including all kinds of amazing rebellious and subcultural content – you have to actively seek them out. And it's not just travel, it's all aspects of how we express ourselves: décor, weddings, how we dress, the art we like, the food we eat, even our politics.

Social media has become an echo chamber of mainstream and predictable content through a process which has been described as the "memeification of human experience". For older users who have seen the world through different lenses, it's easy to dismiss the social media window as just one take on the world. When you're a teenager who spends every possible waking minute scrolling, the understanding of what exists outside these limited trends is increasingly lacking. The impact this can have on identity formation is obvious: expectations, benchmarks and important signifiers of individual identity are being channelled through a very narrow funnel.

Happiness and fulfilment also feature heavily in this funnelled vision. While not a traditional identity marker, in the same way as, say, sexuality or ethnic background, being identified as happy is one of social media's ultimate status symbols. Conversely, admitting struggles with contentment can lead to different character labels spanning "authentic" (to fans) to "difficult", "attention-seeking" and "unstable" (to trolls and, worryingly, life insurers). Happiness is something that nearly everyone wants to project, whether they feel it or not. The "smiling depressive", described as a person whose inner turmoil is masked by outer cheerfulness, has found a new platform to display a "winning at life" front. Nearly 20 per cent of two thousand women surveyed in a US mental illness report said the stigma they felt about their depression or anxiety had led them to share a photo on social media for which the caption didn't match what they felt inside. The procession of bright smiles, #blessed captions and blissful family shots are pretty much the exact opposite of what you see staring back at you on your Monday morning commute. But it's easy to believe that everyone else is joyful when you spend too much time scrolling and forget that another, somewhat bleaker, real-life context exists. Happiness is not a medal to be showcased; it ebbs and flows, and no-one can keep hold of it 100 per cent of the time. The fact that social media obscures this and treats happiness as if it's part of our personal brand is wildly misleading and sets a dangerous yardstick for those still seeking to discover who they are.

Multiple Identities in the Digital Era

Over the course of writing this book, I've spoken to scores of women who make their living from creating curated images and have heard countless accounts saying that *they too* find it difficult to take social media images with a pinch of salt. Lauren Alexander, LA-based fashion designer and co-founder of casualwear brand LNA, explains: "I know a huge proportion of images that I consume aren't real – I work in the business and I know how much gets retouched, edited and even Facetuned before it makes it on to social. But even though I know that, it's still difficult to remind yourself that those images you are comparing yourself to don't actually exist. It's like you know and don't know at the same time."

Questions around fakery are a huge theme of our zeitgeist, and how they affect our identities is intimately wrapped into the contemporary crisis of trust. As Sara Melotti expands, "The way my life looks on Instagram is not even a close approximation of my real life. It's the same for every other travel blogger too. As a photographer, I know what goes on behind the lens and I know that those pictures take hours to set up. They're planned, staged and not a reflection of anyone's holiday. We *make* these images. None of them are spontaneous shots of my real life. I'm creating them for art and I want to make things pretty. But that doesn't mean everything in my life is pretty – far from that. I know a lot of people are so clueless about what's behind a picture or how the whole social media industry works. A normal person is very vulnerable and it can be a dangerous space for them to be psychologically. When I wrote a post on my blog talking honestly about my experiences, I received something crazy like three thousand messages from my followers. Most of them said, 'I don't feel OK,' or 'I feel like shit.' 'When I open Instagram I want to cry.' There's a reason behind that."

One thing that's worth considering is the idea that these online personas are no less "real" than our offline selves. When discussing the difference between the on- and offline identity with Professor Nicole Ellison she raised a pertinent point: "The phrase 'in real life' always bothers me because the insinuation is that there is this authentic face-to-face embodied reality and then anything that happens through mediated channels is somehow fake or deceptive or un-connected to our offline self. The online realm is not a separate sphere of activity in the 'virtual' world, as distinct from the 'real' one. Rather, online activities are as 'real' as those that take place offline (face-to-face). After all it's a person sitting at the computer typing; it's not a robot."

This idea has plenty of research support. There are studies which prove we're unable to hide our personalities online in the long run, that extroverted or introverted tendencies can be determined from our Facebook likes, and emotional stability can be inferred from our tweets. Whether on- or offline, we can't entirely hide from who we are. As Tomas Chamorro-Premuzic, professor of business psychology at University College London and Columbia University, and an authority in psychological profiling, wrote in the *Guardian*, "Although our digital identity may be fragmented, it seems clear that our various online personas are all digital breadcrumbs of the same persona; different symptoms of our same core self."

When it comes to living multiple realities and struggling to locate this "core self", I can certainly relate. My twenties were a process of coming to terms with my current identity, which has really ended up being an amalgam of all the different versions of myself – a sum of constituent parts. It was also a time for shedding shame and embarrassment about where I'd come from and where I'd been in between. Like lots of upwardly mobile people, I've had my fair share of identities over the course of my 34 years. As a teenager living in suburban south-east London, I was constantly trying on tribal identities, desperate to find one that fitted. By the turn of the millennium, I was firmly part of the garage music scene, dressed every Friday in skin-tight jeans by Moschino, sparkly going-out tops and loafers with no socks. I could not wear enough gold, use enough gel in my fringe or make my acrylic French tips any squarer. My accent was heavily accented estuary and the guys I liked were all "bad boys done good". From a cultural and aesthetic perspective, my identity was firmly working class and very much related to my childhood and teenage experiences within my family context.

University changed all that almost immediately. A large part of it was because I was ready to shed my suburban skin and become a new version of myself. I definitely didn't want the same life as my contemporaries back home and in that vein quickly realized that certain social airs and graces would help me get closer to what I wanted in life. My accent changed. I was basically a mid-2000s Eliza Doolittle and I worked tirelessly and consciously to develop a new identity for myself. Whereas social mobility is seen as a positive – something politicians write lengthy manifestos about promoting – the idea of leaving your roots behind and trying to climb to the next rung of opportunity is conversely seen as something shameful and inauthentic. While we like to preach the idea that you can "be anything you want to be" in our real lives, the truth is that there is a social stigma attached to self-invention as if it's a con.

There's no doubt that along with my new identity came a fear of being found out. Of course, there was no digital trail in 2002 to point to my true beginnings and no online shots of all that gold jewellery I used to wear to suggest my previous identity. No-one really ever "found out" about where I grew up or what my family was like. As far as anyone I met in my new circle knew, I came from the same background as them and I was keen for them to continue to think that. I was definitely conflicted about the modesty of where I came from, mostly because at the time I felt it would close off the route to a future I aspired to. So, I exaggerated my skiing abilities and hid broad elements of my "true" identity from the rest of the world. It was, of course, a phase and, as I matured, several other versions of who I am were thrown into the mix. But ultimately, I truly believe there is nothing wrong with playing slightly loose and free with your personal history, especially when you are a young person incubating your adult sense of self – a little bit of creativity is totally normal rather than calculated or "fake".

Curating Yourself into Anxiety

Aside from the tensions in trying to conceal the trickier elements of our lives, there are other potential problems when you're not projecting your "offline self" online. For some, the differences between their "lived" life and their perceived life start to undermine their grasp on reality, leading, for example, to huge overspending to keep up the façade. For others, a perceived shortfall in the offline self in comparison to the online version can unravel their self-esteem: six in ten girls now say they feel prettier online than they do offline. I'd argue this is because they're so deeply involved with their digital projection that they've lost track of what *is* performance and what is *not*.

When you invent your own narrative, the issue of exposure also becomes an understandable anxiety and this is the case online as it is in offline life. Of all generations, millennials are those most likely to have feelings associated with inadequacy, and 70 per cent are said to display traits of what is known as impostor syndrome (the persistent feeling that you don't deserve your achievements or success). One of the reasons attributed to this prevalence is social media comparison; in a 2014 poll conducted by the UK disability charity Scope, 62 per cent of participants said that social media made them feel inadequate about their own lives and achievements. But these feelings of fraudulence are also being caused by the projections of our own relentless perfectionism. Comparing your offline self to the online self you've created has added yet another layer to self-critique, leading to what can only be described as "self-curation anxiety". This is a type of disquiet generated by attempts to live up to the edited version of ourselves we project online.

Professor Nicole Ellison notes, "When individuals ignore their face-to-face environment or community and pour all of their energies into ersatz, fake connections it can be problematic for their identity construction. And if, for instance, they feel like their online self is not authentic, it can also be deeply distressing." A blogger who asked to remain anonymous told me that scrolling through her feed made her feel deep feelings of worry because all she could see was the pretence; her "mediocre and uninteresting" offline life was so far away from what it seemed on social media that she felt constantly ill at ease whenever she posted in case someone "found her out".

As vast numbers of people are opening themselves up to unprecedented levels of public scrutiny, that "unmasking" can come from several corners of the web. "Calling out" people online has become a whole culture in itself. From comments boxes to internet forums, entire communities exist online to keep us in our place and reveal what we are "really" like.

"YouTube audiences are incredibly engaged and perceptive, but a lot of what people say about you and assume isn't accurate at all," explains Lizzy Hadfield, a British blogger and vlogger with over 190k followers on Instagram and over 110k subscribers on the video sharing site. "Of course, it's only natural to speculate, but it's definitely strange reading other people's ideas about your identity. As an example, I recently addressed a comment which accused me of having my lips 'done'. The comment accused me of lying to my audience and basically said that I wasn't a trustworthy person – and that really got to me because that's an important part of my identity. The idea that other people might think I was a liar made me feel really paranoid. When you read forums like Guru Gossip [a site for fans and haters to celebrate or take down YouTube stars] and see all these comments about who you 'really' are, it can be so hard not to respond when something has been said that's way off the mark. The truth is that you're allowed to create whatever persona you want online – there's no law about being a carbon copy of your offline self. When it comes to YouTube, the viewer is always two steps removed, in the sense the camera is the first removal then you have the editing process. There is so much that can be changed and altered about the way you want to present yourself, so people have to realize they don't actually know everything about you."

Cynthia Johnson, a personal branding specialist, says that it's virtually impossible to reflect an entirely accurate version of yourself online. "In the digital age, we have to consider the technology that can lead to miscommunication and misunderstanding about who we are and what we want". Feeling anxiety around other people's perceptions of us is entirely understandable, but more often than not it's something that is out of our control. And that's worth keeping in mind, whether you're on- or offline.

You Don't Own Me: The Evolution of Identity Perception

The idea of "familiar strangers" – people within your community who feel they have a claim to you, or that they know you *even when you haven't met* – was first introduced by American social psychologist Stanley Milgram in 1972. Back when he was writing, the concept was tied to the people that you regularly share a physical space with – your daily commuter train, for example. You wouldn't call them acquaintances, but if you ran into them out of context you'd feel a quasi connection and a sense of who they were. Today, his theory has been applied to the digital realm, with Theresa Senft, senior lecturer in social media at Macquarie University in Sydney, describing a related "strange familiarity" among those who have shared a *digital* space arising from "exchanging private information with people from whom we are otherwise remote". She suggests that social media connections with people we don't know offline, "rework the old question 'Who am I?' to read 'Who do you think I am?' Identity, once believed to be the property of the bearer, now belongs to the perceiver." Basically, other people who have consumed your identity in a public digital space feel a sense of ownership over who you are. They believe that they know you inherently and are both elated when their assessment of you rings true and deflated when you behave in a way they didn't expect. By performing for them you can also give up a sense of responsibility for who you are, instead leaning on a model of how others see you. This is our generation's version of living for your family's expectations rather than your true desires.

For me, personally, the early evolution of my identity didn't really happen on social media – sure, you can scroll back through my

Facebook, but by the time I'd signed up, I was in my final year of university and had tussled with lots of my demons. While the photos from my teens and early twenties might be a bit embarrassing, none of them have had any bearing on how people see me today or could be used to prove who I "really am". No-one can stalk my accounts and accuse me of having "changed" (as if that's a bad thing). Now I have the maturity and self-confidence to feel incredibly proud of where I come from and have no shame in the steps it took me to get from there to here. The fact that my parents grew up in council houses and that I'm the first of my family to go to university is something I wear on my sleeve, and the experiences and friends I've made through my different identity phases have enriched my life and created a truly eccentric circle of people from all walks.

It's easy to say that from this side of the journey, and I don't doubt that some of the doors that were opened to me might have stayed closed if I'd been less opaque about my background and identity at different stages of my social and working life. And there have been blips. For most of my twenties, my identity was wrapped up in my life with my ex-husband, and rebuilding who I was after our divorce was tricky. In some ways, I find it hard to identify with the young girl I was back then, and it does sometimes feel like it was a totally different person who walked down the aisle and struggled through an unhappy marriage. However, in lots of ways the early setbacks have enabled me to rebuild my identity as an adult, free from the misdemeanours of my youth.

Living with someone or being in a circle of people who have known you since you were an adolescent can hold you back from continuing to develop your identity. Everyone has friends who want to remind them of things they said or did back in the day. In a similar way, acting as an open record of our past identities, social media binds us to the previous incarnations of our former selves. Whereas once a battered photo album or yearbook would have been the only proof of who we once were, now the whole world can back-stalk and pass judgement on our "true" nature with a simple scroll of the thumb.

Ultimately, we are all products of our pasts, presents and futures, and our identities combine both our roots and aspirations. Very few of us are facsimiles of our parents and many of us want the ability to construct our own sense of self, liberated from the people we used to be and know. That process is something which happens throughout our lives. Indeed, Harvard psychologist Daniel Gilbert has gone so far as to suggest, in his 2014 TED Talk, that "human beings are works in progress that mistakenly think they're finished", and that our "who we are" is much more fluid than we could ever guess. Identity, in his reading, isn't a fixed point, but an ever-changing concept, which we tinker and tailor over our lifetimes. I'm lucky that my identity growing pains have had no lasting impact on how authentic I'm perceived to be, but children and young adults no longer have that luxury. Looking back, I just didn't know who I was yet in my twenties – for the majority of us it takes years of experimentation and introspection to come to any solid conclusions on our own identities, and that is a process we should all have the right to go through without others' perceptions muddying the waters.

LA-based blogger and influencer Courtney Trop is known for her originality, but she found the journey to self-expression on social media fraught with challenges: "When you change on social media people have a hard time accepting it, because they fell in love with you at one point – or who they thought you were – so they feel a sense that they can count on you to be the same. If something shifts, it's like they are almost offended by it, as if there's a sense of betrayal. For example, whenever I change my hair some of my followers freak out and I get people saying that they wish I would keep it the same or that they preferred who I was or how I looked before. From a social media perspective, if you change your identity you have to accept that you may lose some of your audience who no longer identify with you – that's the price you pay for being yourself. But the alternative is just doing what your followers want to see, which is basically living your life for other people. The idea that you can be consistent to one identity is crazy, and kids growing up now – even the ones with huge followings –

are going to change. Yes, with the internet things are there forever, but they shouldn't have to define you. The sad thing is that for some people it's hard to see past your past."

We all have reputations – within our industries or social spheres – whether we like it or not. What makes a personal brand different is the conscious projection and positive manipulation of our skills and achievements and the focus on consistency and repetition. The problem with commodifying your identity is that "personal brands" are subject to all the rules that normal brands are. Authenticity is established through consistent and reliable values; a flip-flop in attitude or aesthetic will lose audience trust and affection. When we construct a social media persona or brand, to be recognized as authentic means creating a very clear and unwavering USP. You're either a hippy, beachy girl with a penchant for vegan treats or a fitness fan with a proclivity for sharing gym gear. If you've built a personal brand on wellness then start posting about KFC, people won't believe in you. If we all only have this 15 minutes of fame, we can't be confused about what we stand for or how an audience perceives us.

Offline life, however, is consistently inconsistent and throws us curveballs along the way. Whether it's something negative or positive, your reality can change on a heel spin, and so can elements of your identity. You can fall pregnant or experience a change in financial circumstances. You might change religion or sexuality, split from a stable family unit or simply alter your hair colour. All these things could be seen to change your identity and your personal brand, and if that suggests inauthenticity to those who know or follow you, that's something that can "damage" both your digital reputation and your brand equity. The desire to be authentic yet appeal to as many people as possible seems to be inherently contradictory, and the pressure that "personal branding" is putting us all under is sure to shape identity construction over the next decade. As Cynthia Johnson rightly argues, "You cannot spend every day trying to be authentic. Trying to be authentic will push you to lose your authenticity, and your mind. Brands strive to be more like people and not the other way around. My advice is don't try to be a brand, because every person is already better than the best brand out there."

Incubating Identity:
How Social Media Can Foster Self-Expression

It would be remiss not to mention the ways in which social media can play a positive role in identity formation. The relative ease with which marginal groups can connect in comparison to the offline context has to be one of the digital world's biggest selling points. As Nicole Ellison says, "There's a clear case to be made for social media in terms of supporting young people doing identity work. A good example would be an adolescent struggling with coming to terms with their sexual orientation living in a small town with no-one to talk to. The fact that they can go online and access people who share elements of that identity and get questions answered has huge potential to be positive for identity construction. The ability to express an aspect of the self which may feel very important and fundamental to a person's identity but isn't able to be expressed in a face-to-face environment is a game-changer." There's no doubt that social media, and indeed the internet, has forged new bonds of subcultural and minority-culture belonging, bringing people from disparate backgrounds together and offering a sense of hope and understanding for those in a normative cultural environment.

The key to finding confidence in your identity through social media is all about vulnerability, as blogger Freddie Harrel explains. "When I started out, I wasn't immediately so honest and upfront about who I was. At the beginning, I shared less of my personal life and career, but this platform has encouraged me to speak up more about my personal experiences. It's very easy to let Instagram turn [your identity] into something which works against you. If you display a life or identity that isn't your own – that you're always happy and you have everything you could every want – then you have to be able to maintain that. Obviously because you are human and have a normal life and have your mental health to look after, it's nearly impossible to keep up the lie and it's definitely not good for you. But by showing my vulnerability, I've found like-minded people who are going through the same things as me and their support has changed my life and how I feel about myself. If you are able to face your insecurities and your lows and your struggles, face them head-on and not feel ashamed by them; that's how you become stronger and more confident and truly start to find out who you are."

Research proves that having a high level of comfort with our weaknesses is fundamental to our happiness, yet in many ways social media can encourage a culture of invulnerability. Stepping outside that appears to be paramount in accessing the positive aspects these platforms can offer.

✕ ✕ ✕

Social media can offer a place to articulate who it is you want to be, and that should never be underestimated. But walking the new tightrope of digital identity can also lead to the creation of an online persona which highlights the mundane mediocrity of your everyday. As voyeurs into a realm of best-life scenarios, who doesn't feel that they need to focus on their best angles? The conclusion I hope we can all soon come to is that social media is not the place to go for a 360-degree insight into anyone's life. Struggling with how you define yourself on the new media platforms is something that everyone is grappling with, and worrying about how you are perceived digitally is part of the 21st-century human condition. Who you are is one of life's great questions, and no matter how many self-help books you may have read, the journey to that "core" self is a universal challenge in any and every environment.

Takeaways

1. You can never fully control people's perceptions of you
However aware and careful you are with what you share online, and however well-managed your digital portfolio might be, you can never

stop people forming their own opinions on your identity. Each and every single one of us has a unique lens on to the world, coloured by our personal experiences. Individuals have prejudices fostered over decades, and their attitudes to elements of your makeup often say more about them than you. We know that you cannot please everyone and we've heard that it's impossible to judge unless you've walked in another woman's shoes – but it can be hard to accept that no matter what you do and how you behave, people might form an inaccurate impression of you. This is as true in life as it is online, but the difference in the digital world is that your identity is up for public scrutiny.

Criticism in any form can be hard to take. When it seems entirely unjustified and it's coming from someone who has never met you, it can be even trickier. In the online environment, the key to dealing with judgement starts with separating the constructive from the plain mean. If someone replied to one of your Facebook posts touching on your identity with a thoughtful disagreement complete with considered merits, give it the time of day. If instead you get a barrage of criticism or messages which reveal discriminatory attitudes, ignore them. Either delete or disregard unconstructive criticism, because engaging with aggression will only fan the flames. Make sure you always respond to positive feedback and put the negativity into context – if you've received countless supportive messages, focus entirely on those.

2. Don't let your digital persona overwhelm you

How close is your online identity to your offline identity? Are you merely tinkering with the digital version of your life, or is it pure fiction? Take a long, calm look at what you are curating online and be honest with yourself. Does it feel like hard work to keep up the pretence? Does posting on social media make you feel stressed and under pressure to perform? Do you constantly feel like you have to emphasize some elements of your identity and hide others? Of course, there are benefits in being aware of your digital reputation and identity, but if maintaining a façade is coming at the expense of your mental health it's time to re-address what you are posting.

By all means share what you are passionate about and content that you can relate to. And it's worth reiterating there are no laws against the world you curate online. But if you look at your digital profile and have trouble connecting it with your real life, or, worse, prefer who you are online, this could be adversely impacting your happiness.

So, take time to consider what makes you feel discontented with your current life and identity and try to discover exactly what it is about the online version of you that is so appealing. That is your starting point for potential changes you need to make to your life in order to get to a place where you feel more fulfilled. If you have exaggerated your financial status, your qualifications or interest in certain areas, what can you do to square the circle between the "truth" and the projected reality? Perhaps look into taking a course which could bolster your diploma count or join an offline group to explore your interest. Does an over-emphasized image of your working life actually suggest that you're unhappy in your role and that it might be time to look for the next step? All of these idealized identities that we have created online are a useful window into our aspirations and can often give us pointers to our true goals.

However, if you do feel anxiety about the world you have created, remember you can do something about it, simply by being as true to yourself as possible. If you're going through a rocky moment with your other half, don't feel you have to post a smiling selfie of the two of you; if you're struggling with your career, perhaps rein in the #GirlBoss posts. To a certain extent, you are in control of the pressure that you put on yourself in the pursuit of perfection, so do yourself a favour and keep it real.

3. Cut yourself some slack

If you're only sharing the positives of your life and the socially attractive sides of your identity, you have to be aware that so are the vast majority of other people. It can be so hard to consciously consume other people's projections of their identities and very easy, especially when you're being inundated with imagery, which resonates much more deeply than words, to believe everything you see. But just remember how straightforward it was for you to be selective with what *you* shared and remember everyone else is under the same pressures to present the very best versions of themselves.

Consider interspersing your positive spin with occasional more realistic posts and admissions of challenges. Not only will the people who follow you be more likely to appreciate your candour, but having a more balanced profile will avoid anxiety around having to live up to a constructed ideal. Basically, cut yourself some slack. While I'm not suggesting that you use social media as a platform for a meltdown, showing your humanity won't suddenly make you an outcast either.

4. How to change your identity online

If something life-changing has happened and you wish to reflect it in your online persona, you have two choices. Firstly, you can address the shift and share the experiences which have led to your altered identity – a process which would be recommended by personal brand managers, as it conveys authenticity. "It would be naive to think that you could sweep something under the carpet and that your followers – whether they're friends, family or acquaintances – wouldn't notice," says Lizzy Hadfield. "Often if you don't say anything at all, you can promote more speculation and you do have to protect yourself from things like that getting out of hand." She advises, "If you introduce something online, you have to close the door online too. You don't have to share every detail, but you can be very clear about what's happened and then say, 'We're not talking about it again.'"

A second option is to apply Courtney Trop's school of thought: "My whole thing has always been to change and not even address it. You shouldn't feel that you owe anyone an explanation. Some people will hate on it, but you just have to ignore it and be confident with who you are. The people that are meant to come along with you will and the others... There's an unfollow button right there."

Whether you face an identity shift head-on or refuse to comment, you have to acknowledge that people will speculate and those who were naturally drawn to you may no longer be so interested. That is a natural, logical consequence and not something personal that should feel hurtful.

5. Remember you're only human – and that's *your* asset

What we do and say on the internet can last a lifetime and the ways in which we communicate our identities in the digital environment are definitely important. However, mistakes are a part of life and, for anyone actively engaging on a public platform, there will be times when you make a misstep. Protecting your digital identity from those slip-ups is a whole industry in itself, but if you do feel like you've screwed up and you want to clarify your position on something you've said, you can always apologize. Remember that the online world is only one facet of your existence; the offline world is still out there, and no matter what type of reaction you're experiencing in the digital world, it is not the be all and end all.

To avoid making missteps in the first place, aside from thinking before you tweet, it's worth having some kind of idea how *you* feel most comfortable projecting yourself. Rather than focusing on other people's reception to your posts, try to consciously consider if you are happy with your own digital contributions. What are the causes you are really engaged with? What are your personal values? Are you happy with who you are online? It's also worth considering common courtesy, empathy and not being entirely tone deaf to the context. If a close friend has just been made redundant and she shares it online, perhaps don't immediately post your promotion update. Instead reach out to her and see how she's doing – your news won't be any less impressive next week.

Kindness, whether on- or offline, never goes out of fashion.

Chapter 2:
Why Social Media is Ruining Your **Body Image**

Of all the changes that social media has wrought on modern womanhood, it's the impact on our body image that gets the most press. And little wonder: who hasn't felt the often-daily sting of body inadequacy when scanning feeds chockablock with flawless examples of the female form. The inundation of "perfect" bodies and faces is probably the most prominent issue that any of us using social media has to deal with, and it's often the first issue that women will highlight when describing their social media anxieties. The fact that social media can make you feel bad about how you look is hardly a newsflash – in fact it's just assumed to be part of our new reality. And how could it not be when nearly everyone seems to have the body of a Victoria's Secret model, the wrinkle-free skin of a teenager and the facial features of an A-list leading lady?

In 2015 we uploaded approximately 24 billion selfies to Google's servers. According to recent research, teenage girls in the UK spend on average 84 minutes preparing for selfies every week, and it's estimated that the average millennial will turn their phone camera on themselves over *25,000* times over their lifetime. The impact of consuming and creating these hundreds, thousands, millions of images is only slowly being addressed, but the academic, medical and anecdotal consensus is that we are sitting on a huge health, sociological and psychological time bomb. The sheer scale and volume of images we now view and internalize is fundamentally altering our relationship with our bodies.

Traditional media was previously accused of increasing body image dissatisfaction with its persistent depiction of thin, attractive models –

and it was regularly blamed for the rise in eating disorders. However, the new social platforms have supercharged this situation – we are now so immersed in images of perfection that we have almost no realistic idea what other people look like. And, perhaps even more worrying, we've lost a grip on our own mirror image too.

The use of both in-app tools and Photoshop software to modify our appearance means that the images we upload bear increasingly little resemblance to our actual faces and bodies. How many of your friends do you not really recognize on social media? I'll bet you can list at least a handful who are either a completely different size, or have a different jawline, skin or facial features from the ones you'd find scrolling through their feed. The issue is endemic. When you factor in that it takes less than a second to scroll an image on Instagram and that in five minutes you can consume two to three hundred images, the fact that a good proportion of the pictures featuring a body or face has in some way been edited is obviously going to have an impact on our benchmarks. What we're creating through these images is a pressure cooker of comparison, with unreachable levels of perfection. Is it any surprise that all this self-documentation is sending us into a pit of self-loathing and body-dysmorphic despair?

But for some reason we aren't addressing the issue head-on. Somehow the crisis has become so normalized that, among the girls and women it affects, it's almost a cliché to mention the extent of its bearing – more likely to elicit a reaction of "obviously" than a critical appraisal. Conversely, among older generations, policy makers and those not au fait with these platforms the issue seems overblown. They think it can't really be that bad – after all it's only a few bikini pictures, isn't it? Neither of those vantage points enables us to tackle the very real problems which are having such a profound impact on women across the globe. It is neither normal nor exaggerated. It is in fact one of the biggest contemporary challenges that women in every country that has Wi-Fi are contending with. And it's time we all wake up to it.

You Must Love Yourself to Post That...

There's a common misconception that posting images of yourself – especially body shots and selfies – means you're a show off who thinks you're the shit. However, a slew of recent studies actually proves the opposite is more often the case. A 2017 research paper on the experience of taking and sharing a selfie lays bare the psychological factors at play: the actual act of snapping a selfie has been shown to make us immediately more self-conscious and more aware of how others view us. At the same time, respondents revealed a drop in self-esteem at the very moment of taking the image of themselves. The combination of increased feelings of pressure around how people view you and a process which dents your self-esteem makes for a complex cocktail of emotions far removed from "showing off".

While posting a provocative shot of your cleavage and abs may appear to be the height of vanity, it's often more a reflection of a shaky sense of self-esteem. Elsa Godart, author of *Je Selfie Donc Je Suis* ('I Selfie Therefore I Am'), writes that: "What may look like straight-forward narcissism can often be insecurity and a craving for reassurance: a reassurance that you can only ever get from 'likes'. But you're chasing the dragon, because far from calming any neuroses down (although it may do this for a second), posting another selfie will only amplify them." A narcissism which is about desperately *wanting* to feel good about yourself isn't the same as actually feeling good about yourself. And really isn't that what everyone's searching for when they post a picture of themselves? Isn't that truly the Holy selfie Grail?

Tune It All Out

How far can you really go with retouching your own images these days? The answer is as far as you want – and you don't even have to have any Photoshop skills, or a computer. Today you can do it all on your phone on the go. Up to 57 per cent of women say that they crop, filter or doctor their pictures, and Dr Pippa Hugo, a leading eating disorder consultant at Priory Hospital Roehampton, says as many as nine out of ten teenage girls now digitally enhance social media images of themselves – with filters or specially designed on-phone apps before they share them. With names like Perfect365, Facetune, ModiFace and Visage Lab, these apps can dramatically doctor body and face images, whitening your teeth, slimming your nose, smoothing your cellulite and nipping in your waist until you've created a Barbie-fied version of yourself.

The first time I saw the app Facetune, I thought it was a laugh – the kind of thing you'd play with to turn yourself into a Pokémon character. But I soon realized that it could be insanely dangerous. What could start out as a tweak here and there might soon evolve into a highly skilled operation of skin smoothing, waist trimming and leg lengthening until any average woman is suddenly transformed into a professional model with an Amazonian physique. Over six million people downloaded the first version of the app and it was the fourth highest seller in 2016. Facetune 2 allows you to enlarge or shrink your eyes, nose and mouth and reshape your entire face. You can change the colour of your irises, add studio lighting, while refining your figure in a manner which won't distort the backdrop (often a telltale sign of retouching). It is startling how much "better" you can make yourself look. As for how many people are using it, Facetune 2 costs £32.99/$20 for the year at the time of writing, so no-one's downloading it for a one-off giggle any more. It's an open secret among influencers that nearly *everyone* uses it to some extent, though admittedly some are more subtle and skilful in their use of it than others.

One issue is that the use of these apps is creating unrealistic "memories" of your own face and body. The images stored on your phones never actually happened. You never had thighs that slim or skin that glowing – but it can be easy to start believing that once upon a time you were that "perfect". This leads to a world where young women are holding themselves up to scrutiny not just against the images that other people have edited and posted, but also against the images of *themselves* which they have edited. In this context, it's no wonder that the consumption of these visuals can make women feel overweight and unattractive: the mirror can never compete. "Social media has made us want to look like other people – but those people don't even look like that," influencer and mental health campaigner Roxie Nafousi says. "What we're lusting over is so blurred and edited and, even though we know that to an extent, it can still distort our frame of reference."

The use of these "cosmetic surgery" apps is also creating a "list" of flaws in our physical attributes, and making us all hyperaware of what we feel we could change about our appearance. Lauren Alexander explained to me: "Social media has brought a lot of LA culture to the rest of the world. Here it's completely normalized to want to change your body and your face – we have a phrase, 'you're not ugly, you're just poor.' There is such an emphasis on self-improvement and striving for perfection. Growing up I would never sit around a table with friends and talk about Botox or peels or plastic surgery, and now that's entirely usual. When I first moved here, I remember being asked why I didn't do Botox, have a nutritionist or a personal trainer. Those things were just assumed, and now social media has made the rest of the world feel they need it all too. It's impossible not to wonder: if everyone else is doing it, why aren't I? When you add up the personal trainer, barre-method classes, gym membership, hair appointments, the supplements, Botox, facials and lasers, it becomes a full-time job just to keep up with it all."

Going one step further, Beverly Hills expert in rhinoplasty Dr Deepak Dugar (who was trained by Dr Raj Kanodia, the surgeon known for his work on A-listers, reportedly including Cameron Diaz and Jennifer Aniston) says, "social media has definitely normalized plastic surgery. Before, people used to think, 'Oh, plastic surgery is just for these LA people or London people, but that's not for us.' There was a sense that it was only for an elite. What these new platforms have done is pull back the veil to show that anyone can do it. You can see the pre and post videos and the before and after results on average people – not just celebrities. The entire world, from Russia to the Middle East to Europe and across the States, has seen a shift in accessibility and availability of procedures – simply because social media has made it seem more accessible and available. There's a new sense of democracy."

However, the selfie culture, particularly the use of editing apps, has also led to a worrying trend, Dr Dugar explains. "Apps like Facetune have given an unrealistic expectation of what we want to look like. We've all had times when a friend has taken a photo and we don't like the way we look. The problem is that if you take that to a deep level where you don't like any photo of yourself and you find yourself editing every single picture of yourself, you end up creating unrealistic expectations. And often surgery can't address that. There's no way to 'fix' a face. If you don't like your nose and lips – then I think it can be very healthy to address it, conquer it and move on and feel empowered. But the problem is that social media breeds a situation in which most people don't have a specific issue they can pinpoint – it's generally that they don't like the way they look *overall*. At that point, I truly believe it's unhealthy to be doing any procedures."

If She Can Have It, Why Can't I?

In the case of body image, social comparison certainly plays an important part: a 2014 study for US *Glamour* magazine found that 64 per cent of women said looking at pictures on sites like Facebook and Instagram made them have negative thoughts about their body. Comments from the study include this insight: "With actresses, I know they have a personal chef and trainer and it's their job to have the bodies they do – I don't have any real expectations of looking like them. With people I know, it's like, well, she did it. Why can't I?"

LA clinical psychologist Dr Jessica Zucker explains: "The anonymous woman [on social media] could be anyone, so your expectations change. It's hard not to go straight to 'I wish I looked like her,' or 'what can I do to look like her?' All the self-loathing and hatred this generates could even trigger issues around what someone is eating – or not eating – that day. It can be very complex. On social media, you'll also often find a focus on specific body parts. Women are chopped up in general in the media – and we're all aware that some areas of society only value women as tits and ass. But now it's thigh gaps, clavicles and bikini bridges under the microscope. We typically see images of flawless female body parts tailored to titillate the opposite sex as if they're not full people and we've internalized so many of these ideas. We live in such a patriarchal world, there's no way around the inherent bias. It's almost impossible not to soak up these viewpoints then express them in a way that leads us to survey ourselves and have negative feelings about our bodies."

And this is where the millennial experience is distinct from previous generation's issues around magazine retouching and altering. It is the omnipresence of these seemingly "relatable" images of myopic perfection which defines their consumption.

One of the most challenging aspects of digital body image is that these women with perfect figures that we're aspiring to are women and girls all around us. They go to our gyms, they work in our offices and they date our exes. For millennials, it's the girl next door who has the thigh gap, her BFF's sister who has the washboard abs. It is this systemic peer-to-peer comparison and false sense of reality that makes us feel we're failing if our life doesn't match up to what we see. The closeness which we often feel with our favourite YouTubers and Instagram stars, and the fact that they seem so resolutely "normal" and "just like us", further reiterates the fact that our lives and bodies are lacking in some way. Social media has created an intimate window into the female form, but those that rise to the "top" (gaining the most likes from their communities and thus boosted in feeds by the platform's algorithm architecture) are those that fulfil a popularized, mainstream idea of what a "good body" is. The bombardment of specific body types in the media is nothing new, but the reaffirmation of those often unattainable shapes via social media is more pernicious in its omnipresence than ever before.

Lucy Williams, a London-based blogger, is known for a particular brand of effortless cool with a side of wanderlust. But even as a #BikiniInspo pinup, she feels the pressures of perfection and comparison: "Like everyone else, I am totally impacted by what I consume on social media and I look at those girls on Instagram with minute waists and endless limbs, comparing myself and coming up short – it's impossible not to. There is no such thing as a perfect body, and I am 100 per cent not an owner of one, even if it did exist. The perfect that people usually think of is basically the Photoshop look: no stretchmarks, no cellulite, no rolls. I have rolls on my tummy, I have dimples on my thighs and the more women I hang out with the more I realize that everyone has the same to a certain degree. Confidence doesn't come from the numbers on the scales, it comes from acceptance – and social media can make that hard to find, no matter what your size."

So how deeply does this crisis penetrate? A 2016 study found that out of 1,765 Americans aged 19–32, those who spent more time on social media were 2.2 times more likely to report eating and body-image concerns. Among the most active users, that jumped to 2.6 times more issues. What's more, a study of 960 college women found that even *20 minutes* of scrolling on Facebook was associated with higher levels of disordered eating. Unsurprisingly, it was the women who placed greater importance on receiving comments and "likes" on their status updates and untagged photos of themselves who reported the highest levels of disordered eating.

Claire Mysko, CEO of the New York-based National Eating Disorders Association, said in *USA Today*, "We live in a culture where eating disorders thrive because of the messages we're exposed to. Social media heightens that exposure. Before [a girl or woman] would do [disordered eating behaviour] in isolation or with a classmate. Now you can log on and see what thousands of people are doing. It changes the game." In 2015 the UK's National Health Service released figures showing the number of teenage admissions into hospital for eating disorders had nearly doubled over the previous three years. When you consider that anorexia has the highest mortality rate for any mental illness – one in five anorexics will die either from physical complications associated with the disease or suicide and in the US every 62 minutes someone dies as a direct result of an eating disorder – the magnitude of the issue becomes apparent. And there's no fudge here; healthcare professionals are *directly* blaming social media for the increase in admissions. This is something that we should not just be aware of but should be actively campaigning to change.

A Personal Obsession

My list of newly adopted hang-ups is something that I've only developed because of looking at social media pictures of myself that bit too hard. I've actually never been one for too much mirror gazing – in fact I'll often get home in the evening and find a smear of newsprint across my cheek – but when you take so many pictures of yourself and have them stored on a reel of thousands of zoom-able shots on your phone, it's easy to start to identify "problem" body parts. From there it's a simple step to becoming consumed with tiny body and face features, which in the bigger picture are almost entirely inconsequential. But social media culture can make us ultra aware of all sorts of things we wouldn't have batted an eyelid at before, and if that imagery is the first thing we look at when we wake up in the morning and the last thing we see before we go to sleep, it takes a steely confidence not to be sucked into the vortex.

In truth, I have spent the vast majority of my life obsessed with my weight. Over the course of my 34 years there have been times when this preoccupation teetered over the edge into the abyss of self-destruction, at other times, especially during my thirties, it subsided to the dull ache of an omnipresent worry. Although I'm well-aware I'm not the first person to feel this way, it's deeply embarrassing to admit quite how much I've thought about my body over the course of my life. While boyfriends and jobs have come and gone and I've moved across continents and scaled career ladders, worries about my BMI have remained a steadfast theme, consuming my thoughts whenever I'm at a low ebb.

Growing up, health wasn't just a distant concern to be dealt with in middle age; it was directly correlated to how I looked. As a teenage smoker and obsessive calorie counter, exercise was what you did to fit into jeans, not to feel strong. Higher education offered few chances for reform, and during this period I ate one single, specific meal every night – a "Salmon Cottage Pie" ready meal with 348 calories per serving. Ironically, I also regularly consumed entire bars of chocolate and bottles of white wine, so to say my diet logic was faulty is somewhat the understatement.

Post-university, my supermarket shopping became a little more varied. Instead of just one meal, I bought all the meals. My weight fluctuated dramatically, which unsurprisingly made me feel appalling. I can remember when my mum got married we had to lop the bottom of my bridesmaid's dress off and stitch the fabric up the sides as I'd gone from a size eight to twelve in the three months between fittings – I'd gained more than 15lb (6.8kg) and couldn't fit into a single pair of my jeans. I'd then skip meals, smoke a lot and lose a stone (6kg) just as quickly. The whole sorry yo-yo thing consumed my every waking hour; my looks oscillated from bloated to sickly, and I suffered from near-constant stomach gripes. While my weight was never a medical concern, and I'm aware that, at 5ft 3in (160cm), a UK size 12 (US 8) is close to the average size of a 22-year-old woman, it was my whole attitude and the anxiety that came with it that was truly unhealthy. I could wake up at 2.30am and spend the hours until my alarm went off devising ways to get thinner. Or else just use the time to hate myself. Thinking about it now makes me feel incredibly depressed.

While I managed to quit the daily pack of cigarettes, as for exercise, that went out the window completely as soon as I left high school. Any vigorous movement was absent from my life until I was around 29. It was at this point that I realized that a part of my bottom no longer fitted into my knickers; in fact both cheeks had begun to slide inexorably down towards the backs of my knees. My calves were totally lacking elasticity and I couldn't do a single sit- or push-up. Combined with grey, congested skin and a pain in my hips that nothing, not even four G&Ts, could cure, I finally made the decision that it was time to seriously do something about my lifestyle.

This story might be hard to believe if you look at my Instagram page. People have often commented in the past that my body looks great on social media and said how envious they are, which makes me feel both validated and uncomfortable. Because, while it's true I'm happier with my body than when I was in my twenties – though see below for caveats – it hasn't been a straightforward road to get to where I am now, either psychologically or physically. I started small and over the past few years have significantly changed my attitude to my wellbeing. While my nutrition obviously needed an overhaul, it was exercise that really started the whole ball rolling. Sometimes I've loved it, sometimes it's felt like a drag, but overall fitness has provided a positive anchor in my life and helped me weather all sorts of emotional storms. Due to exercise, I've had periods when I no longer thought or talked about food all day long and, for about three years before my pregnancy, my weight stayed within a 5lb (2.3kg) range – something which helped exorcize a lot of demons (no pun intended). During those times, I've felt proud of parts of my body and how far I've come and have been able to let more things go. I haven't obsessed about exactly how thin my legs looked in a picture or worried as deeply about my cellulite. But I've never stopped being critical – no matter if I weighed under 7st (44.5kg) or over 9st (57.1kg), there have always been flaws I've perceived with my body.

The things I fixate on now have become increasingly bizarre, and without a doubt that's down to the fact that I've started taking so many pictures of myself for Instagram. For example, I'm obsessed with my knees – specifically the pocket of fat that sits at the thigh and knee join. It is the only thing I look at in pictures and I'm continually conscious of the strange "knee vaginas" or "knee baby faces" I can see in them (both terms coined on social media). Back in the day when I was a calorie counter, I had no specific problem with any part of my legs – but now I'm in better shape than I ever was in my youth, I'm endlessly googling "knee liposuction". I also want a brace for my "Nanny McPhee" teeth (which I used to see as British and charming), I've just got my eyebrows microbladed (I certainly hadn't considered this in the pre-selfie era as I have a fringe) and I can imagine a world in which I might have a different nose – all because I turn the camera on my face more than once a day.

Objectively speaking, I know that there is nothing wrong with the way I look. But this isn't about objectivity. I'm talking about the impact that a barrage of images of "perfection" can have on your subjective standards of beauty and the result these standards can have on your self-perception. Social media has changed our notions of beauty and created a culture in which we are blitzed with this ideal. "There is an onslaught of beauty pressures that bombard girls' daily lives," says Laura Choate, author of "Swimming Upstream: Parenting Girls for Resilience in a Toxic Culture", in *Psychology Today*. "If they listen to these messages, they come to believe two things: (a) I should look like this and if I did, I would be happier, and (b) practically anyone can look like this if they work hard enough and buy the right products and merchandise. So not only do many girls start to believe that they should be focused on attaining the 'perfect physique', they also believe something is wrong with them if they are somehow unable to reach this goal. And they develop a negative body image as a result." Who can't relate to that thought process?

And it's not just comparing your body against other people's bodies that can cause issues. Before, we only had our "thin jeans" to taunt us and perhaps holiday snaps to remind us of when we were in good shape. Now our iPhones and iCloud accounts are packed with photo diaries of our own looks captured on a near-daily, if not weekly, basis. I got my first iPhone five years before I had grey hairs or wrinkles. Aside from being able to see myself age 27, I also have a record of what my body looked like, offering ample not-so-flattering compare-and-contrast opportunities. This digital record of thousands of pictures, as opposed to the 26 or so we printed at a time from our disposable cameras, means we are locked into a battle with reality and construction, which would have been unthinkable in the pre-digital, pre-social media age.

Girl on Girl

An interesting departure here is that in many ways the male gaze has been moderated by the advent of social media sites like Instagram, which have a female-heavy demographic. While there's no doubt that social media still acts as a platform for us to showcase our attributes to potential partners (not forgetting the identities we create through images selected for online dating profiles), it's often female-to-female validation that women are looking for with their posts. My personal profile has an 85 per cent female demographic, and I've found that the "sexier" images create less engagement. Of course, that doesn't mean that you can't find pornographic or hyper-sexualized images of women on Instagram – it's just that the main audience is less concerned with cleavage. While there are, of course, pockets of communities across all social media platforms in which more curvy, Kardashian-esque (usually equally unobtainable) figures are increasingly aspired to, there is one body type that continues to be ubiquitous: fit, thin and rigorously gym-toned.

Some of this can be blamed on the advent of #fitspo. We've all seen the #FitNotThin hashtag so beloved by fitspiration and wellness bloggers, and it's clear that social media has helped up the level of muscle tone now considered to be necessary for an ideal physique. However, while this development has been applauded, the influence of "fitspo" bodies has been more complicated. In a 2016 study, researchers coded a set of six hundred "fitspiration images" taken from Instagram for body type, activity and objectification. The results showed that the majority of images of women contained only one body type: thin and toned; the 2.0 body may be masquerading as something new, but it's still the extremely limited version of beauty we've been consuming for decades – just with a 21st-century tweak. In a 2015 study, researchers found that viewing images of this new beauty standard of athleticism is just as bad from a self-worth perspective as exposure to simply thin women if the athletic women pictured are "*both* muscular and slim". The mantra "strong is the new skinny" is a misnomer. What we really mean is "strong but *still skinny* is the new skinny".

The truth is that these images don't make most women feel empowered and motivated; instead they just make them feel depressed. A survey of 276 Australian and American women aged 18–25 found that the more often participants looked at "fitspo" images, the more likely they were to be unhappy with their own bodies, and a 2017 research article showed a clear link between orthorexia nervosa (an obsession with "clean" or healthy eating) and fitspiration image consumption.

"Of course, social media has played a massive part in the shift in recent attitudes to fitness – and health," says Pip Black, co-founder of London-based Frame gyms. "There are a lot of beautiful, slim girls on social media who are naturally toned and lean. Yes, they work out regularly, but the truth is that they'd look great either way. And they are followed by thousands and thousands of other women – many of them young, impressionable girls who see that body shape as the norm. It's not like back in the 2000s when everyone wanted to be super skinny – now we all have to have a six-pack. But this time around, a lot of disordered eating and excessive exercise passes as acceptable under the banner of 'fitspo'."

Pip explains how a focus on matching up to the bodies we see on social media can totally transform a woman's life. "Exercise today is always, always about getting 'the body'. For us that's something that's really discouraging. Often you will find that people in their peak 'super slim' shape are working out like that and not eating enough because they're not happy. They're putting all of their efforts into being totally internalized and thinking they can control at least this one area of their life. It's not anorexia, but it's disordered eating to varying degrees. That's just not something anyone should aspire to, no matter what it looks like on social media."

There are other dangers to this new body type for women's health which go beyond self-worth. Joan Murphy, Pip's co-founder at Frame, highlights an issue which we are definitely not talking about enough, and one which I can definitely relate to: "When it comes to striving for a six-pack, people are often only considering the now and what they see in the mirror in front of them. They're not thinking about fertility, bone density or gut health. The sorts of things that go along with cutting out major food groups and stripping things out of your diet. And, even more worryingly, women are taking their cues from people in the world of social media who don't have either the experience or training to advise others."

Last year I experienced a knock to my battle to conquer my body issues because of a struggle to conceive. The first advice from my fertility doctor was to ease off the exercise routine because – something that we don't think of when we're rabidly consuming Instagram bikini shots – too much exercise can harm your fertility. And, for some people, too much exercise doesn't mean doing an Ironman. Achieving the "fitspo" look of a flat tummy with defined abs, long, lean arms and legs, a gravity-defying bum and a photographic clavicle – basically all the things that look good on Instagram – can come at a cost to your monthly cycle. While every woman is different and will be affected differently by exercise, for me personally, whenever I've got closest to achieving all those things at once, my periods stop. While some super-toned, slim women, including models, dancers, athletes, gymnasts and #fitspo girls who look great on the beach, may not find their fertility is impacted by their workouts, others – like me – will. Just because a body can look fit and aspirational on social media doesn't mean it is actually functioning in a healthy way.

If I do a lot of cardio, I don't ovulate. It makes sense in the context of fight or flight – if you've got all that cortisol and adrenaline running through your body, it doesn't exactly suggest, "Time to get up the duff," to your highly sensitive reproductive organs. My low fat-to-muscle ratio and exercise routine may also have contributed to a condition called luteal phase defect, which often combines late ovulation with a shortened second half of your cycle. Without treatment for this, I wouldn't have been able to ever conceive. It's hard not to blame myself, and my relationship with health and food, for the fact that I struggled to get pregnant. Of course, there's nothing wrong with trying to get fit and feel great about yourself, and of course, some people naturally have a body type which will easily build muscle. But that is not everyone – and striving to achieve a look beyond your natural body shape can be deeply unhealthy.

We need to learn to see our bodies for what they do as much as what they look like. Exercise in a social media context can be one big competitive sham. Wellness should be about feeling "well". Which means not being totally exhausted or killing yourself. As fashion and health blogger, Niomi Smart, explains, "Real health is about the feeling of wellbeing rather than the way you look. It's so easy to be deceived by looks – you can have the fittest looking body but not actually be particularly healthy. I personally don't have a defined six-pack or bulging biceps, but I feel the best version of myself and I know that I'm healthy."

What *does* make you feel good is exercise that is fun *and* manageable. While you might think that isn't possible, it's really a case of trial and error. If you hate something (beyond the moderate burn) don't do it again – but focus on what it is you hate. Was it the pace? Was it the intensity? What would have made it better for you? The first few tries at exercise after a break will inevitably make you feel exhausted – but when you leave, do you feel uplifted?

While I haven't entirely got it figured out, I do believe it is possible to feel a sense of insecurity and reasonably realign your thoughts to a more positive place. If seeing a beautiful girl in a bikini or lingerie makes me feel envious, I try to think about something that I *do* like about my body. If I look through a set of pictures where I see something about my figure that I hate, I try to take a breath and put it into context with the rest of myself and my achievements. Sometimes I fail and go into a spiral. Other times I manage to keep it in check.

It's easy to forget that your own thoughts construct your own reality. If you keep focusing and thinking negatively about something, in the end it will eat away at your esteem and confidence. Exerting discipline over your mind's wanderings is an exhausting task, but it's one of the only ways to recast your frame of reference when it comes to body perception.

#BodyPositivity Rules?

One area of hope for change has been in the body positivity movement led by legions of women disillusioned with the one-size-fits-all standards that social media (as well as other media and society at large) perpetuates. In an attempt to unlearn social stigmas, the body positivity movement is about recasting every body type, shape and size as equally valuable. While the roots of body positivity can be found in the fat acceptance movement, focused on the prejudice that overweight people experience, it's come to encompass all body types. Social media has been integral to the spread of the message, simply because visual platforms like Instagram and Facebook have allowed women to see other women posting confident images of what they really look like, "flaws" and all. From scars to stretchmarks to cellulite, alongside less conventional body shapes, the movement has helped undermine the idea that only slim, toned bodies have a place in public life. Take body activist Kenzie Brenna's #CelluliteSaturday to plus-size blogger Simone Mariposa's Twitter campaign #WeWearWhatWeWant – social media has also encouraged women who struggle with their imperfections to stop endlessly beating themselves up about their bodies.

Callie Thorpe, a successful plus-size blogger, describes how body positivity and digital media completely changed her attitude to her body and dramatically enhanced her self-esteem. "Weight was always an issue for me," she explains. "At the age of nine I was put on steroids and my nan, who raised me, was always a comfort feeder. After she died when I was 13, my problems developed further, because I turned to food to deal with my grief. I was on a diet from around the age of ten and over the years I've punished myself in every way you can imagine. At university things escalated and I was using laxatives and going on ever more extreme diets: cayenne pepper, cabbage soup, just plain starvation – you name it, I tried it. The level of self-hatred and anxiety I felt over those years was just crazy. After trying to lose weight unsuccessfully for a holiday, I finally decided to google 'Plus-Size Swimwear' as I'd never bought a swimsuit before. A plus-size blog called *GabiFresh* popped up and it's not an exaggeration to say that finding it completely changed my life. For the first time in years it felt like I could breathe a bit and I realized that it was time to stop punishing myself."

The body positivity movement has been accused by some of "promoting" obesity, however, as Callie explains, it's more about a sense of pragmatism and a realistic approach which fosters a belief in your right to happiness, no matter what the body you inhabit: "I'm just saying that if you are the size you are, you don't have to kill yourself every day or hate everything about yourself. You can wear a nice dress to your wedding, go to the gym and feel confident in your fashion choices no matter what you look like – and social media has given me the platform to challenge those assumptions. People often accuse me of promoting obesity just because I'm putting myself online. But that just isn't the case. It's also worth saying that my life isn't all buzzy, buzzy self-love, body positivity, bloody perfect every day. Some days I feel shit and worry that an outfit is too tight. Or I'll go to an event and I'll feel out of place as I'm the only woman of my size there and end up leaving. I just have to keep coming back to the truth that I'm trying to be the best version of myself both mentally and physically. If someone doesn't like me because I'm a size 24 [US size 20], I can only feel sorry for them."

Rather than just being confined to the blogosphere and social media, there are signs that the body positivity movement is starting to make inroads into wider attitudes. In 2016, Ashley Graham, a US size 16 (UK 20) model, was featured on one of three *Sports Illustrated* covers in celebration of their annual swimsuit edition, and the insanely unrealistic proportions of the Barbie doll (36-in/91-cm chest, 18-in/46-cm waist, 33-in/84-cm hips) were finally, after nearly 60 years, addressed. As 92 per cent of American girls aged three to twelve have owned one of the iconic dolls, the release of petite, tall and curvy body variations (alongside diverse skin tones and hair types) has been heralded as a win for the body positivity movement. However, it's not all been good news – what the digital world giveth with one hand, it taketh back with the other.

"While social media has changed so many things for me for the better – I've modelled for plus brands, I was the first plus-size columnist for *Marie Claire* and I've managed to build a career around my journey – I've also dealt with a lot of negativity," explains Callie. "Recently I've had a shit ton of abuse because I was featured in *Vogue* and someone wrote an article about it which was shared in a fat-hating forum, leading to more than nine hundred abusive comments. People said I should be tied to a car and dragged along the road. They told me to kill myself, to die. That I'm disgusting, that I don't deserve to be a model or in *Vogue*. That I make them sick. That I'm going to die of diabetes and my husband is going to bury me... Anything you can think of was said. While it's definitely brought me opportunities, social media has also brought me a lot of pain."

The rise of fat-shaming has been the flipside of the "body positivity movement" coin and highlights the issue of cyberbullying, one of the very worst ravages of the digital world, which will be dealt with at length in the next chapter. Needless to say, the negative experiences that women like Callie and other plus-size women go through can have a serious impact on their mental and physical health (it's been proven that stress around excess weight actually encourages over-eating). While communities have increased the visibility of multiple body shapes on social media and can provide a solid support network, we're a long way from liberating women from either social stigma or the beliefs that we've all internalized over years of prejudice.

However, that is not something reserved for just plus-size women or indeed those whose body shape falls outside the accepted standards. It's also worth pointing out that there's a vocal and equally vile "skinny-shaming" mob out there, adding to the truism that no matter what your body, there will be people who reduce you to a set of measurements, which are apparently up for criticism. As Callie articulates, "The truth is the majority of women struggle with their weight no matter what size they are because we are never told that what we are is acceptable. There's always something new that we need to change. When women are slim, but not quite there in terms of the images that are presented by social media – maybe they're a curvy size 10 or 12 [US 6 or 8] – then they can have even worse problems with body image than I do with mine. It's crazy to acknowledge that, because there's obviously a disparity in terms of privilege, and the way people are treated in the world as a thin woman in comparison to being a fat woman. But I can completely see that thinner women can go through equally distressing experiences as I have. For me, I know I will never look like those stick-thin images and I guess there's a sense of liberation in that."

✗ ✗ ✗

The sad reality is that social media puts pressure on every woman, even if you are the one that others are #BodyGoals-ing over, because social media is a hyperspeed reflection of our *prejudiced society*. Fat, thin, toned, soft, pregnant, tall, short, narrow, wide, flat butt, bubble butt, whatever. No-one is immune. Feeling empowered and proud of your body isn't something that is found by fitting into your "thin jeans". A single digit dress size doesn't protect you from the sticks that we use to beat ourselves with – and dealing with issues around body image isn't something that is reserved for tall, short, curvy, over- or underweight body shapes. So, next time you start hating on yourself or let an image of a "beautiful" body torture you, just think: that girl is quite possibly lying awake in bed thinking about her baby face knees at 4.30am. You are *definitely* not the only one struggling.

Takeaways

1. Pause the screens

If you are starting to feel the pervasive effects of social media on your body image and self-esteem, take some time away from your devices. Will social media disappear if you don't look at it for 24 hours? No.

As hard as it might feel to be severed from your social lifeline, regular breaks are good practice in order to regain some perspective and balance. Delete the apps from your phones, tablets and laptops (rather than actually deleting your accounts) and re-download them when you're ready to come back. Nothing will have changed, I promise you.

2. Admit your feelings

Another theme that has cropped up time and time again during my interviews with women working across social media is envy. Jealousy and envy are dirty words in female culture, and to admit you covet what someone else has is tantamount to admitting that you're a bitch. But envy is only an issue when you let it fester and morph into something negative, whereas the pang you might feel when confronted with someone else's achievements or beauty is entirely natural and certainly no indication of meanness. It is completely possible to be happy for someone's fortune while envious of it at the same time. And it's not unusual for another woman's beauty to make you feel inadequate.

"I'm only human and of course when I see an image of Alexis Ren or other models prancing along a beach in skimpy bikinis with the most incredible bodies, I obviously then feel like a potato," says Niomi Smart.

"But then you have to remind yourself that everyone's body is different and comparing yourself to someone with a totally different body shape is such a waste of energy. I'd rather aspire to have the work ethic and ambition of other women rather than their physical appearance."

It's not bitchy to want a different or better life, and ambition can also be an incredible force for good. The issue is when you try and pretend you don't have those feelings and when you replace them with resentment or rejection.

3. Know you are not alone

If you only take away one thing from this chapter – or indeed from this entire book, I would hope it's the fact that *we are all in the same boat.* Or at least in the same fleet of slightly different boats. The pressure that you feel when it comes to body image isn't exclusive to you – it's a broad societal burden that we all have to bear.

This isn't just an issue for one generation – it's for all social media users across extensive age, economic and regional demographics. No-one is immune. Those who have grown up after the social media and mobile phone revolutions won't have experienced a world in which body images *weren't* shoved down their throat, all day, every day. Yet those who were exposed to this new world after they reached adulthood can still be affected in just as powerful ways. If, as we see from the testimonies above, influencers themselves are under the influence, what hope have we all got?

"I'll find that I put up a picture on Instagram looking like I'm really confident, but a day or the week or even an hour before that I might have been crying my eyes out, thinking, 'Oh my God I'm so fat; I'm so disgusting; I want to rip my skin off. I hate myself...' influencer Roxie Nafousi explains. "But then you post a picture and maybe it gets likes and comments and then you get to feel good for a moment. But it's a vicious cycle, because then someone else is obviously going to look at your image and think, 'Oh, she feels great about herself, she loves herself – Why don't *I* love myself?'"

While it's true there has never been a halcyon time when all women loved their bodies, it was inarguably easier to find some context before the onslaught of social media imagery. But this is where we are now, and all you can do is arm yourself with tools to protect yourself from both the new and old body anxieties and strive to find acceptance. Grab a true girlfriend, open a bottle of rosé and share how you're feeling. You're not weird, you're not a loser, you're not a narcissist. You're just a woman living in the 21st century.

However thin, curvy, toned, tight, bodacious or booty-ful you may become, you will never be able to measure up to a body blueprint that often doesn't even exist in real life.

The magic solution isn't some newfangled starvation dirt or food-group elimination method. It's boringly and predictably only an acceptance of what you have that can set you free.

4. Feed your confidence, not your demons

One of the first steps of this practice is to identify the things that you are proud of or else feel a sense of acceptance about. If you can't think of anything, ask a good friend to help you highlight your assets. Write them down and keep them somewhere you can access them – I have mine on my iPhone Notes. Every time you feel those body anxieties creeping in, refer back to the list and say the words to yourself either out loud or in your head. It's all about stopping the thoughts in their tracks and rebalancing the assessment of yourself. Dwell on those things and swirl the positive words around until you feel the "hate-me"s subsiding. It sounds pretty esoteric, and I'm the first to raise a red flag for scepticism, but this one does actually work.

It's also worth remembering that everyone has a completely different lens and vastly varied standards when it comes to ideal bodies and faces. For example, I am relatively flat-chested – something some people feel insecure about. For me personally, however, the opposite is true. I love having small boobs and would never trade them for a larger cup size, even if it were safe, painless and free to do so. A plastic surgeon

I met last year said that in her game you're immediately taught to rid yourself of presumptions about other people's insecurities – a woman might come in with a huge mole on her face, but start talking about unnoticeable stretchmarks. What you see isn't what I see, and vice versa. That's another thing you have to hold on to – in the vast majority of cases, no-one else thinks your hideous flaws are hideous. In fact, they probably don't even notice them at all.

The one thing that is guaranteed to drive you cray cray is endlessly denying yourself pleasure (and that actually applies to everything in life). Managing your diet in a bid to change your body is sensible if you are unhealthily overweight and perhaps understandable if you've been on an indulgent trip, gone through an injury or just fallen off the wagon of your normal routine. But if you live on a *never-ending* diet, spend your life obsessing over going up or down a few pounds and this state of affairs is making you desperately unhappy, you have fallen into the self-esteem danger zone.

The inevitable truth is that there's no one catch-all "secret". You are not going to suddenly discover a diet that lets you enjoy all the food you want but somehow magically also makes you slim down a dress size. Over the years I've done: Slimming World; SlimFast; Weight Watchers; Atkins; the high-fat, low-carb diet; the low-fat, high-carb diet and the 5:2. I spent nine months entirely sugar-free (not even an apple crossed my lips) and I've been Clean & Lean and under control. And not one of them changed my figure substantially or for long. No matter what the diet industry tries to sell you, there is no regime that will change your bones, melt your fundamental proportions or insert an overnight thigh gap. And that reality is the same for every individual you follow on Instagram – Facetune or no Facetune.

Chapter 3:
Why Social Media is Ruining Your **Health**

Of the many accusations made against social media, it's the impact on our health – or more specifically, our mental health – that's really making us sit up and smell the matcha latte. It's certainly the issue which inspires the most hand-wringing among parents, psychologists and educators. And little wonder: the research is starting to make Facebook, Instagram, Pinterest et al. look like the next generation of Big Tobacco.

Certainly, when it comes to our wellbeing, there's an argument that social is the new smoking. Sounds laughable? Well, just consider that Justin Rosenstein, the engineer who created Facebook's "like" button, has equated Snapchat to heroin; Shirley Cramer, the chief executive of the UK Royal Society for Public Health, said in a statement that "social media has been described as more addictive than cigarettes and alcohol"; Instagram has been accused of manipulating exactly when users receive likes on posts in order to keep them hooked; industry kingpins have admitted that certain features have been explicitly designed to take advantage of our neurological vulnerabilities; and that the vast, vast profits from this culture of addiction are lining the pockets of Silicon Valley's very few. Sounding more familiar?

On a cultural level, we are beginning to contend with the darker side of social media. A number of recent feature films have addressed the new pressures on our mental health; check out Elizabeth Olsen in *Ingrid Goes West* and Ben Stiller's *Brad's Status* – two standouts among a glut of Instagram-inspired titles (the majority of which are teen horrors with spooky titles like *Friend Request*). Alongside the Hollywood treatment, journalists around the globe have taken up the issues, casting light on the once untouchable world of tech. Elsewhere, governments and schools are increasingly attempting to regulate the apparently un-regulatable, demanding safeguards, fines and contractual assurances that improvements in the social media environment will be made. The big worry is: are we too late?

Digitally Depressed?

No matter where you come from, how much money you have or whatever your age, you or someone close to you has experienced mental health issues, whether you realize it or not. It is a universal experience and part of the fabric of all our lives. In the UK half of all cases of mental illness start before the age of 15 and 1 in 4 girls is now clinically depressed by the time she turns 14. In the US as a whole, approximately 44 million adults will experience mental illness in any given year. Just imagine if we were talking about a physical disorder here: if 25 per cent of British teenage girls and 20 per cent of Americans adults had bird flu, we'd be in full end-of-the-world-is-nigh panic. Instead, because it's an "interior" health issue, something that can be kept "secret", it's been allowed to spiral out of control in plain sight. While there are other factors at play, it's widely accepted that social media has been a major reason for this epidemic. As the *Harvard Business Review* succinctly states: "The more you use Facebook, the worse you feel." And yet we still log on and allow our kids to do so too.

Yes, it's unquestionable that social media has acted as a platform to enact change for the cause of mental health. It has brought people who are suffering together and provided a space for them to share their experiences and connect with others who can empathize and offer considerate advice. Social media can prove invaluable to people going through health crises by introducing them to people who have overcome issues and moved on to thrive even when illnesses are chronic. There are certainly silver linings. But in this area what we're all trying to figure out is the weight of the cons vs the pros. How can we use social media to connect, articulate and come to terms with the issues that we're experiencing but avoid the near and present danger to our mental health that every social media platform has on an *architectural* level? And who can we trust to make the changes needed to improve a space which clearly has never had our best interests at heart? That answer, quite obviously, can't be the very firms who are making a mint off our misery.

For the over three hundred million worldwide sufferers of depression, social media has provided support but also led to desperation. While there's been plenty of research to link increased levels of depression with higher levels of social media use, there's also the argument that the more depressed you are the more you choose to use social media, skewing the stats. Reaching out to your friends and followers online for a hit of validation to try to improve your mood is an obvious motivation, and really who hasn't been there?

From a depression perspective, I've generally been pretty resilient when it comes to feeling low. Even in the midst of challenging times I have always kept a sense that, no matter how much I may be going through a level of hormonal despair, I'll always be able to pull myself back from the brink, seek help or rationalize my experience into something manageable. However, I have had first-hand experience of being with someone who didn't have that ability and know how destructive these issues can be, not just for the individual who is suffering, but also for every other person around them. Depression can blight lives and lead to desperate experiences which can be so far away from what you would ever want to publicly share. When I was a lot younger, I was in an abusive relationship with a partner who suffered from anger-management issues and depression. To be clear, my ex-partner never hit me. He threw plates of food at me, smashed up furniture, punched holes in walls next to my head and once in a rage ricocheted his fist into my cheek, but it wasn't like you see on a soap opera. It was generally everything but physical contact. I'd be called a whore, a cunt, a piece of shit; I'd come home to him sitting in a darkened room just waiting to explode. While I didn't go through the pain of physical violence that so many women suffer, and in no way do I seek to equate my experience with theirs, I do understand what it feels like to hide the truth of living with a mental health crisis from the rest of the world.

How the hell did I get there? It's a question I've asked myself endlessly over the years and I still don't really have an answer. I was very young, I'd fallen in love and equated having a "short fuse" with being male. This was something I had, for one reason or another, come to accept as the norm. Every time there was an outburst, there would also be a heartfelt apology, an assurance that he would see a counsellor and that it wouldn't happen again. Because alcohol was often involved in the early days I wrote it off as a "boy blowing off steam" kind of thing, as if that made it OK. Back then, these flare-ups would happen rarely, and in between we had what felt like the most adoring relationship. I felt secure, that I was in something special and no-one else really mattered. He completely and utterly spoiled me with affection and constantly complimented me. Looking back, that level of intensity and co-dependency obviously wasn't healthy and I was certainly addicted to the affection and validation. Our lives revolved around each other and, from the outside, it seemed like soulmate love: deep and emotionally connected – like two pieces of a jigsaw puzzle. When he downloaded an app on my phone which would "always let him know where I was", I was sanguine about being traceable at all times. When he'd leave 27 missed calls and aggressive voicemails on my phone, I'd rationalize it and felt guilty for being in an underground venue without checking my messages. When he told me I was only "allowed" to go out twice a week, I reasoned that it was reasonable. I walked into a web of control and recriminations blindly and willingly because I was, like so many of us, needy for love and scared of being alone.

Of course, it wasn't all one-sided when it came to the arguments. I could be extremely cutting and often undermined him – a product of a total loss of respect and patience for his problems – and I pretty much always stood up for myself (mostly because the accusations were so completely ridiculous). That was perhaps what fanned the flames of the outbursts. Over time, the fact that he couldn't control his aggression and was constantly losing his shit then grovelling meant I became extremely contemptuous of him. Because I argued back, I convinced myself that I wasn't a victim. However, the truth was that I'd often cower in the cataclysmic rows. It's impossible not to be wholly intimidated by a full-size man in the midst of red-eye rage, and I'd often run out the house or lock myself in the bathroom to try to escape.

From a treatment perspective, we researched anger-management courses and he went through a few bouts of CBT and other therapies, but generally nothing seemed to help – that was just the way our life had become: unpredictable, aggressive and full of trauma. Over time I became so used to the eruptions, which by then were rearing their heads on a weekly basis, that I became numb to it. It's far easier than you can imagine to pretend that things aren't happening, to close in on yourself and armour against them. I normalized the situation and told myself that everyone had issues. By ignoring the destructiveness and persuading myself that it wasn't unusual, I facilitated the continuation and escalation of the behaviour 100 per cent, and from the outside, I was entirely complicit in the charm offensive. I remember a girlfriend once telling me, "never say anything bad about your boyfriend to your friends, as that's all they'll remember," and I followed her guidance to a T, keeping schtum and never confiding in anyone. After it was all over, I confided in a few close friends about what had really been going on and they were totally stunned and appalled. They would never have forgiven him, so the stakes really are high when you share this kind of experience.

It wasn't me that ended the relationship but when it broke down, though I was crushed, there was definitely a sense of relief. In lots of ways I emerged seemingly unscathed and was lucky in the fact that I never actually thought I was a slut or a whore. I was also, thankfully, young enough to move on and learn from my mistakes. Basically, I always thought I was going out with someone with problems and it was my job to help him through it. He was the broken bird, I was the one to fix him. In hindsight, of course I know you can't repair anyone else; they have to heal themselves. And you are *never* in love with someone who scares you. Although I do bear some scars, the relationship taught me a huge amount. Today I'm also much warier about compromising my independence, in a good way. I make much more time for my friends and, as much as I love him, my boyfriend isn't the only person I need in my life, which is obviously far healthier. I'm not looking for drama or that full-on desperate-yet-destructive love because I know it's nothing but two people dragging each other through hell. I also know that your sense of validation should come from within, otherwise it's not real. Esteem and security aren't things that can be conferred on you by other people, they're things you have to work on building and maintaining from inside. What people think of you will never be as good at providing support as what you think of yourself.

I feel this is worth sharing because we tend to have a distorted image of what a woman who has been through these kinds of problem looks like. But that just isn't right. One in three women in the US and Australia experience domestic violence in their lifetime. In the UK the police receive a hundred calls an hour relating to domestic abuse. And in Italy, 40 per cent of women report suffering psychological abuse from a partner or ex-partner. As shocking as that is, it's the reality of being a woman living in the 21st century for so many. Of the hundreds of women you're following on social media, a third of them will be in a violent relationship at some point in their lives. Women who look like me. They could have everything that you think you want, at least on the surface. Their lives could look entirely aspirational from the outside. Living with mental health issues is so often hidden from view and our screens and isn't always all about the person that is suffering with the problem. While social media didn't exist when I had my experiences, I know there is absolutely zero chance I would have ever let anyone know what I was going through on that kind of platform – instead I would have been using it as just another tool, a particularly effective one to publicly paper over the cracks.

"Social media is still rife with seemingly 'perfect' lifestyles, but I feel it's becoming a collective responsibility to be more honest," says Charly Cox, a poet and writer who has been vocal on her blog and social media about mental health issues and her Bipolar II diagnosis. "Sharing the banalities and extremes of mental illness can be liberating, community-building and powerful – all things far beyond a perfect aesthetic. For me, it's become about giving a sense of reality to what's going on outside of the parameters of the square in a digestible, honest and approachable medium." While she praises the platforms for offering an opportunity to articulate her issues and campaign for de-stigmatization, Charly also blames the environment for encouraging unhealthy attitudes. "As a 22 year old, I think most of my insecurities have been bred from bad online behaviour. Once you're online, you're out there, aren't you? Reading comments made me quite unwell for a while. I've done some mad things off the back of a stranger's opinion. I genuinely once put extra strong Veet [a chemical hair removal cream] on my face because someone said I looked like Bradley Wiggins. It was the aftermath of having scratchy little carpets grow back on my face that [stirred me to] develop healthier mechanisms to attack how I looked at social media. The biggest and most positive change was being more honest. I unfollowed all the accounts I looked at in a midnight slump, clawing at my love handles wondering why I couldn't look like them, and suddenly found it became a more positive meditation. I found myself scrolling for information, inspiration and decent well-meaning conversation, instead of a warped reality and ideas that I didn't need."

As for the response to her social media honesty, in the main, Charly says, her experience has been positive: "People, generally, are less cruel and judgemental than you believe they might be. I hold a lot of reassurance in knowing that those who are following or engaging in mental health content have been so subjected to their own levels of judgement, that they're unlikely to want to offer it back at you. There was a time when I was inundated with comments that perhaps I was an alcoholic because I'd had a particularly heavy week of events/parties and that stung. In a wave of people uniting in community and forum sometimes you do find yourself in a space where others feel they're equipped (or worse, doing you a favour) to give you an unsolicited diagnosis, but it's best to shrug that off and see it as a way of people caring. I've come to accept that what I'm going through, whilst difficult and hard and frequently excruciating, is actually quite normal. I'm sharing stories and thoughts and feelings that have been felt and experienced hundreds of times before, that now, whilst they have my own personal spin on them, don't leave me feeling naked but united. I struggle with the word brave, but I know it's said with kindness; hopefully one day we won't see people being honest as a brave act, but one we all partake in daily as part of normal life."

The real point here is that more people than you can know live with secrets that they edit out of their life projections to the world. Mental health struggles have long been part of this "interior" and often domestic experience. However, today we have the power to share our experiences and use honesty on social media to shine a light on even the darkest days, and hopefully, by doing so, we can start to change the story for everyone. If we could tell the truth rather than curate what we wished to be true, it would serve us all. There is no shame in struggle, but if there's no mention of it in our perfected digital lifestyles, we only feel all the more shamed. Life is messy and complicated, and sometimes really ugly, and if we want social media to be a healthier environment, it needs to reflect that too.

Marketing Your Mental Health

Social media firms have transformed how we relate to each other, and they spend a huge amount of time, energy and money on understanding how each of us tick, so they can extract maximum engagement – read profits – from us. Their very business model is based on our behaviour and they have been quietly gathering information on our habits for over a decade. Will regulators ever be able to catch up with the body of knowledge that has been gathered as a result of billions of dollars of investment in order to curtail – or even understand – the extent of these firms' power? Unlikely.

It's disheartening, but hardly surprising that social media platforms seem reluctant to change anything which could dent their share values. Facebook's revenues of $40.6 billion in 2017, and the sheer economic force that these firms wield, seem to make them impenetrable and exempt from any outside scrutiny. Even in the light of the recent data scandals, the world's biggest social media site continues to churn out advertising profits. These tech giants may pay lip service to making incremental improvements, but by operating under the guise of "making the world a better place", and preaching social utopia while making profits off the back of our unhappiness, they've effectively gaslighted billions of us. Why would they limit the impact their products have on our feelings of insecurity, envy, anxiety and inadequacy when all these things are apparently marketable?

So how does it work? An internal Facebook document obtained by *The Australian* in 2017 sheds some light on the level of manipulation. It explains to a lucrative advertiser that the Silicon Valley-based social platform can monitor posts and photos in real time to determine when young people feel "stressed", "defeated", "overwhelmed", "anxious", "nervous", "stupid", "silly", "useless" and a "failure". They can provide information on young people's more rudimentary behaviour: their relationship status, number of friends, location and rate of social media use on smartphones and desktop. Disturbingly, they have also mined data on users who have discussed "body confidence", "working out" and "losing weight" and can serve that up to advertisers too. If you've ever felt like social media kicks you when you're down, that may very well be because it has been programmed to do so. As former Google ethicist Tristan Harris says, this level of detailed emotional information offers "a perfect model of what buttons you can push in a particular person". By targeting people at a low ebb – say with weight-loss products, cosmetic services, loans or holiday offers – conversion will undoubtedly be increased. Ultimately, Facebook is selling the emotional levers of its users to the highest bidder.

Everyone's looking for a pick-me-up sometimes and social media provides you with the instant opportunity for retail therapy to cure your deflated feelings – it's just hard to swallow that these platforms can strategically collect information on when exactly you appear at your most vulnerable then peddle it on to companies unscrupulous enough to take advantage of your weakness to make the sale. While Facebook was highly critical of the information obtained by the newspaper and has pledged to "do better" at prioritizing its users' mental health, we know from countless behavioural studies that people often compensate for low mood, feelings of failure and insecurity by consuming more. Keeping us feeling down about ourselves is good for business, no matter what any CEO might say. Ever wondered why social media sites are free? It's certainly not for any altruistic purpose. Instead it's because you – or your data – *are the product* and advertisers are the customers. If all this time you thought Facebook et al. were programmed to serve you, it's time for a rude awakening.

The kind of insights that social media platforms have on you are generally kept under wraps – very few people ever get to work with the algorithms which learn to read your mind then feed you what advertisers know you want to see – but occasionally there's a slip-up. Like in 2014, when a study was released showing that Facebook had used a newsfeed experiment to see how they could control our emotions. By manipulating the feeds of 689,003 unsuspecting users, the site assessed the impact of surfacing more negative or positive stories and hiding certain emotional words. The study showed that "emotional states can be transferred to others via emotional contagion, leading people to experience the same emotions without their awareness." Basically, your friends can depress you without you even having to interact with them, and Facebook at any point can engineer what you see to mess with your mind. A representative released a statement defending the ethically dubious experiment (which they hadn't felt the need to notify those nearly seven hundred thousand users it was carrying out, by the way), saying they had undertaken the test "because we care about the emotional impact of Facebook and the people that use our product," and "felt that it was important to investigate the common worry that seeing friends post positive content leads to people feeling negative or left out." Perhaps the intentions were good, but make no mistake: social media platforms are entirely aware of where you are at emotionally and that knowledge gives them the power to persuade you to click on that designer dress which, yes, might blow your bank balance but will probably make you feel – at least momentarily – better. Trying to save for an apartment? You'd be wise to swerve social media and keep your emotions to yourself.

The Millennial Malaise: Anxiety Strikes

Growing up I'd never really heard of the word anxiety. I knew what teenage angst was, but I didn't realize it was part of anything wider than wearing a Nirvana T-shirt and being fractious with your parents. I was aware that I had problems dealing with stress, that exam season would trigger a bout of IBS or skin rashes (little mini blisters across my cheeks and cold sores), and that I'd often feel a deep sense of panic and feel I couldn't catch my breath. But there was never a sense that it was anything psychological, or even treatable. Being so driven at such a young age had made me obsessive about being "top" at everything at school. When I was six years old I suffered from glandular fever and spent nearly a month out of school in and out of hospital. My biggest concern was that I didn't miss any work. By 16, I was organizing three after-school academic clubs, taking extra GCSE lessons in free periods, working 20 hours a week at a supermarket, running 3 miles every morning, competing on sports teams and had dropped about a stone in weight from meticulous dieting. Another bout in hospital, this time for pneumonia, didn't stop me in my tracks. There was absolutely nothing my parents or teachers could do to stop me – I had to be perfect at everything. Looking back, I was, quite obviously, a classically anxious child, who often pushed herself to both mental and physical exhaustion. But when I was a young, there just wasn't the same cultural understanding that "nerves", "worry" and relentless unease were a particular mental health issue: I was just a precocious and stressed kid.

Today things are very different. Anxiety has been identified as *the* biggest mental health threat facing young people. Around 17.5 per cent of female college students in the US have been diagnosed with or treated for anxiety, and the blame for this drastic uptick has been laid squarely at the door of perfectionism – the layers and layers of pressure that is the millennial generation's undoing. A recent study of over forty thousand Canadian, British and American college students found that "multidimensional perfectionism" (which includes the pressures of social media ideals) is the main driver behind the surge in anxiety issues. These encompass generalized anxiety disorder, panic disorder, phobias, social anxiety disorder, obsessive-compulsive disorder and post-traumatic stress disorder. During my school days, of course there was a certain level of competition. But it totally pales in comparison to the overwhelming levels of perfection that can be consumed on social media today.

Aside from how they look and who they're friends with, millennials are struggling with the demands to achieve perfect grades, secure perfect jobs and nail down their life partner at an increasingly earlier age. Not to have achieved all these goals by certain stages of their life is often treated as a catastrophe. Through consuming information about each other digitally, the pressure to conform to increasingly normative and restrictive targets – the idea that there is only one very narrow path to success: great job, nice home, six-pack, hot partner – is creating a collective sense of inadequacy.

Fashion blogger Lindsey Holland, better known as @RopesOfHolland, who runs a YouTube series tackling mental health, explains how benchmark anxiety got the better of her. "My feeling of anxiousness started in a relationship I was in during my early twenties. I'd never felt secure, because I wanted to pin him down for all those expectations I had at the time – the perfect wedding, kids – and he just wanted to run 10,000 miles away from me. Social media can make you feel like there are deadlines passing you by, and there was a time that I'd be pretty upset if someone around me got engaged – I'd find myself obsessively looking at their pictures on Facebook and thinking about what kind of ring I'd have. I was only 25, but I really felt that I needed to achieve those life goals. For me, anxiety is like going into fight-or-flight mode with massive surges of adrenaline which you just can't stop from coming, and looking at Instagram or Facebook used to really fuel my anxiety. It always made me feel that I was less than someone else – you can literally drive yourself mad with comparison. I'm not in the same rush to achieve all those goals as when I was younger, but it's taken me to get to 30 to become more relaxed about what other people are doing – I still want to be married and to have babies, but I now know it's not a race."

Anxiety is an issue which can be treatable, and many, many people recover from its worst ravages, either with or without the help of medication. While my pregnancy brought my anxiety back into sharp focus (more on this in a later chapter), I've spent most of my recent life without any anxiety at all – helped mostly by going through lots and lots of failure. Not getting a place at Oxbridge was the first step to dealing with anxiety. Perfect grades and a perfect UCAS application didn't equate to a perfect university acceptance for me, and while it was the first major botch-up of my life, it definitely helped to take the pressure off. When I received my rejection letter, I also had my first moment of teenage rebellion, cut my afternoon classes, took a train into London and went straight to Tiffany's on Bond Street to spend my supermarket earnings on lots of jewellery... If only Facebook had been there to facilitate that emotional transaction... More failure followed: the seven job interviews I got rejected from to get my first full-time job, my inability to ingratiate myself with my first boss, getting divorced before I was 30, failing my driving test, the long list of other men that have broken up with me... While at the time these things felt insanely stressful, overcoming failure can make you fearless, and mine, over time, certainly cured me of my relentless perfectionism. However hard you work to be perfect, life has a habit of getting in the way.

I don't need to be "top" any more and I'm definitely not so fixated with being a good schoolgirl in every circumstance. Sure, some old habits die hard (I'm anally tidy and won't let anyone visit my apartment unless it's in showroom state, I can feel a deep sense of worry vis-à-vis my body image and I struggle with confrontational social situations), but one of the reasons that social media doesn't – in the main – make me feel anxious is that I've become comfortable with my heavily flawed, imperfect self. I would also say that the defective version of me is far, far more likeable than the one that was straining to be an A* student in all aspects of her life.

One of society's biggest problems at the moment is that modern parents have become so risk-averse that they're no longer allowing their offspring to fail – at anything. As "enmeshment" parenting (a highly involved parenting style in which the parent literally lives for a child's success) grows ever more intense, young people aren't being given the opportunity to deal with their own screw-ups, which fuels an even deeper anxiety that they must not deviate from their prescribed script. But the truth is that we all need to fail sometimes, in order to learn that perfection isn't the be all and end all and that the sky doesn't fall in if you don't ace every element of your life. Also failure doesn't necessarily lead to failure. It can, in fact, enhance your success and make you able to enjoy that success to the full – it is a blessing that we shouldn't all be trying so hard to disguise. So many things have gone "wrong" for me and my life has not met the benchmarks I had once hoped it would. But being able to release the standards that I had set for myself I've dodged a life of anxiety and ultimately found my own individual version of success.

The anxiety of failing #LifeGoals can cripple a student's ability to perform in exams, interact socially, impede their ability to graduate and then hamper their attempts to enter the job market. It's long been thought that perfectionism is a motivator and there's no doubt that it can spur you on to push your limits. But it's also an affliction which can lead to serious health consequences. Perfectionism got me to the top of my class, helped me run 1,500m (1 mile) in under five minutes and definitely spurred me on to achieve top grades throughout my education. It also drove me to starve myself until I was a stone underweight and found no enjoyment in any of my accomplishments, led me on to the path of insomnia and caused stomach issues that took years of acupuncture and alternative therapies to deal with. It did not make me happy in any way.

Over social media's lifetime in the UK there's been a rise of self-poisoning by girls of 50 per cent, an increase in hospital admissions for self-harm among girls by 68 per cent, and a 400 per cent increase in girls being treated in hospital for cutting themselves. Over the same period there hasn't been the same spike in difficulties with boys. In the US suicide rates have been back on the rise since 2010, after two decades of decline and, while rates for girls remain significantly below that of boys, they've doubled between 2009 and 2015 to hit a forty-year high. A San Diego State University study shows the increase of young people taking their own lives directly mirrors the surge in social media use, pointing to a correlation. Another study has shown that teens "overusing" social media with five hours or more of daily engagement were 70 per cent more likely to have suicidal thoughts or actions than those who reported one hour of daily use. *All* of these issues have been linked to the dramatic increase in the amount of young people suffering from anxiety.

This barrage of statistics may feel overwhelming. But for some reason we're not overwhelmed enough to do much about it. It's easy to think that we don't have any agency to change things, but we need to keep reminding ourselves that these sites didn't exist a generation ago. For starters, it seems a no-brainer that every social media site should have parental controls and effective age regulation and that each user should have to prove his or her date of birth to enable them to a) log on in the first place, and b) have their access level determined. You can't smoke, drink, drive or have sex until you reach a lawful age, simply because these activities are potentially harmful for young people. Social media has proven over and over again to have destructive effects on the malleable minds of early adolescents, so the same legislation and safeguards should apply in the digital world too. Every social media site should have easily accessible support systems for those who are having depressive, anxious or suicidal thoughts, and it should be each platform's responsibility to make sure that these services are effective. There should also be very clear warnings that images can be distorted, edited and curated to suggest a level of faultlessness that doesn't exist.

Elsewhere, the perils of perfectionism both on and offline should be taught as a mandatory part of every school syllabus, and we all should be conscious of our own social media use and actually set a good example. Every single person should be aware that in 2018 a shocking 25 per cent of teenage girls in the UK have been diagnosed with mental health issues. But instead, we're touching our phones on average 2,617 times a day and letting the money-making social media machines operate with impunity. WTF are we doing here?

Relationship with Ourselves:
Popular, But All Alone

Think about the last time you sat with nothing but your thoughts. Shunning all distractions, confronting what was going on in your head with nothing else except for your own mind to bounce off. Personally, the only time I really am totally "alone" in that way is when I wake up in the night. Although I always start these wakeful periods with mindfulness exercises, I often end up having some of my clearest thoughts in the dead of night. But while my musings may be razor-sharp in the wee hours, they are also punishing and sometimes overwhelming, and the relief which comes with dawn break is palpable. Why? Because I can pick up my phone, relax and stop spinning around whichever crisis – practical or existential – was filling my mind. Scrolling through my phone makes me feel entertained, distracted and safe; on days when I'm feeling particularly low, exhausted or overwhelmed it calms me and allows me to switch off the stream of consciousness snaking around my brain. It also eases my passage to actually getting up, something which, as a person who struggles with sleep, is no mean feat.

There is zero doubt in my mind that I'd prefer to be with my phone than just my self. Aside from the fact that I find it easy, familiar and less stressful, it also stems the intense boredom of self-exploration and alleviates the intensity of my thoughts, dialling things down to a manageable level.

An often-cited 2014 experiment led by Timothy Wilson of the University of Virginia examined how able we are to sit with and entertain ourselves over a short period – six to fifteen minutes – of time. Aside from the majority reporting that they hadn't enjoyed the experience (and several hiccups as subjects found literally *anything* they could do to distract themselves – from stealing a pen to writing a to-do list to using the instruction paper to practise origami), it was the participants' response to the "shock experiment" which most dumbfounded the researchers. Each of the subjects was wired up and given the opportunity to shock themselves whenever they wanted over 15 minutes. Despite the fact they'd already had the opportunity to test the level of shock, and despite the fact that many of them said they would *pay money* to never feel the shock again, a quarter of the women and two-thirds of the men did indeed opt to shock themselves again when left in solitude. One subject pressed the button 190 times in 15 minutes – they felt *that* uncomfortable with their own thoughts, that anything, even physical pain, was better than a quarter of an hour's reverie. Interestingly, the study found that the results were not dependent on age or smartphone/social media use – it isn't just millennial tech addicts who have problems sitting with just their own thoughts.

"Solitude is where you find yourself... If we're not able to be alone, we're going to be lonelier," says Sherry Turkle in her TED Talk, and in many ways, I can relate. Working on my own at home every day has definitely changed my perception of solitude, and for a time I became pretty much incapable of escaping some kind of screen or device. If I was a little more than a hand's reach away from one of them, I got twitchy. Aside from being in the shower (with my phone perched on the sink, just in case), my day ended up being a catalogue of screen segues – from my laptop to tablet to phone to TV. It takes proper discipline to unplug.

Whether or not avoiding time with myself in the day is having an impact on the intensity of my insomnia episodes at night is something I've definitely considered. While there's a solid body of research proving the link between high levels of social media use and disturbed sleep, it's usually blamed on the "wake up" signals created by blue screens, or not switching off early enough. But what if it's because our brains haven't had a moment to reconnect to the self, or sufficient time to come back to our centres? Solitude allows our bodies to catch up with our minds, allows the brain to rest and side-step burnout, and triggers the parasympathetic nervous system, which slows the heart rate, reduces blood pressure and relaxes our muscles. It also allows space for creativity and aids concentration. Without solitude, we are naturally wired, and that's even before we put stimulating screens in front of our faces. Today Americans average only 6.8 hours of sleep a night (less than the health recommendation of 7–9 hours a night), with 40 per cent logging less than 6 hours, according to a Gallup poll. How much is that to do with the collective aversion to solitude? When you consider that a lack of sleep is associated with – take a breath – higher levels of diabetes, heart disease, obesity and depression, as well as a reduced life expectancy, it's easy to see why turning our backs on ourselves threatens not just our mental but also our physical health prognosis.

Zero Escape:
"Screenager" Cyberbullying and Harassment

One danger to mental health that parents *are* more conscious about than ever, is the menace of cyberbullying. This school-gate scourge has commanded so much media attention that parents and teachers alike are hyperaware. However, the threat of online intimidation and victimization is certainly not just reserved for kids: cyberstalking and harassment has become part of the tapestry of digital life. One in every twenty-five Americans online (about ten million people) have either had explicit images of themselves shared against their will or have been threatened with that exposure. For women younger than 30, it was 1 in 10. Another survey found that 47 per cent of Americans who used the internet had been victims of online harassment. Online persecution of black internet users and people that openly identify as lesbian, gay and bisexual was significantly higher. Hate, harassment and hounding aren't just niche www.com experiences – instead they've become worryingly normalized.

The 2.0 bully has distinctive features, especially because social media never sleeps. Our 24/7 connection means that there are no safe spaces – not even locked in our houses or bedrooms. Just think of all those hours we spend plugged into the matrix and imagine that every minute links you to your tormentor, or at least to the threat of torment. There's also the potential for a much greater degree of anonymity for bullies and the difficulties that come with trying to remove bullying digital content – whether it's statements, images or video footage from social media platforms. Once the information is out in the digital ether, stopping it circulating can be near impossible. One of the most horrifying aspects is that you may not even know who these trolls and bullies are – it can just be the bad luck of the draw that you've inspired someone to unleash a personal hell through their keyboard.

Reports suggest that up to 50 per cent of school-age girls go through some level of digital harassment (though for extreme cases it's under the 10 per cent mark) and up to 40 per cent don't tell their parents. While the vast majority of cyberbullying of young people occurs in tandem with the traditional schoolyard tactics of ostracizing, name-calling and physical intimidation, even a short period of digital aggression can, it has been proven, have severe effects on mental health, including rates of depression, anxiety and self-harming behaviours. A study of 2,215 students concluded that cyberbullying can lead to problems processing emotions, disruptions in socially appropriate behaviour, an impaired ability to interact successfully with others and a significant decline in normal levels of concentration. Although there is a level of healthy scepticism about the true impact of cyberbullying – as a hot, zeitgeisty topic among already over-cautious and fearful parents, some teachers and psychologists say that it's been used to mask other issues – the UK's National Society for the Prevention of Cruelty to Children has said it recorded an 88 per cent increase in calls about the issue in the five years between 2011 and 2016.

It's also not just traditional social media platforms providing the theatre for this new upsurge; a host of new "honesty sites", including the much-maligned Sarahah app, have been embroiled in stories of intense digital harassment. Sarahah allows users to send anonymous messages and describes itself as a tool to "Improve your friendship by discovering your strengths and areas for improvement; Let your friends be honest with you." While honesty may be the best policy in some instances, it seems not so great when you don't know where the feedback is coming from. Instead of a two-way street, Sarahah doesn't allow you to know who has so thoughtfully revealed their candid appraisal of your character and you maddeningly can't respond to messages – though you can thankfully block anyone who sends offensive or unwanted posts. Initially programmed for workplace feedback, the app has proven a hit with teens desperate for validation. The goal is to receive positive messages, which they can then share via screenshots on Snapchat. While it sounds convoluted, it's yet another example of the ways in which social media can compound our feelings that we are not worthwhile unless someone else says so and we can share that with our community. Last year Sarahah reached the top of Apple's App Store in 30 countries, including the UK, Ireland, the US and Australia. Already banned in several schools, due to its use in anonymized digital bullying, the site echoes the fears around other anonymous platforms like Ask.fm and Sayat.me, which have both been implicated in teen suicides. While Ask.fm is now under new ownership and has developed a more rigorous response to abuse, Sayat.me, which once had 30 million users, many believed to be teenagers, was taken offline after a British 15-year-old boy took his life. Investigations continue but it has been reported that abusive messages it is believed he had received through the app may have contributed to his death. It can be hard to understand this burning desire to know what people "really think about you", but it's the crucial question at the heart of all insecurity and certainly related to a drive for perfectionism in friendships. Sadly, it also welcomes trolls with open arms.

Cyberbullying of teens is one area where social media sites have responded to concerns. Notably, Facebook has a transparent process for removal of content, which is aided by a support dashboard. However, the social platforms have had constant criticisms of slow response rates and a lack of staffing and investment, which is needed to make the facilities function effectively. Yet again it seems that these sites are failing to put their money where their mouths are. Equally, when digital abuse moves beyond simple user-to-user attacks (with fake accounts being set up and rerouted IP addresses being employed), victims – both young and old – have found that getting social platforms and lawmakers to take them seriously is an uphill battle.

The impact on mental health that this often long-running abuse can have is significant, and it's not just for vulnerable teens or children. A recent Australian study showed that over three-quarters of women under thirty had experienced digital harassment and one in five of them felt depressed, with 5 per cent feeling suicidal because of it.

And these women seem just as reluctant as the schoolkids to report their experiences, most probably because the police have such little sympathy or power to support them. In the UK, in all digital harassment case files reviewed, care for the victim was deemed to be inadequate. *Every single case.* As our law enforcement agencies struggle to contend with the issue, the number of tracked offences has, concurrently, been rising sharply. To give an idea of the extent of the problem, a terrifying 20 per cent of women aged 15–29 have been digitally stalked in some way in the US.

There can be no discussion of cyberbullying without mentioning the exploitation of sexual imagery of women and girls which they have either shared of their own volition or felt pressured into doing so through sexting. Half of all millennials in a 2015 survey said they'd uploaded a nude shot via social media, with Snapchat leading the charge. The problem is that once the picture has been sent, you have to trust that the recipient isn't going to pass it on without your permission. If things turn sour in a relationship, "revenge porn", or the digital dissemination of sexually explicit images or videos, is rife. The charity Childnet International found that more than half of UK teenagers have friends who have shared intimate images of someone they know and 14 per cent of girls say they have been pressured into sharing nude images. To say things can get nasty is an understatement – whether the images are sent to your family members in a direct message, streamed on YouTube alongside commentary about your figure, or shared among your work colleagues with a supporting hashtag, the result is the same: a deep feeling of inescapable shame. Little wonder that US campaign End Revenge Porn found that 51 per cent of US victims have contemplated suicide.

Social networks don't allow the sharing of naked images of people under 18 – it's one of few red lines that they won't allow to be crossed and is seen as strictly a legal matter. But if you're over 18, it can be soul-destroyingly difficult to get such images taken down, especially as they will often be linked from vile revenge porn site to site in an apparent digital quagmire. From a judicial perspective, while it remains illegal in principle to share an explicit image of another person without their consent, in practice, it's painfully difficult to prosecute. Data obtained from the Crown Prosecution Services between July and December 2017 showed that 61 per cent of reported cases in England and Wales resulted in no action being taken – and the same data showed that some victims were as young as 11.

Around the globe, governments have tried, often in vain, to respond to the phenomenon. In Israel, the offence is punishable by five years in jail and those found guilty are prosecuted as sexual offenders, while the targets are recognized as victims of sexual assault. The Japanese Revenge Porn Prevention Act imposes a potential ¥500,000 fine or three years in prison. But no matter where the initial sharing of imagery happened, all legislation is beset with complex difficulties in successfully prosecuting or removing the content from the internationally disparate digital addresses. With the advent of "deepfakes" – AI computer-generated pornography whereby people use artificial intelligence to very convincingly swap the faces of actors in pornographic films with people they know – the need for strident measures from social media sites has never been more necessary. But once again, they will take no responsibility for the damage wreaked through their platforms.

One of the big issues is the sheer amount of personal information we are all sharing – material which can be manipulated by both unscrupulous criminals and digital trolls to take harassment beyond a crappy comment here or there. Ask yourself, how often are you geo-tagging your images on social media? Do you openly celebrate your birthday and disclose your age every year? What about that risqué snap you sent to that guy on Tinder after a couple of rosés? Perhaps you congratulate your mum or your friends on their birthdays? What about your place of birth? Is that accessible in your basic info? Even if you trust that your private details will be kept private, how much could be gleaned if someone really wanted to take advantage of you? Have you ever posted an image with your road name or house number visible?

Do you post your holiday journey to the airport on Stories or Snapchat? The exact address of your hotel? Social media can be a hunting ground for thieves, trolls and stalkers – and while you're flaunting the very best sides of your life to your legitimate friends and followers, you're also opening yourself up to people who can exploit you. Conscious social media is about being aware of how all our projections of perfection can come with a price tag – in the very worst cases an empty bank account, an invaded and ransacked home or a relentless tormentor who has the power to publicly disseminate your private information, including the most intimate of imagery.

In the UK last year, five hundred people a day were impersonated by a criminal trying to steal their money, buy items or take out a loan in their name. Home alarm specialists ADT say up to 78 per cent of burglars use social media to target properties, and according to research at Bedford University, cyberstalking is now more common than physical harassment. This isn't hyperbole, instead it's a moment to check ourselves and consider just how much information we've leaked along our digital footprint – and how much of it might hurt us mentally, both in the long and short term. Don't get paranoid, instead get protected.

Sharing Ill Health: A Blessing or a Curse?

Sickness is bleak, depressing and colossally sad. In the ceaselessly upbeat world of social media, anything that's a downer can feel out of place and, for those dealing with chronic illness or physical health episodes, navigating the unwritten rules about how to share their experiences is still tricky territory. Not every internet user is compassionate: some will see sharing about sickness as attention-seeking, and continual updates with bad news may end up being ignored by those who are unable to cope with the realities of ill-health. This, understandably, can be incredibly hurtful to those who are suffering.

How or why people decide to go public about their medical conditions has always been a matter of deep personal choice, though as with all elements of our lives, social media is rewriting the relationship between privacy and disclosure. These days it's almost impossible to evade exposure of obvious ailments, from losing your hair to broken bones, unless you stay clear of all digital documentation – no birthday group shots for you. There are also clear risks in sharing sensitive health information online, especially when there are stigmas around particular illnesses, not least the impact it might have on your insurance premiums due to woeful gaps in the law. Professionally it may also be problematic, leaving a traceable record of your illness and setting off alarm bells for an employer that you might be unfit for a position. Discrimination is very difficult to prove when you've served up the information in the first place, and the fact that people can access elements of your medical records without even talking to you can have widespread implications for your digital reputation.

For a generation of oversharers, there are other hazards to take into consideration. When you're so used to airing your laundry online, it can become habitual to do so, even when the stakes are higher and the potential for "sharing regret" increases. While you're in the midst of illness you may feel compelled to reveal intimate details of your experience, but on the road to recovery you might feel less happy to have that information and those images of yourself available to the public at large. The problem is, of course, that online they are practically indelible.

What's more, sometimes in the world of digital health, not all is quite as it seems. High-profile cases of sickness fraud – including the now-notorious story of Belle Gibson, a wellness blogger who falsely claimed to have cured her brain cancer with only natural remedies and nutrition – have proven that these communities are vulnerable to fake-news violations and misinformation by immoral charlatans. Building a social media empire off the back of the sympathy she found online for her phony diagnosis, and raising money for charities which she failed to donate, Gibson is an extreme example of how, even in the sensitive realm of sickness, there are con-artists at work.

However, these concerns don't seem to be stemming the tide, and a significant proportion of people *are* sharing their medical issues, with up to 40 per cent of people saying they have posted online about a health-related issue. One of the biggest reasons is that there is a wealth of information, advice and support out there, just waiting to be harnessed. Collective experience of health, and information around specific conditions, is so much more diverse and broad than one person's journey, meaning that for those struggling, there's a wealth of intelligence, treatment plans and specialist recommendations ready to be accessed through peer-to-peer support.

In 1983, a study of people with epilepsy found that only 6 per cent had ever spoken to anyone who shared the same illness. Today 4.5 million people a week use apps like HealthUnlocked, a social network which matches you with other people dealing with the same health issues. Patient empowerment has changed the terms of the medical game, and advocacy around specific illnesses has helped develop what has been termed "sickness subcultures", with some of the most highly engaged communities anywhere online. These support groups can be a lifeline to those who have been housebound by their illness, especially if there is functionality for digital social interaction, so it's little wonder there's been such a boom in health-related social applications – there are currently thousands of apps available on Apple's App Store, covering everything from haemophilia to asthma.

Lauren Mahon, a blogger and social media manager, was diagnosed with breast cancer at 31 and used her platforms to both document her experience and campaign for greater awareness. Her journey highlights the unbelievable power as well as the challenges of sharing a health account online. "Cancer is such an unknown," Lauren explains, "so when I was being sent off for scans, bloods and egg-freezing, I remember wishing I'd known what to expect, just a little bit. That was one of the reasons I knew I wanted to do something to raise awareness online in the hope it might help another woman like me. It wasn't until the week before my treatment started that I actually found the confidence to say what was happening and go "public" on social media. I know it sent a shockwave through my following, especially as I was a young, healthy, happy woman – it just wasn't the serious news that anyone was used to hearing. When I made the decision to be honest and open about my experience, I knew I had to do it the whole way. Warts and all – or, in my case, pooping in the bath. It's a grim reality, but by normalizing the conversation we make the world a slightly less scary place for all those facing or who will face this disease. For me, the very hardest part is definitely dealing with your own mortality on a daily basis. Being in the cancer community is incredibly powerful, and the experience binds you and means you're never alone. However, it also means that you make friends with people who may not make it and see spread and recurrence coming from every corner, and that can make it a difficult space to exist in sometimes."

Social media communities who have followed an individual's illness can also, she explains, add a level of complexity to moving on once into recovery. "I lost a fair few followers when I went on holiday to Sri Lanka this year, and I wondered if it was because people were only interested in the gritty, sad side of cancer and now that I feel as though I'm on the up, it's boring? My good friend Laura, who has also just kicked cancer's butt, posted something recently that said, 'They want to see you do well but never better than them,' and that does ring true." Other worries have included the reaction from others in a professional capacity. "I have worried that I'm not desirable for potential employers because I'm perceived as this 'cancer girl'," she says. "But I also know I'm so much more than that, and any person or business that wouldn't want me around because of it isn't worth my precious time anyway. Honestly, I truly have no regrets because launching my campaign, GIRLvsCANCER, gave me a space to curate and show my own experience, my way, rather than the clinical, scary way shoved down our throats in the media. I'm also so proud that my coping mechanism is helping others cope too."

Another subject for debate centres on how much you share about someone else's health issues – however much they might impact the reality of your life. Traversing this complicated line, Claire Marshall, the content creator behind the beauty and lifestyle blog and YouTube channel *Hey Claire*, has tussled with what to reveal and what to conceal about her mother's declining health to her audience of nearly a million subscribers. "My mom was diagnosed with early-stage dementia in 2011, but we didn't know how quickly she would deteriorate," Claire explains. "I've always tried to be very open and honest with my followers and I'm so appreciative of them. When I first started out and everything was happening with my mom, I didn't really have many friends or a solid support network to lean on, so my audience really became my family. Those few hundred followers were the closest I had to a network, and I shared a lot of what was happening in my life. For example, the first time my mom forgot my birthday. Nowadays, I think there are times when some of my followers feel I'm holding back, but it's really just out of respect for the other people who are now in my life, including my mom."

✗ ✗ ✗

Social media has revolutionized our experience of health and fundamentally changed the way society treats both mental and physical conditions. There is no going back: what was once incredibly personal has become incredibly public. In so many ways this can be liberating and life-affirming. But while social media has facilitated changes in cultural attitudes, fostered communities and undermined the stigma around both mental and physical health, it also has been a significant trigger for the contemporary mental health crisis.

Not everything or everyone online are there to help you, least of all the social media firms themselves. There can be long-lasting consequences to what you share about your wellbeing, as with all aspects of your life, and if you've been sleep-walking into spending untold hours on social media, it's time to wake up to the damage it may be doing to you. Consciously consume, know your rights and stay awake to the information that you are sharing, because the truth is: your very health depends on it.

Takeaways

1. Learn your triggers

One of the first steps to dealing with anxiety can be to accept that it's an element of your makeup. "As soon as you acknowledge that anxiety is part of your reaction to certain triggers, you can start to learn to manage it," explains Lindsey Holland. "There will be some situations that you go into that will cause a strange build-up of feelings and emotions, but the key is to recognize them because you can then begin to talk yourself down. After a while you realize that everything comes from pressure that you're putting on yourself, and that means that only you are capable of reducing that burden."

There is no catch-all cure for feelings of anxiety, but more than anything it is vital that you work out what sets you off personally. For lots of people that will be something that they consume on social media, so the way you use these digital tools is fundamental to managing issues.

Start by adopting best-practice tactics:

* Unfollow anyone that makes you feel inadequate.
* Limit the amount of time you spend on your phone.
* Push yourself to engage with social things outside your online life.
* Try to work out why certain triggers are setting you off – what are you actually worried or nervous about?
* Begin to identify things that are actually dangerous (say, a risk of injury or death) rather than just scary.
* Remember that there is a difference between those two things – and that difference is your perception. (Something that might seem scary, like starting a new job, is definitely not a risk to your life, whereas something that might not seem frightening at all – like deciding not to use sunscreen on the beach – may actually be dangerous.) This is a technique I use a lot to try to really drill down to how I'm actually feeling and stop my automatic anxiety response. For example, writing this book is scary but not dangerous, so it shouldn't fuel my angst.

To use myself as an example for the last point, I have an active, worry-prone mind and I've taken a lot of gambles in my life: leaving jobs without another one to go to, moving country with no real plan, deciding to set up my own business in a new and unproven market... These leaps of faith have been terrifying and have certainly caused me turmoil. But understanding worse-case scenarios and acknowledging that they are generally not *dangerous* has enabled me to take them while relatively keeping a lid on the anxiety.

2. Let go of the milestones
If seeing other people hit milestones makes you feel inadequate, ask yourself why. Why do you need to be on a timeline? Who says so? Life is generally not compliant with your plans: that's life, and it's just the way it is.

I'm 34, unmarried with a baby and still can't drive. I didn't get to edit a magazine, I don't have a garden or stairs in my house – my deadlines have come and gone years ago. Seeing that other people do have those things could get me down, but knowing I run my own business instead – something I never thought would be part of my life – and have a solid, healthy relationship that doesn't require a ring or a bouquet to make it complete makes me realize that there are better things out there than what I thought I wanted and needed. Happiness and success aren't one straight line or a ladder of equally spaced rungs. It's a topsy-turvy, unpredictable journey of highs and lows. Feeling anxiety about going off course is entirely misplaced because there is no course. I'm still happy and successful in my own way, even though most of the things I had on my life plan didn't work out.

3. App yourself happy
One of the issues with social media is that we can feel out of control of our consumption of it. We know our constant scrolling is making us feel bad, but we're not sure how to police ourselves. One solution is to use technology to help you get to where you want to be. Today there are a

host of new tools out there to help you break bad habits and can help you develop a healthier – and happier – relationship with social media. Here are a few examples:

* The iOS app Moment tots up every minute you spend on your phone and allows you to see exactly which apps are draining your time.
* AppDetox (for Android) allows you to create specific rules for access to certain apps with time-based limitations, as well as an option which requires you to walk to get access to more screen time. By literally locking your apps it forces you off social media and back into real life.
* The Freedom app can block distracting apps and websites across your computers and any Apple devices at once, allowing you to schedule in specific times of the day when you just can't access them. You can also block the whole of the internet if you really need to focus on a task at hand.
* Need something a little more extreme? Check out Off the Grid, an app for Android phones that completely jams your phone for however long you ask it to. Whether you're heading out for dinner with friends or are adamant that you want to put your phone down at 9pm every night, you can entirely check out. You can also be safe in the knowledge that people attempting to contact you will be informed that you're currently "off-grid", that loved ones can be added to a "whitelist" to ensure important calls can still get through, and that you can still access your camera, because, well, you know why.
* If you'd rather not rely on apps, you could even connect your router at home to an outlet timer to cut off access to the internet for your whole abode at a set time every day.

These aids may sound dramatic, but they are definitely effective. Self-control can be an issue for everyone, but there is a whole host of technology at your fingertips to help you protect yourself.

4. Schedule some solitude

Just thinking that you want to spend less time on your phone is not enough. When there's something that's as attractive as social media on offer, your habits don't just change – you actually have to make a concerted effort. One of the ways that you can help yourself is to timetable daily, or even weekly, moments of quiet. As we know from the electric shock experiment above, a lot of us struggle with alone time and sitting with our own thoughts. Guided meditations are one way of learning to be relaxed in our own company, but it's not for everyone. Start by taking just five minutes every day to sit up in bed before you run to the shower – and make sure your phone isn't reachable. You might like to make a cup of hot water and lemon, or else just take a moment to scan how you're feeling. Mindfulness exercises can help if your thoughts become overwhelming, and knowing that there are only five minutes to get through can help make it more manageable. Over time, try extending the length of time you spend with yourself. Remember the aim is not to run away from your thoughts but confront them. It's not meant to be easy, but over time you are more aware of how you feel about things, and as a bonus, it might even help you fall and *stay* asleep.

I'm definitely working on this one as we speak.

5. Get real about digital security

Using the same password for everything? Have no idea what two-step verification means? Time to start getting serious about your security. Aside from giving cyberbullies and trolls potential access to your information and identity, slack digital security can open you up to all kinds of fraud. I have two girlfriends who have had their social media accounts hacked and all the images deleted, and of course, the perpetrators gained access to all their personal details too.

These days profiles can be used for all sorts of services and site logins way beyond just social media, so keeping control of yours should be a major priority.

Sounds boring? It is, but it's also so worth it. I've spent untold hours sweeping through my profiles removing any images which might point to my address or personal information. However, it can be tricky to encourage others to be as mindful as you are – if someone posts a birthday ode to you on their profile, for example, it can be difficult to ask them to take it down. But think of it this way – would you tell any stranger on the street your date of birth? It can be hard to scrub information from the internet, so the best practice is to never reveal it in the first place. And just remember, however much effort it might take to protect yourself, it's just a fraction of the headache you'll have if you let someone else get their hands on your info.

It's also crucial to think carefully before you send any images to anyone. The rule is: don't trust anybody with imagery which you wouldn't be happy posting on your own Instagram. If you don't want to be sorry, be safe.

6. Know the risks as well as the rewards

Community, acceptance and support are just some of the benefits of sharing both mental and physical health issues online, but it's important not to be blind to the realities of the risks too. Your digital footprint is crucial to the professional recruitment process and, sadly, no matter how much attitudes *are* changing, discrimination against those battling health issues remains rampant. Indeed, half of people with diagnosed mental health illnesses say that they had not been hired because of it. You should consider that if you disclose your problem to the internet, you are disclosing it to any potential employer too. This is not a reason not to share, but it is a reason to be conscious about the way you do it.

Charly Cox explains her rationale: "This issue used to be a constant struggle for me, but now ultimately it boils down to the truth that if a future employer has seen me talk openly about my mental health and found issue with it, it's not going to work out anyway. But there's definitely a way to go about it. Keeping things conversational is a good rule of thumb; anything too self-confessional or worrying which has potential to spark concern suggests it's not something you're dealing with well. By no means should you feel the need to make it light or limited, but try to find an overarching message or point through sharing your own experiences, as it makes it look less like a plea for help. Always think: why do I want to share this particular story? Will someone find solace within it? Will it make someone feel less alone? Stigma is still there, and it will take a while for those with judgement to see it for what it is. Ultimately though, pushing through a fear of judgement has been much more rewarding and boosting for me than sitting silent and knowing nothing's changing. Strangely, it's also made me feel more in control of my own mental health."

Chapter 4:
Why Social Media is
Ruining Your **Relationships**

*Man is by nature a social animal; an individual who is unsocial
naturally and not accidentally is either beneath our notice or
more than human.*
– ARISTOTLE, *POLITICS*

How would you define a friend? Is it someone you could turn to no
matter what? Just call my name and I'll be there? Or is it someone
who you're in near-constant contact with, speaking to all day, every
day? Is it the person you've got the longest "Snapstreak" (chatted on
Snapchat for over three days straight) with? How much one-on-one
time do you have together? And what are your conversations like –
deeply engaged and empathetic, or more interrupted and punctuated
into bite-size snippets?

The impact that social media is having on all of our relationships,
spanning our families, friends and romantic couplings to our very
relationships with ourselves, has been fundamentally altered by the
way we use our devices to communicate with each other. What we
now need from our networks is in flux, and the very nature of friendship
and the foundations on which we believe they should be based have
changed almost beyond recognition. The question is: *is social media
enhancing our social lives, or is it doing the exact opposite?*

Humans are by definition social beings. From a genetic perspective,
we have evolved to live in social groups for both protection and
reproduction. Being social makes us buoyant: connection to a group
makes us happier; social exchanges reduce the stress hormone cortisol,
while simultaneously raising feel-good oxytocin and serotonin. Being

social is basically like biological crack – so is it any wonder that we've become so very quickly, so very deeply infatuated with *social* media?

"As humans, we thrive by building relationships. It's very primordial. Social media plays right into what really makes us tick as human beings," explains Dr James A Roberts, a professor in marketing and an expert on digital consumer behaviour. And who can argue? Logging on to read thoughtful comments and messages from friends, seeing what loved ones are busy getting up to and reading insightful stories which make us feel connected to our digital tribe can create an instant sense of belonging.

It can also relieve any feelings of loneliness and reduce the geographical differences between us that are part of modern lifestyles. But it's no panacea and the very reasons that it's so seductive have also become causes for concern. "As relationships are so important to us, there's an argument that the more we use social media, the better. But that's only if we're *actively* interacting with other people – sending messages and pictures and connecting," Dr Roberts continues. "But really what we're finding is that much of social media use is *passive*, characterized by 'lurking' or 'creeping'. We're spending hours not actually socializing, but merely viewing other people, consuming sanitized, best-case scenarios of each other's lives. Instead of the feel-good hormones we might expect to be pumping through our veins instead, we're torn between feelings of FOMO and inadequacy."

The tech companies have jumped upon this distinction between active and passive social media consumption as the new paradigm for determining "good" vs "bad" social media relationships. The argument is that if you're actually using platforms to meaningfully connect, then you'll reap the positive rewards that digital socialization can offer. On the other hand, if you stay schtum and just lurk, stalk and creep, your mental health and happiness will be at risk. As an admission that social media can be bad for us, it's a start, but there are many, many other factors at play when it comes to the ways in which social media has changed our relationships. The distinction between active and passive use is too simplistic to nail it. Essentially, our phones and social apps haven't just changed how we make relationships, they've also changed what we believe relationships to be.

Quantity Over Quality:
Friendships in the Digital Scape

With our phones by our sides we are never alone. Even though I work from home on my own I speak to lots of different people via social media, email and messaging services. In fact, I'd say I have some kind of exchange with at least 50 people a day, about half of whom are people I know and half are those I don't know at all. In the olden days, speaking to 50 people would be an über-social day, but now, in our mediated world, it's pretty unremarkable. Being alone with technology feels markedly less alone. In 2008, Clive Thompson coined the term "ambient intimacy", a description of the cumulative impact of comforting pieces of micro-information which we're all consuming daily about each other. Instead of having to make an effort to meet with friends in person, we can skim "weak ties" to get those little hits of connection which we crave. By plugging into our phones we can escape ourselves and the strain of solitude and swim in a simulated sea of social interaction.

This state of affairs has an interesting impact on widely accepted psychological theories. For example, "Dunbar's Number", named after anthropologist Robin Dunbar, suggests that there's an upper limit on how many people we can know before connections start to fray. In 1998, he published his beliefs that the human brain can only manage a finite number of relationships, somewhere around the 150 mark. Other psychological studies have supported the reasoning by showing that social human groupings generally taper off around that number. I currently follow 838 people on Instagram, I've got 848 friends on Facebook and 303 on Twitter. And that's before we even get into the responses I give to comments from the approximately fifty thousand followers across all my platforms. And I'm not unique in this; most of us are now connected to a veritable ton of people. So how are we doing it when our human brains can only apparently cope with 150 contacts?

The answer is simple: *most of these people are not your friends*. They can't give you the connection you seek, and the apparent intimacy they offer is all an illusion. This is harsh but true, and what's more, the research proves it: teens who visit social-networking sites daily yet meet up with their friends less frequently are the most likely to agree that "A lot of times I feel lonely," "I often feel left out of things," and "I often wish I had more good friends." A 2014 study showed that a quarter of people didn't feel they had *one person* they could confide their personal troubles and triumphs to. Loneliness has been shown to be as damaging to our health as smoking 15 cigarettes a day, and it's become worryingly normalized across all ages and social backgrounds. The UK government even just appointed a "Loneliness Minister" in an effort to tackle the issue.

Spending my days alone but constantly connected doesn't stop me from feeling isolated. It doesn't stop me from jumping on my boyfriend the moment he walks in the door, desperate for some kind of human contact. It really just makes me feel alienated in my little silo, working as a one-woman band. And the people I'm connected to? Apart from those I'm genuinely intimate with, most of them are what has been termed "parasocial friends" – remote connections similar to those we can form with celebrities or even fictional characters. Keeping up with their movements can use up some of the emotional space in our Dunbar number, pushing out the people with whom we have authentic connections. Spreading myself thinly over hundreds, if not thousands, of people means that I have less time for my real-life mates. One of my new year's resolutions was to devote some of the four and a half hours per day I'd been filling with screen time to face-to-face meetings instead. Yes, it takes a chunk out of your day, but only a chunk you'd be wasting on your phone. More connection doesn't mean less isolation. It just means we're using our social time on shallow and non-meaningful snippets of friendships – or ambient intimacy – rather than the real thing.

Filtering Our Communications

I wasn't a popular kid in school. By the time I got to secondary school, this time a selective, private girls', I'd developed a loner status and being left out was just what I expected. To be honest, it made me feel a bit miserable, but not inconsolable – I had my hobbies and my books and I was nerdy enough to enjoy going to school for the learning. I always looked forward to exams and got on very well with my teachers. Need I say any more? Not really having any friends was part of my young life until I was 14, when ditching my glasses, getting a "Rachel from *Friends*" haircut and picking up a new smoking habit somehow gained me entry into the popular group at school. It was an extraordinary teen film-esque moment and the feeling of being accepted by a *clique* changed the rest of my school experience. Even though I was never really properly "in" (I still had a roster of deeply uncool after-school activities, including clarinet lessons and greenhouse monitoring), it was also when the troubles started. Girls can be mean and running with a crowd of high-achieving, pretty adolescents led to the start of a life-long anxiety around female friendships.

One of my biggest problems used to be that I often put my foot in it. "Saying what you see" is a good skill for a writer and journalist, less so a teenage girl trying to navigate a complex and highly strung set of social rules. I regularly made blunders which could come off as tactless and the result would often be an ejection from the social circle for an unbearable period of weeks, sometimes months. Each and every time it happened, it was like my world fell apart. Even today I'm highly aware of how my words could be construed by friends and I deliberate over ways of approaching issues, avoiding conflict at all costs. I still find it nearly impossible to contend with any difficult conversation in person and, while I'm good at hiding it, the amount of hand-wringing, tears and nausea that confrontation both in the workplace and in my social life causes me is off the charts. Social conflict has the power to paralyze me and completely take over my life: I can't think, I can't eat, I can't sleep. And

I definitely cannot just "let it go". If a friend is upset with me, it hollows me out, and while I've got much better at accepting that not everyone *in general* is going to like me, issues still emotionally floor me.

Over the ensuing 20 years, I've learned to be more diplomatic, but those youthful experiences have certainly impacted the way I prefer to communicate with friends today. One of the big attractions of conversing via mediated technology – whether it's text, email or social media – is that you have the power to review and edit your words until you get them "just so", something I find hugely comforting. I'm actually also massively telephobic (talking-on-the-phone-averse). However, like most millennials, I'm entirely at ease emailing anyone to ask for anything and feel both articulate and confident communicating via the written word. WhatsApp is an entirely stress-free environment for me. In fact, everything about communicating via technology appeals, whereas a lot of face-to-face interaction – especially anything awkward or potentially aggressive – brings me out in a cold sweat.

In this, according to Sherry Turkle, professor of social studies of science and technology at MIT, I am not alone. In her 2012 TED talk, which has been viewed more than four million times, she explains how technology has eased our path to connection while undermining our ability to have face-to-face conversations. As she says, "Texting, email, posting, all of these things let us present the self as we want to be. We get to edit, and that means we get to delete, and that means we get to retouch. Human relationships are messy and demanding, and we clean them with technology." When I look back at the social struggles I experienced in my adolescence, I know 100 per cent that had I had the option to use my phone to communicate with my teenage circle, to present myself through a filter, I would have used it as exclusively as possible. I was so scared of saying blunt things and what people might think of me that the ability to perfect my conversations would have been far too alluring.

A survey of American millennials by OnePoll found 65 per cent don't feel comfortable engaging with someone face-to-face, and 80 per cent prefer conversing digitally. As today's schoolkids increasingly prefer to connect remotely, there's little reason to leave the house. The number of teens who get together with their friends nearly every day dropped by more than 40 per cent from 2000 to 2015. We want access to each other – but crucially we want it in a controlled environment. Of course, there are potential drawbacks to digital communication – the fact that everything you say is "on record" adds a sense of pressure and the threat of cyberbullying is rife. But in general, digital communication allows us to sterilize our relationships and avoid the challenge of looking someone in the eye when having to say things which feel tricky. Avoidance is part and parcel of the way we connect today.

"In the past I've got into heated discussions with a friend and I've said something in the moment because I was so emotional. Whereas I find if I message my friend saying, 'I feel upset about what happened,' it gives them time to digest that message and think about what they want to say back, which often helps to calm the situation," explains Lily Pebbles, a blogger, YouTuber and author of *The F Word*, a book on modern female friendship. "I know I sometimes hide behind a screen – I've definitely decided to go to WhatsApp before calling a friend in person. It's almost like a pre-warning, so I'm not just coming from out of the blue and having a go about something. The idea of just calling someone or turning up at their doorstep to have an argument – I'd be terrified!"

At this stage of my life, the majority of my significant relationships (aside from that with my partner) happen through technology. My immediate family all live abroad. While my mum was living in Cape Town it was typical for us to only see each other at Christmas. My brother lives in Germany so it's easy to go year to year without having any physical contact. However, the three of us message each other approximately 467 times a day on our WhatsApp group chat. I know pretty much everything about their lives. Sometimes it can feel like a burden to keep up with the thread, but it's completely transformed our family dynamic. My brother and I didn't get on when we lived together as kids and we grated each other's gears during a two-year stint sharing a flat in my early thirties. Online, however, we are perfect, respectful siblings. Equally, my best girlfriend Beth lives in New York but we maintain a daily connection via technology. We have discovered each other through our screens, and while face-to-face conversations established and solidified our early friendship, now as our lives keep us closer to home, technology serves as a more than capable conduit. For me, on a personal level, social media and advances in communication technology have offered me an incredible opportunity to keep in touch with the people I most care about. I have become the perfect long-distance friend and feel authentically invested in my digital relationships.

However, and this is a *big* however, I'm aware that by reducing how often I do something I don't like to do (any type of tricky face-to-face conversation), my skills have become further depleted and my anxieties around them have heightened, and then some. The types of conversations I now rate as tricky have become more and more extensive. I also find it extremely difficult to be spontaneous and would rarely just pick up the phone to catch up with a friend or ask them over to my flat on a whim. There's a feeling that I can't interrupt them by asking for their time at too late notice, or that it's intrusive to call at the weekend, or during their evenings. Far better to text so they can get back to me in their own time.

It's not that I actually lack social confidence in terms of face-to-face meetings – my job is so sociable that it would be impossible to do if I didn't like meeting and talking to people, and I make acquaintances very easily. It's more I've become very used to the social media age pre-agreed boundaries for developing and maintaining those relationships, even among close friends. One thing that I've noticed is these confines often keep things shallow in real life – sharing is not quite the same as actually caring. Gone are the days when I'd have DMCs (deep and meaningful conversations) into the wee hours, listening intently to my girlfriend's struggles. The intensity of those friendships has simply worn off, and communication via technology has certainly had its part to play. It's definitely hard to type out heavy feelings among the emojis; far easier to gloss over it all and keep things light and message-digestible.

If I'm feeling these issues in my thirties, is it any wonder that there are reports of young people entering the workplace entirely lacking in basic interpersonal skills? Making eye contact, small talk, picking up the phone and performing in meetings are all areas that young millennials are said to be failing in. Michaela Launerts, author of *#GirlCode*, explains that young office recruits are "so used to being able to filter themselves before they post something online that they get stuck in a kind of real life stage fright."

From personal experience, I'd also say that favouring digital communication in all cases is something that is catching – you don't have to have been born after 1990 to have altered the way you get in contact with people. The first magazine office I worked in at the *Sunday Times* was a loud, boisterous cacophony of phone calls, with colleagues interviewing, cajoling and sometimes outright screaming down their handsets at poor, unsuspecting PRs. At my last office job, a fashion-tech company, I didn't even have my own phone. In fact, there was only one landline on the whole floor. Work progressed in monastic silence, or else punctuated with intense music, and it was easy to avoid face time for days on end. Of course, we did chat, but it wasn't a prerequisite to functioning in the workplace – you could use the social and work-related Slack channels to connect to your colleagues, and for everything else there was email. While there were plenty of millennials on staff, the screen communication culture was common to everyone, no matter what their age. It's just how offices are these days. It's easy to say, "So what?" – as long as we're still chatting and able to work and build relationships, even if it is only through our screens, really how much has changed? Isn't this just evolution in progress? However, it's worth considering: a) why we've been so keen to adopt this new way of communication, and b) what we miss in the process. The first answer is simple: it's easier and quicker to communicate with a screen than with a person who might stammer and stutter their response, and we love convenience more than anything. The second answer is thornier, but also more profound.

In the 1960s and 1970s Alfred Mehrabian, currently professor emeritus of psychology at UCLA, put forward research on the relative importance of verbal and non-verbal messages in the context of communication of emotions. He suggested that only 7 per cent of successful communication is in the words we use, 38 per cent in our tone of voice and 55 per cent in our body language. Although this research is clearly focused on face-to-face interactions and has been widely critiqued over the ensuing decades, it points to how important non-verbal cues can be for the delivery of our emotions. This will not be news to anyone who has been *seriously* misunderstood through digital communication. How many times have you made a joke via text only to get a "?" back from your friend? Or suggested something by email which has been received as being aggressive or thoughtless when that was the last thing you meant? How much less likely would the confusion have happened if you'd been there in person to add a wink, a nudge and maybe a sardonic smile at the end of your memo?

It's not rocket science to understand why we might feel more bonded to our friends in person rather than via text, but it's depressing how often we're happy to substitute the ersatz communication for the real thing. In *Reclaiming Conversation: The Power of Talk in a Digital Age*, Sherry Turkle makes a striking case for the need to preserve conversation. Aside from surveying the worrying lack of social development among school-age children, she makes the ultimate point: "Face-to-face conversation is the most human – and humanizing – thing we do. Fully present to one another, we learn to listen. It's where we develop the capacity for empathy."

Without empathy, we can't tell when we hurt each other; we lose the ability to read our colleagues', parents' or children's subtle cues; we forget each other's emotional ticks and nuances. Hiding behind a screen makes us regress in our levels of emotional and social intelligence. And over time we become more and more a mystery to each other, degrading the quality of our human connections until we feel deeply alone.

And when it comes to romantic relationships, the behaviour of those who've grown up in the anti-social social age is especially poignant. Dr Jean M Twenge, a professor of psychology at San Diego State University and author of *iGen* (defined as the generation born between 1995 and 2012 who can't remember a time before the internet), notes that in her 25 years of research there has never been such an abrupt shift in behaviour between generations. Let's take dating as an example. In 2015, only about 56 per cent of US high-school seniors went out on dates, whereas for baby boomers and Generation X, that percentage was around 85 per cent. Why go out on dates to get to know each other when you can just send each other snaps and lurk on each other's stories from the comfort and physical and emotional safety of your own bed? Aside from not dating, teens also aren't having sex – the number of sexually active teens in the US has declined by almost 40 per cent since 1991 and the teen birth rate in the UK has halved since 1998. This generation doesn't drink or take drugs in the same way either – in the UK levels of alcohol consumption have plummeted to their lowest levels in over a decade and teens in the US are less likely to be taking illicit drugs than their predecessors. So, what are they doing instead of sex, drugs and rock 'n' roll? I'll give you two guesses and they both start with the smartphone.

Romance is Dead: Break-Ups in the Digital Era

Romantic Instagram relationships are perhaps the easiest to fall for. However cynical you might be, and even if you manage to avoid every Katherine Heigl romcom, the dream of "happily ever after" stares back at you, seemingly from every screen. And this is especially true when it comes to social media. When I got married eight years ago, I was pretty culpable when it came to projecting only the good side of my relationship online. That wasn't because I was trying to manipulate what the outside world thought of me (at least consciously) – it was more that I only took and shared pictures when we were happy. But still, no-one could ever have guessed that it wasn't a fairy tale, and I was more than happy to perpetuate that myth.

Even though I view them with a heavy dose of cynicism, gushingly romantic gestures on social media can still make me slightly bereft because they play to our deeply internalized ideals of happy ever after. Nearly half of a Pew Research study group of teenagers (47 per cent) agreed that social media offers a place for them to show how much they care about their significant other, with 12 per cent feeling this way "a lot". I think we all know someone who falls into that 12 per cent – somebody who spends most of their time posting dreamy love scenes, or writing heartfelt messages to their partner on social media (check out @TheCoupleGoals on Instagram, currently boasting over four million followers. Warning: not for the faint- or broken-hearted). Their love seems to be the core of their social media existence and identity, with "I" morphing into "we" progressively with every "Relfie" (yes, that's a relationship selfie). Of course, in the same way that we've learned that individuals present a hyper-idealized view of themselves and their bodies on social media, the same thing happens with the way we present our partnerships. Just think, when did you last see a shot of an argument in progress or one of the not quite so thoughtful things (underwear left on the floor, loo seat up, every cup in the kitchen used and unwashed...) that all our partners on occasion annoy us with? But contrary to expectations, research has proven that those who post the most about their other half are in fact the least secure in their relationship status. A 2014 study showed that when people felt more insecure about their partner's feelings they tended to make their relationships visible on Facebook on a daily basis. The truth is you never know what is actually going on behind the screens or those closed doors.

To use my own marriage as an example, having presented happy images of wedded bliss on social media, I was just as shocked as anyone when my husband left me a couple of weeks shy of my thirtieth birthday. With just the shirt on his back he was gone overnight, and aside from one brief meeting later when I said goodbye to our terrier, I've never seen him again. It is to this day the most shocking thing that's ever happened to me and marked a definite juncture between being a person who believed in a world of controlled rites of passage and someone who understands that life is often messy. After eight years of sharing the same bed as someone, a shock break-up is always going to send you a bit bonkers. When you've been married in front of all your friends and family, and implicitly in front of today's broader social media network, it's a whole lot worse. I was – how can I put this – stark, raving, off-the-charts deranged. Googling "Divorce before 30" (obviously my first step at day zero), served up countless news stories replete with stats proving the high likelihood that youthful "I dos" will end in Splitsville. You can find pieces that explain, "You still have a chance" (thanks, *Elite Daily*), advice blogs telling you that your divorce will be "one of the best experiences of your life" (spoiler alert: not until well down the line) and a few nicely written anecdotal accounts (*HuffPost* has a heartfelt series if you find yourself in a similar position). But there's no guide to surviving the bat-shit period, no conversation about how to keep it together and very little mention of the deep, gnawing shame that comes with a failed marriage so young, in a world demanding perfection.

After a few days of trying to work out how I could change myself so he would want me again, everything became a haze. I was immediately adamant that I had to keep it together and only took one day off work. I stopped sleeping almost entirely. A few moments from that time are clear: my miserable birthday dinner where everything tasted of cardboard; the first Christmas on my own with my family distraught to see me in such a state; and the well-meaning private messages sent to me via Facebook and Instagram, from married friends who "couldn't believe" that it had happened but who very soon I would never hear from ever again.

From the social media perspective, I had approximately one thousand images on my Facebook profile of my ex-husband and they tortured me for months. Whenever I was travelling, or up awake at night, I would look through them all in a manic, masochistic binge. The wedding shots obviously cut deep, but the most painful were the early-day unglamorous shots – the pictures of us falling in love. As Ira Hyman, professor of psychology at Western Washington University, explains in *Psychology Today*, "Facebook holds everything in an unchanging past. All those happy pictures. All that togetherness. The version Facebook retains is the idealized version of that old relationship and the glorified, impossible version of your previous partner. Only the good times reside in the network's memory." Social media kept my rose-tinted specs well and firmly on, and plugged into a past which was, to every intent and purpose, completely over.

After a couple of months of mooning, I nipped it in the bud and deleted every image of him – and yes, it took hours. Also, when I packed up his stuff, I sent off every photograph of us, every keepsake, every love note. I donated my white dress and its associated veil to charity and wiped the flat clear of anything that would set me off. When you're trying to keep your dignity (which really means being able to leave the house and not end up in hysterics), it's important to be totally ruthless. I fully deleted him from both my online and offline lives, which was a massive wrench at the time but definitely helped the grieving process.

When your audience, be that three hundred Facebook friends or thousands of YouTube followers, has consumed your relationship online, it can feel like a huge pressure to explain where the hell this other person has gone from your life. I kept quiet about it, but then at the time I didn't have the kind of following I do now. Lizzy Hadfield, a YouTuber who regularly shared posts featuring her ex, had a lot more pressure to deal with the public fallout. "I was really, really nervous about telling my followers about my break-up last year," she explains. "So much so that I put a proper plan together because I was so worried about how it would be received. I did feel responsible for protecting my ex, and it was definitely frustrating to feel I had to justify things, because breaking up is hard enough to do behind closed doors. But I knew I had to do it in a respectful way. There ended up being a lot of negativity towards him, which is horrible because *I* put myself out there online, and while I've weighed up the repercussions of that, other people – your friends and family – shouldn't have to deal with it. But I guess that's just the way it is and part of your privacy that you sacrifice when you live your life on screen."

My break-up rock bottom was spent in The Bowery Hotel during New York Fashion Week, February 2014. I was lonely, in terrible debt, terrified of the logistics of my divorce and had burned my face with hair straighteners, creating five shiny blisters on the side of my face. During *fashion week*. I still wasn't sleeping and had a huge workload ahead of 12-hour days, 2am deadlines and 5am wake-up calls. I still had to get up every morning, put my face on and pull together a chic outfit. I had a photographer shooting my looks for a social project I was working on for my magazine's channels and, of course, felt the pressure to post on my own social platforms too. When I look back at those images I can see the pain in my eyes, but no-one really would have ever guessed what was going on and I certainly wasn't telling. Instead, from a social media perspective, it just looked like I was having a glamorous time at New York Fashion Week wearing lovely clothes and staying in a five-star hotel... Yet another example of how entirely inaccurate social media perceptions can be.

The biggest thing with any break-up is that you have to keep somewhere in your muddled mind that you will come out the other side. My "other side" moment happened on my first ever trip to Los Angeles, one of the reasons that the city will always be dear to me. It was a mere seven weeks after my break-up and things were pretty bleak. I was in town to interview two towering female names in international fashion – Diane von Furstenberg and Tory Burch – and both of them were incredibly inspiring. Halfway through my interview with Diane, she stopped me and asked, "Is there something going on with you?" While I thought I'd been hiding the black hole that had taken residence within my heart, it seems the subterfuge wasn't enough to fool DVF. I ended up giving her a précis of my situation, and in turn she gave me two pieces of advice which have stuck with me ever since.

Firstly, she told me that, "the body has no memory for pain", something which seems impossible to believe when you're in the depths of despair, but is one of the most useful and accurate pieces of counsel I've ever been given. Even now, as I'm writing about that time, it's as if it happened to some other person. I can't completely connect to that pain – my body bears no physical scar of that emotional sucker punch and, while I'm not saying I don't have some psychological echoes from that time, in the main I've just moved on. However hard things get, you have to hold on to the fact that the pain will pass and you *will* come back to yourself. Secondly, Diane said to me, "It's time to change the lenses in your glasses. You think he left you, but the truth is he set you free."

She was right: my ex actually did set me free, but I felt entirely unequipped to deal with the new world of romance. Dating after you go through any kind of break-up isn't straightforward, but the lie of the land had completely changed since I'd last been single. And that was because of one thing – Tinder.

Digital Dating: The Stats

The technosexual revolution has been developing for decades (I actually found my mum's husband for her on Match.com nearly 20 years ago when I was 16), but it wasn't until Tinder hit in 2012 that *everyone* got swiping. Racking up 1.4 billion swipes a day, the fact that the app is loosely connected to your Facebook account (drawing profile images and making connections apparently based on people you already know) and now also Instagram-integrated makes it feel more like a social media platform crossed with a game than the more dorky dating sites (requiring endless personal statements and multiple-choice surveys).

My personal experience of app dating is similar to those of lots of my cohorts: terrifying at first, a few LOLs in between, but ultimately really only a place to get your head back in the dating arena. When your confidence is way down and someone has made you believe you're unfanciable and unlovable, even having a single "match" on a dating app can boost your self-esteem. Reintroducing the idea that someone, somewhere, might want you (even if only for a moment), the apps can definitely help you start to find a way back to your mojo. Sure, I was stood up on dates, had an odd encounter with a chap who excused himself after the starter and didn't return until the dessert course (Like, seriously, where did he go? And why did he come back?) and got ghosted by guys who I'd kissed on the street in drunken clinches. None of those things were fun, but they were fundamental steps in my romantic rehabilitation. What can be harder to deal with is months of app-exclusive dating, something which has been shown to lead to a decline in self-worth, esteem and body-image security, according to a recent study. "Tinder users report having lower levels of satisfaction with their faces and bodies and having lower levels of self-worth than men and women who do not use Tinder," explained Jessica Strübel, co-author of the research.

The truth is that digital dating can be an excruciatingly slow process. Aside from the fact that most people you meet sadly will not be Mr or Mrs Right, keeping up conversations long enough to meet up with someone when you have the rest of your life going on can feel an impossible challenge and lead to "dating burnout" – where all the conversations and dates become a blur. When you have Bumble, Hinge, Tinder and Happn notifications buzzing on your phone all day and all night, there's not much room for anything else – like, say, a normal social life or, you know, work. In the 2017 Match.com "Singles in America" survey, 15 per cent of singles said they felt addicted to the process of dating and 54 per cent of women felt exhausted by the whole process.

Dating apps are now even more closely linked to social platforms, and there's even been a recent shift to moving proceedings directly onto social sites themselves. Instagram is now a dating app, if you choose to use it so. Views of Stories are often seen as the first preamble to a romantic connection, and I have scores of girlfriends who are attuned to *exactly* who has been viewing the snapshots of their day, even if that means scrolling through thousands of followers to find that hot-guy handle in the haystack. Someone interested might then take the next step of the "casual like", which could actually be casual, progressing on to multiple likings of posts, culminating in the attention-seeking "back-stalk like" (liking an image more than three weeks old). At this point you would be assured that you have an admirer, and could feasibly expect a DM (direct message) to come through. Moving off Instagram to texting or WhatsApp would be the next logical step, before potentially, maybe, hopefully arranging a date. If this all seems like an insane social media dance with weird and unintelligible rules, that's because it is. If it takes this long to get a guy to meet you, is it any wonder we're constantly glued to our phones?

"It's definitely disconcerting to see a guy watching your stories when you thought they were out of the picture. You start thinking, 'Is he into me again? Does he miss me?'" explains Kelly Agnew, a New York-based senior fashion and beauty editor at Refinery29. "If you let it, the search for a romantic partner online can take over your entire life, because in a big city, it's really the only way to meet a guy. Over the years I've definitely had to take some time off from the apps, because I couldn't fathom spending another night in bed swiping left and right – who has the time, let alone the finger strength, for that? Plus, my workload is pretty full-on, I have a Thursday night dance cardio class I hate to skip and I value my time with my girlfriends and self-care way more than drinks with some random guy. Sometimes you just have to get back to the rest of your life. That said, I definitely have got the whole first-date thing down, perhaps *too* pat. I vet most guys before I right-swipe with a deep internet background check, order the same tequila cocktail [on a date], hell, I even wear the same outfit nine times out of ten. When I'm really focused on dating, I might see two guys a week. Not that it doesn't have its fun moments, but in general the word I'd use to describe it is gruelling. But of course, you keep going back to it, because one day one of those guys is going to be 'the One'. Or at least that's what you tell yourself."

In the end, I did meet someone new, but not on a dating app. In fact, even though we were both Tindering hard, we'd never have met digitally as he was four years too young for my age filter. One of the biggest problems with digital dating is that most of us have no idea what we actually want. In my mind, I was looking for an "adult" 30–45, someone who had made their way in life and was at least 6ft (183cm) tall. Instead I fell in love with a 5ft 9in (175cm) 26 year old who lived in a shared rental without a sitting room, worked weekends and definitely didn't have it all figured out. Our lifestyles were not instantly compatible and it took some serious work to iron out the kinks between my relationship expectations and his relationship experience. But he did – and still does – give me a run for my money, and that's really the only thing that matters.

While wild horses couldn't keep me away from him, I'm not sharing daily pictures of him on social media or making endless status updates about my levels of adoration (and hell would have to literally freeze over before he did either). We've been dating for four years, own an apartment together and are about to have our first child – yet we're both still "single" on Facebook. This reticence to share isn't only because I know what it feels like to read the gushy stuff when you're heartbroken (and I wouldn't want to be the cause of pain for someone else), but also because I just don't feel the inclination to do so. I don't care what anyone thinks about my relationship or my sweetheart; he doesn't need to be "visible" to be important, and on the odd occasion that I do post something public, it's really just for him. I'm still a hopeless romantic, but the prism through which I view couplehood has changed completely.

Green-Eyed Detectives

We've discussed the power of envy to turn our social media experiences into compare-a-thons, but the related feelings of jealousy really crank things up a notch when it comes to the realm of relationships. Have you ever kept tabs on someone through social media? Maybe it was a crush or a new romance and you were trying to scope out their single status or your relative attractiveness to their previous flames? What about a proper partner? Perhaps you've had a quick look at who they're following and liking on Instagram? Or the slightly less acceptable sneaky read of their private messages when they forgot to log out of your iPad? How about your exes? In truth, could the secret service actually do with hiring someone as expert at digital reconnaissance as you? If so, you are part of the new *social surveillance* culture, a world in which every step we take and every move we make is being monitored by people we know and love.

Over a quarter of young people – 27 per cent – say social media makes them feel jealous or unsure about their romantic relationship. As soon as you connect with, or indeed pre-stalk, a new lover on social media, you are served with a huge amount of information on his or her interactions with their community, which may or may not include a lot of people they've hooked up with. Aside from being able to scroll through a decade's worth of photos and associated comments, you're constantly updated with their "current activities", broadcasted for all to see. If they so happen to innocuously like a picture of their ex, their gym instructor or work colleague, you know about it immediately. And you can start to stew. The very fact that you are consuming information about your partner outside his or her physical presence totally upends the normal context of romantic relationships. If you'd been there when your other half complimented someone, you'd more than likely brush it off immediately. Reading it in comment form can somehow make it feel like a betrayal, or perhaps the beginning of a secret conversation chain that *may* one day lead to you being dumped by text. Again, it's the lack of non-verbal cues which can really mess with your perspective and your mind. Innocent engagement can be easily construed as suggestive, and even the very fact that your new partner is connected to his past paramours can feel like a dagger to the heart. If a picture of him at a drinks party you didn't know about suddenly pops up on your newsfeed, it's easy to think, "Why wasn't I invited?" Then, "Who was he there with?" when, in fact, it could have been a spur-of-the-moment post-office quick pint which just so happened to get uploaded to social media. It's our public and constant access to things which were once private that can set the green-eyed monster into overdrive.

However, it's not just in the emerald eye of the beholder. Social media has definitely increased the opportunities for flirtation as well as emotional and physical adultery. The fact that the screen is there, acting as a filter, can mean appropriate relationship lines are easily blurred; it's easy to think it's just messages online and not really anything to do with real life, right? Actually, not so right. As many as a third of all divorce cases in the UK now report the words "Facebook" in the proceedings, and more than 80 per cent of US divorce lawyers say the role of social networking in irretrievable marital breakdown is on the rise. If we add in the stats on social dating sites, it starts to become difficult to believe that anyone's keeping it in their pants. A report last year showed that 64 per cent of people had "seen somebody on Tinder who they knew to be in an exclusive relationship", and 56 per cent reported that they had female friends who used Tinder while in relationships. What we know is that social media is very good at making us feel that our lives are inadequate and that the grass is greener pretty much everywhere else. No relationship is perfect, and rocky patches are par for the course. During those moments, it's almost too easy to lose sight of your ethical compass and turn for comfort to the seemingly endless supply of alternative, idealized partners available at the swipe of your iPhone screen 24/7... Is it really any wonder that so many of us have come to the conclusion that tweeting must mean cheating?

It's Either Me or The Phone

Even if you're not playing away from home, social media can cause strife in your relationships. "Phubbing" or "phone snubbing" is the term which best describes what we're doing when we use our phones excessively instead of engaging with our romantic partners, and it's been shown to have a huge impact on the success of a relationship. "What we found was the more often your partner uses his or her phone in your presence, the higher the level of conflict in your relationship," explains Dr Roberts. "This conflict isn't always voiced – sometimes you might say, 'Put down your phone and talk to me,' but other times it's a silent feeling of rejection. Either way, being 'phubbed' leads to conflict and lower relationship satisfaction, and if you extend that out it can be connected to divorce and certainly to one's happiness."

It's hardly rare to feel that your partner is ignoring you in favour of a glowing screen. Of course, usually it's entirely hypocritical. Reviewing my Moment app, which tracks my iPhone use throughout the day (my average is four hours and twenty-six minutes per day, with about one hour fifty minutes on social media as part of that colossal use of 26 per cent of my waking life), I can see that a significant part of my screen time is during the evenings when I'm sitting next to my boyfriend. It's exceedingly easy to point the finger when you feel that you're being neglected in favour of something more interesting on your loved one's phone, but there are few saints left when it comes to digital distraction. It's easy to say, "Let's talk more," but unless the pair of you can commit to phone-free time, that next article or social media picture or email is far too alluring. I get phubbed, but I'm also a phubber. Some evenings we just phub all night, which is sadly not a euphemism.

× × ×

These are just some of the ways that social media has transformed my personal relationships. It's not a stellar list. If you too are dealing with any – or all – of the issues highlighted above, try not to entirely despair, because a lot of them can be dramatically improved by making changes to your behaviour. I'm not going to lie: it's definitely easier said than done. But making a conscious and informed decision about how you deal with some of these feelings really is the first step. As for me, I'm logging off to go and meet a real friend, no offence intended.

Takeaways

1. Connect emotionally offline

I get it; we all have busy lives. But there are few more important things to our happiness than our relationships, and they are *definitely* worth the investment. If time is of the essence, you need to get really brutal and honest with yourself about which of your relationships are priorities and which you're just going through the motions with. Making a cull, however heartless it sounds, will give you the quality time you need to connect deeply with the few instead of superficially with the many. Just remember Dunbar's rule – the more time we give to pseudo relationships, the more thinly spread we are where it matters.

It's true our friends may have got used to the more hands-off approach that you've both probably been following of late. To ensure your more assertive behaviour isn't seen as intrusive or overly needy, it's worth initiating a conversation, which could happen via technology, about how you feel. Tell them that you want to spend more quality time with them both in person and on the phone and that you're missing the real-life connection. If they don't respond well to your suggestion of more offline interaction, they probably deserve a one-way ticket to your cull list.

2. Stop hiding behind your screens

"Do something that scares you every day," is one of those hackneyed Instagram quotes that catches in your gullet. While I believe in the power of taking risks, doing something scary every day is no-one's idea of fun. However, when it comes to face-to-face clashes, the only way any of us are going to get any better at dealing with intimidating in-person situations is, sadly, practice. Conflict-avoiders like me are most often worried about people liking them and the risk of losing favour. In these situations, I often spend hours, if not days and weeks, mentally preparing exactly what I'm going to say, going over and over my words – which is one of the reasons it's so much easier to do it virtually, because you can edit it down to convey the perfect message.

However, what happens when you stop focusing on the things you say and instead concentrate on listening to the person at the other end of the conversation? It's so easy to obsess about the way that our words *might* be received that you can forget that conversations are two-way streets. Try showing vulnerability, coming at the issue honestly and sensitively, but also truly hearing what the person says – this is a sure-fire way to ease the stress. Basically, it takes two to tango, so share the pressure.

3. Forget the pre-nup, it's all about the phone-free agreement
"With relationships, we know excessive phone use is a bad thing because it divides our attention," says Dr Roberts. "To help improve the situation, I always suggest smartphone-free zones and time periods. Try marking out places in your home where smartphone use is forbidden. Some of the obvious ones are not using it in the bedroom – both something that helps with your sleep and sex life – and limiting your use when you're with your children, with your partner on a date, or at dinner. With these little victories, you can prove that it can be done. You don't have to go cold turkey, but if you want to make your partner feel valued and properly protect your relationship, you have to try and balance the time you spend without your phone."

4. Try to meet people IRL
When did you last make a new friend offline? In the past year, have you asked someone (or graciously accepted an invitation) on a date *in person*? It doesn't take long to lose confidence in making real-life connections, and once you're out of practice, it can seem like an insurmountable struggle to approach people you don't know well or at all. While the digital hacks for meeting people can be incredibly convenient, they can also conversely make you feel more apprehensive about making new offline relationships. After all, why should you have to go through that discomfort when you could do it all behind the safety of a screen? The real answer is that, however much technology can

give fate a helping hand, by avoiding opportunities to meet people organically in your environment you are only going to reduce your chances of meeting people that truly mean something to you. The combination of on- and offline networking is a powerful strategy when you want to meet new people. Feeling unable to chat to a fun-looking girl at the end of your Pilates class or feeling so overwhelmed at the idea of speaking to a person you'd like to date who is already – even peripherally – in your life is something really worth working at.

While I am no expert on friend- or courtships, I have over the years met thousands of people through my job. And I can safely say that everyone gets those tingly butterflies when introducing themselves to people they don't know, but quite like the look of. But you have to keep saying to yourself: what is the very worst that can happen? OK, they could look at you blankly and say they are not interested in conversing with you, but that would be highly unlikely and pretty rude. Sure, they might not jump at your attempt to get to know them...but they quite possibly will. Isn't it worth the roll of the dice?

Although I don't have a formula, finding common ground is obviously a great starting point. One of the nicest things about meeting people IRL is that you can often skip weeks of intermittent messaging and progress a relationship far quicker. And you can tell far more speedily if you're both wasting your time on a fantasized version of each other. There's no right way to meet people, but stubbornly deciding *not* to consider the people walking in and out of your life every day is certainly not going to lead to a richer pool of potential relationship candidates.

Chapter 5:
Why Social Media is
Ruining **Motherhood**

Of all the sticks women beat themselves with, perhaps the thorniest of all is that of needing to be a "good" mother. While new narratives around choices of childlessness are breaking through, it's still a truism that the vast majority of women will, at some point, become mothers. Indeed, at the last count of British women turning 45 in 2016, 82 per cent had at least 1 child. While parenting manuals may fall in and out of fashion, discussions around IVF might trend and debates around the pros and cons of different types of birth will rage on, motherhood remains fetishized, scrutinized and pressurized across the globe. Invariably reflecting the issues of society at large, social media has an unsurprisingly complicated track record when it comes to the challenges women go through along the many stages of parenthood.

Polished, pretty and relentlessly positive, the aspirational cult of social media "mama-hood" isn't fundamentally much more than an updated version of her Stepford sister. OK, she may have ditched the Betty Draper nipped-in waists for head-to-toe Isabel Marant bohemia, and her home might be stacked with tasteful Californian casual décor rather than chintz. She might even go on a Women's March. But the sanitized, yet oh-so-stylish, version of what a mother could look like, projected apparently effortlessly across Pinterest, Instagram and Facebook, can be enough to crush the morale of even the most adept of new mums. Organic weaning, matching alpaca sweaters (for your brood of five, no less), tousled beachy hair, "snapped-back" bodies and prolific outdoorsy activities combine to make Gwyneth Paltrow look like a runner-up in the perfection stakes. This is motherhood as a beauty advertising campaign, a staged glorification, both impenetrable and immaculate. And it's a standard which entirely masks the messy, weary and at times monotonous reality which every mother trudges through. It also elevates a sense of complete maternal sacrifice – and idea that with your baby's birth you too have been reborn as a different person without the interests, passions and achievements which once made you the person you were. What you are is a mother; it's your only definition. When we talk about being sold a fantasy on social media, the mama "glow" really takes the proverbial biscuit.

Motherhood, especially the first time around and in its earliest days, can be a time of intense vulnerability for many women. It's also a period which has been highlighted by researchers and psychologists as being particularly treacherous for dealing with some of social media's most pernicious pressures. When we're already sleep deprived and disassociated from our bodies, social comparison and feelings of inadequacy have the potential to rupture self-esteem and identity, and threaten our mental state.

More than a third of British mothers will experience mental health issues related to parenthood, and while social media can provide support in the form of community groups related to pretty much anything you can imagine across the motherhood gamut, it can also put women under even more stress to compete with each other. Watching other mums bake their kids vegan treats, with their pristine homes in the background and handsome husbands just out of eyeshot, can understandably make another mother who hasn't showered in three days and has only eaten take-out noodles for the past two weeks feel somewhat incompetent. How can other women appear so capable? Is it because they can afford help? Or is it just because they're better mothers? If so, how am I getting this so wrong? Did I birth a monster baby? Am I already a...*bad mother*?

As Kat Farmer, a mother and the blogger behind *Does My Bum Look 40 in This*, says, the reality for most women is not characterized by clear countertops and cupcakes. "I had three children under four – and the entire experience was a blur. I do look back and think about how incredibly vulnerable you are at that point from so many different aspects. You're attacked by so many different emotions. Your work is at that point probably in the toilet. Career? What career? You're up to your knees in nappies and you are most definitely not looking at your finest. Your house looks literally like a squat and you're bone-knackered. You also have no money. Really, you couldn't be at a lower ebb. At that point, social media can be pretty tough. It's a very exposed spot."

The "mamas" who present coffee-table versions of the motherhood experience may not be doing anything new: we've seen these interpretations of child-rearing before in magazines and advertising. But in the social media age they're that much more potent as these are *actual mothers,* not models who've been cast alongside photogenic cherubs. You've possibly watched their bellies swell over nine months and probably heard the ins and outs of their (natural, non-medicated, obviously) birth stories. You know how they came up with their baby's name and how they decided to decorate their nursery. You can't deny that they are "real", so you start to believe a little at least of what you see.

Happily, there's also been a sustained and vocal reaction to the sugar-coated version of child rearing, inspired by feminist thought and the strong voices of women who, to put it bluntly, are fed up with being made to feel like shit by the perfect social media mother. The average age of a mum in England and Wales hit 30.3 in 2015, and the number of women over 40 having babies overtook those 20 and under. The US picture is broadly similar, with the typical age for first-time motherhood around the 28 mark and more women giving birth between ages 30 and 34 than 25 and 29. This means that it's increasingly more mature women who are going through the experience, often with established careers, financial independence and a full case of life experience in tow. They have more of an inkling when they're being duped. The "warts-and-all" honest motherhood movement has begun to chip away at the glow approach, with women sharing images of their less-than-perfect postpartum bellies, accounts of their disillusionment and depression, and a raw version of motherhood which exhibits its hardships. True, there are criticisms (seriously there are criticisms about *everything* related to motherhood on social media, so buckle up for judgement) that some of this has gone too far to the point of martyrdom and that honest motherhood is creating an excessively bleak picture for what to expect when you're expecting. But it's definitely a welcome rejoinder to the airbrushed version of motherhood that has dominated the space.

Many women – even those who may present glossy and glamorous lifestyles on social media – are also deciding to join the conversation, as Laura Fantacci, the Italian co-founder of influential digital magazine *Wardrobe Icons*, explains. "Aesthetically, for what I'm doing professionally, showcasing the chaos of real home life on social media wouldn't feel right, but whenever I have a voice, I'm not shy about saying that life isn't always picture-perfect. I don't want to hide behind the 'this is the best moment of your life' message because, for me, initially the experience was overwhelming and definitely not entirely positive. At times, I felt scared to be alone with my baby. Life suddenly stopped having a rhythm designated by day and night and had just become an existence on a loop. I was so sleep-deprived and deeply drained – I found out later that I was coeliac, so that compounded the exhaustion. I remember my husband leaving in the morning and I was just counting the seconds until he came home. Everything was magnified because of my expectation of what it would be like. I had pictured the whole thing to be this glowy, serene, happy time. So, there was a huge element of disillusionment. It was disappointment in myself, in how I handled it and how poorly I'd coped. It was also a disappointment in the reality of motherhood."

While it's encouraging to see these more nuanced depictions, they don't relieve the weight of our ideals. A 2015 University of Northern Colorado study showed that even women who do not subscribe to "motherhood ideologies" are at risk of experiencing increased stress and anxiety, and decreased self-esteem in the face of the pressure to be perfect. Even if we are woke to the fact that all mums deal with explosive nappies, tantrums in public places and the soul-destroying exhaustion of two-hour feeding rotations, there is evidence that we continue to internalize guilt and self-doubt. And that's something that's not good for our kids.

Sarah Schoppe-Sullivan, professor of human sciences and psychology at Ohio State University, has shown in her research that striving to be the perfect mother can actually backfire and make you a worse one. "The quest to be a 'perfect' mother may actually harm a mother's parenting," she explains. "In my lab's research on new parents, we found that mothers showed less confidence in their parenting abilities when they were more worried about what other people thought about their parenting." So much of looking after a baby is about confidence – the countless daily decisions you make all hinge on feeling secure about your ability to make the best choice for your child. Without confidence, you endlessly question yourself, creating a tense, highly stressed environment for the whole family. Feeling calm and sure of yourself has been proven to benefit your child's development, whereas when parents are significantly stressed during their child's early years, one study showed that some of their genes (involved in insulin production and brain development) were affected into adolescence. Social media has not invented the perfect mother. But it has certainly strengthened the façade and turned the screws on what that perfect mother should look like. More than 80 per cent of women in a UK survey in 2017 said that Instagram and Facebook "added pressure to be the perfect mum". Even those who embrace elements of imperfection and project a confidence in their own shortcomings are not immune to the pressures. No-one it seems is impervious to the glow.

Getting Pregnant, Staying Pregnant, Being Pregnant

You might have heard that we're in the midst of a fertility crisis. Everywhere we turn – whether it's our parents, our newspapers or our

GPs – we're made aware that our eggs are passing their sell-by date, slowly, yet inexorably, going bad inside us. As soon as I hit 28, it seemed to be all everyone I knew talked about, and it's still a major topic of conversation among both my followers and friends. The truth is it's no joke: sperm counts among Western men have halved over the past 40 years, and as women have delayed trying to conceive, their chances of having a family have markedly declined. There's evidence that the memo has been received and that women are aware that starting their journey to motherhood at a younger age improves their chances of success, however, there are also plenty of impediments to this trend reversal – many of which I can relate to personally.

At the time of writing, I'm about to give birth in less than two weeks – if our son decides to come on time. I'll be 34 years old and a few months shy of geriatric motherhood. I first started trying to conceive when I was 32, and the monthly feelings of failure were one of the hardest things that I've ever had to deal with. My story is entirely ordinary in many ways. While I required medical assistance and drugs to conceive, I didn't go through IVF and, in comparison to what many, many other couples go through with multiple losses, hardships and the huge expenses incurred by fertility procedures, I know I've been fortunate. However, there's no doubt that social media made a massive impact on my experiences with both my fertility and my pregnancy, and at every step of the way it's had a bearing on my mental state.

I decided to post an "announcement" bump image on social media when I was 16 weeks pregnant, simply because there was no hiding it any more (my belly has tracked at the 98th percentile the whole way through – this hasn't been a subtle pregnancy...and, yes, I'm nervous for my vagina). While my boyfriend and I couldn't have been happier to share the news, it was definitely a bittersweet moment. Because over those months of trying, I had found it increasingly hard to stay upbeat as every woman I seemed to know or follow on Instagram effortlessly produced one bundle of joy after another. I was adamant that my bump wasn't going to add to that tally or compete in the ever more creative "reveals" that we're becoming accustomed to on social media. I just really wanted to be entirely honest and let any woman who was in the same position as I'd been know that she was not the only one going through it. In fact, as around one in seven couples in the UK and one in eight couples in the US are said to have trouble conceiving – whatever social media might suggest – they're part of a significant minority and very far from being alone.

I'm not used to feeling a really deep stab of social media envy. We all get FOMO, but that crushing covetousness has never been my digital Achilles heel, and since my divorce, I've managed to keep a sense of perspective when consuming other people's lives. But the baby thing was different because it wasn't about "happiness" or "success" – it was about a biological process. Motherhood is so tied up with identity and can penetrate to the core of who you are, not just what you have. Unlike other life achievements, there are no halfway houses. You can't ever be nearly pregnant – you either are or you're not, and feeling let down by your body is a different kind of sense of failure than, say, feeling inadequate about your work ethic and career success. Trying to conceive while you're consuming endless images of beautiful babies in fresh cashmere bonnets can feel lonely, bewildering and horribly, horribly self-centred. No-one wants to feel anything but elation for other couples having babies, but while I'm ashamed to say it, I didn't always feel entirely happy for other people. Actually, seeing other women getting pregnant, especially on social media, where I had little idea of their backstory, often caused me pain as well as biting jealousy.

It's no-one's fault. Lots of the posts I can remember feeling hard to swallow weren't at all boastful or smug, just simply poignant snapshots of love. But the experience has definitely moderated the way I feel about sharing my journey to motherhood, as I know that there will be women registering images of my burgeoning bump who feel just like I did. I'm not saying that it's stopped me posting pictures of myself – at the end of the day I don't have a body double that could have filled in for me as I grew outwards. But I am very conscious of the way, if all goes well, that I'll be posting about my baby, as I know from experience that my happiness might strike some other not-so-happy chords elsewhere.

Not being able to get pregnant when you desperately want to is one of the most wretched experiences a couple can go through. The monthly cycle of dashed hopes, the constant questioning (If I had to pay for every time I googled "causes of infertility", I'd be bankrupt. And let's not talk about what I've googled since...) and the insidious feeling of self-doubt can have an impact on all areas of your life. I know I'm by no means alone going through nearly a year of "TTC" (trying to conceive) – but that time has armed me with some really strong opinions on how the medical profession and we as a community deal with it. If I hadn't sought specialist help, I wouldn't be pregnant now – because I've been advised that, due to a cycle condition, I'll probably never be able to get pregnant without the help of drugs. And had I listened to pretty much everyone around me impatiently telling me to be *patient*, I'd most likely still be at square one.

Women trying to conceive are bombarded with two entirely contradictory directives both from the media and healthcare professionals. The first has been endlessly discussed – and involves the ticking clock. Approaching 35 – colloquially known as the fertility cliff-face – we're told that our egg quantity and quality is reducing at a clip every six months or so. When I was 27, a GP told me to start trying as soon as possible as I couldn't "expect" to have children after I was 30. Unfortunately, there was a slight spanner in the works as my husband left me right around that deadline, so baby-making plans were stalled. It took me another couple of years to meet a new, willing partner and if we decide to/are able to get pregnant again, I'll be on the wrong side of that cliff face.

Even if we discount the financial imperative to delaying child-bearing – it's a fact that the older you are when you have a child, the higher your wage-earning potential in the long-run – these guidelines seem to forget that life has a habit of getting in the way. Failed relationships, redundancies, insecure living situations, huge student debt or just not finding the right person in our increasingly solipsistic culture are just some of the endless bumps in the fertility road. But that doesn't mean that the biology can be ignored – by age 40 only 40 per cent of women will be able to have a baby naturally, with that decline in outcome having dwindled swiftly from around the critical age 35 marker.

The other message, which flies entirely in the face of *the deadline*, is that of serene perseverance. GPs in the UK repeatedly told me that I needed to try for 18 consecutive calendar months before we could even have a discussion about my fertility. When I brought up specific concerns from my cycle history – like the fact that sustained exercise often stopped my periods coming or that my ovulation pattern didn't seem to match up to what all the "how to get pregnant" guides advised, I was treated as if I was an entitled brat, impatient for her Starbucks order. I get why the message of forbearance is followed: it takes some time to get your cycle back on track after coming off contraception, then maybe a month or two more to get your dates right. But a year or 18 months of patience, when you're also being counselled that the end of the runway is approaching daily ever nearer, is deeply stressful and makes you feel constantly like you're either a) not doing enough and it's going to be too late before you know it or b) being too demanding and need to lighten up.

One thing that a lot of women who fell pregnant immediately have said to me is that they almost didn't have time to register what they were doing before the magnitude of what was going to happen to their lives hit them. When you've been trying for months, that issue is certainly reduced – the huge life change was everything I longed for – however there is, instead, an additional pressure on the pregnancy, because if it doesn't work out, you know it might take just as long again to get pregnant. Like a lot of women, I had huge pre-12-week anxiety – the stakes are so high and you are so out of control it's almost impossible not to feel that way. Add in the hormones (both natural and the drugs) and the level of research I couldn't help myself doing on my phone during nights of restlessness, I became full of doom.

I was very, very negative and entirely unprepared for the way that pregnancy would affect me mentally. The very idea of me feeling anything but joy sounds bonkers, right? I'd just spent all that time desperate to be pregnant, then all I did was sit around crying about *maybe* losing my baby and spend my nights awake spinning, thinking about all the things that could go wrong. Night times, in fact, have been the worst throughout my pregnancy, but at the beginning especially, I had endless harrowing dreams, filled with dead babies specifically from literature – Tess of the d'Urbervilles' Sorrow, Fanny Robin's unborn child from *Far From the Madding Crowd*. Every time I woke up from one of them, I felt so ashamed. Why couldn't I just be happy like all the other pregnant women we see out there? Why was I letting my mind take me down these terrible paths of subconscious fear and despair?

After my 20-week scan, the low moods and tears did give way and I had a couple of months of feeling pretty positive, until birth anxieties started to kick in as I hit my third trimester. Again, the amount of information that was available to me through my phone meant I could probably write a Ph.D thesis on the risks of childbirth. Being informed is one thing; losing yourself in obsessive googling for days on end is quite another. It wasn't that I didn't know the dangers of excessive search engine use...but I just couldn't stop myself. We all have ways of coping with stress. For some people it's making a spreadsheet, for others it's all about distraction techniques. For me it's always been about preparation, but sadly childbirth isn't an experience you can revise for – though I've definitely given it a good punt. There is zero doubt that having 24/7 access to a limitless amount of information in the form of scholarly articles, magazine and newspaper features, as well as blogs and social forums through my phone, completely and utterly exacerbated my anxieties. My researching was compulsive and it took finally bursting into tears at my 34-week hospital appointment for me to really tell anyone what I was doing and start working on stopping myself. When you're hooked in all day, every day, it's so easy just to stumble across one more article or one more Facebook group with opinions on what you should or shouldn't be doing to prepare for such an intimidating experience – the temptation to look just in case I found out that one vital, elusive piece of information just proved too great.

Although I've been practising mindfulness, listening to hypnobirthing tapes and generally keeping myself busy, it's not like I've suddenly been able to relax and "trust my body". The truth is that there are no guarantees and childbirth is a lottery. I've been incredibly lucky with support from women's counsellors and my midwives as well as friends and family who suspected that something wasn't quite right – and I realize that if I hadn't found the courage to acknowledge that I was struggling, I'd still be on that social media-fuelled self-destructive path. I've found it incredibly hard to be open about any of these feelings, both the downs and the anxieties, even on my own platforms, simply because there is a huge amount of guilt that goes alongside it. How dare I feel overwhelmed, teary or have panic attacks when there are so many women who would do anything to have a baby growing inside them? I also think when you're expecting to feel so happy and you don't, you can't help but implicitly worry that you're losing your mind, which is also not something I'd ever want to advertise – it still takes a lot to admit that we're grappling with anything that could be construed as mental instability.

But we need to be more open about this both personally and publicly, because the truth is not everyone has a great pregnancy and every woman's experience is entirely unique to her own body and complex balance of hormones. If your pregnancy isn't going quite as you dreamed it would be, and you feel both mentally and physically out of kilter (I haven't even mentioned the "morning" sickness – needless to say, my hormones were not kind to my stomach either), social media can present a massive issue, especially over these early months. The fact that you are advised not to tell anyone that you're with child means you can't be yourself in any way and, if you're someone who uses the real-time tools like Stories or Snapchat, you can feel under immense scrutiny. Can they see the bump from this angle? Has everyone already guessed? Does your client or boss know already? I didn't reveal to people that I was being sick, having anxiety episodes or dealing with narcolepsy because it was meant to be a secret. Over the really bad weeks, I stopped uploading content entirely, which in the grand scheme of everything was clearly not an issue, but at the time made me feel stressed. Even if you don't use social media for work, you can feel that constant pressure to share regularly – there's a reason that it's called a feed: it's always hungry for content.

The changes that your body goes through during pregnancy are not only sometimes overwhelming (as well as incredibly impressive), but they can create some issues in the social media environment. By week ten, I was in maternity jeans and my boobs had gone from a 32B to a 34E. Several followers asked me if I'd had a boob job – which while funny also underlines how hyperaware social media audiences are about body shape. But until you have your 12-week, or even your 20-week, scan, culturally it's expected that you keep your pregnancy under wraps. It's an understandable practice: when around 20 per cent of pregnancies end before the 12-week mark, there's the sense that you want to be sure before you share, or else if something goes wrong, you'll be dealing with both the personal and public fallout. During the early stage, every picture I took either used a handbag to obscure my belly or involved me sucking in and angling forward so my dress didn't hug the bump. It's not a new issue that women struggle with hiding early pregnancy, but social media definitely brings a whole new layer to that subterfuge.

After revealing that I was expecting, some of the comments I've received about my body have made my eyes pop out of my head. Unsolicited observations are part and parcel of the pregnancy package, but there's something even more unbelievable when people feel they can put them in writing for everyone to read. Followers have said that I looked like I was ready to give birth at five months, that I must be having twins because I'm so big, that I've got a "BIG BABY" in there. Once, when I posted a Story snap of a pizza I was eating, someone took the time to direct message me that I really needed to watch my diet as I was getting so big. I really do wonder if people think these things are funny, or if it's that they've become so conditioned to expect women to look like Victoria's Secret models that a real pregnant woman boggles their mind. Gaining weight during pregnancy is not an *optional* thing. To make sure your baby is healthy, you need to add 28–35lb (12.7–15.9kg), and if you were slim before, it might be more. Sometimes that isn't glamorous and that weight goes to your chin, your bingos, your saddlebags. Often, you'll find your legs and ass covered in cellulite and, alongside the other pregnancy benefits (for me so far: varicose veins, skin tags on my neck, hormonal breakouts, thinning eyelashes, swollen sebaceous glands under my arms...), you might not exactly feel like Beyoncé.

The advent of the #fitspo pregnancy and the images we see on social media of women lifting heavy weights up to their due dates or keeping their six-packs intact into their third trimester may be the genetic reality for some women, but it's definitely not the norm. I had a seriously fit and flexible body before my pregnancy and managed to keep up with exercise during my second trimester. But between the early months of sickness and later months of pelvic pain, the burpees have been well and truly out of the picture. Again, these were not *options*. With the "helpful" comments, muscular "motivation" bodies and svelte celebrity pregnancy shots, social media can be a tricky space for all pregnant women, let alone those who have suffered from body and eating-related issues in the past.

Another thing I've had a lot of is people asking me how I can *still* be pregnant. I've seen it written on other pregnant women's walls too, and it's something that speaks volumes about the nature of social media: people get bored with the same story – they know you're pregnant, but they're impatient to see the update. But guess what? Pregnancy takes 40 weeks (or, for some heroes, up to 43). That's more than three-quarters of a year. It's not a new campaign or a hairstyle you're trying out, and it doesn't give a shit about social media attention spans. For so, so many women pregnancy is not like falling off a log. Not everyone has a wonderful nine months or has some romantic conception story primed for their YouTube birth video. Getting pregnant can feel like a monthly fading dream. Staying pregnant can feel like a marathon you haven't even started to train for. Being pregnant can feel terrifying and lonely and create a complex web of emotions. Some of us, even if we exercise and eat as well as we can, will have a "massive" belly. Some of us can't exercise because we'll puke if we bend over and can only keep bread and cheese down. You don't get a say in that. Where some feel depressed, others will feel anxious. Of course, there will also be women who breeze through the whole thing, not really even noticing that they've got a bun in the oven. But that can't be the only experience that we feel comfortable sharing on social media, because it is just so thoroughly misleading.

When I did reveal some of the things that I'd gone through, the response was phenomenal. I received thousands of messages from women who said they had felt the same things, or were struggling through the same processes, and all of them thanked me for acknowledging them on social media. While it's every woman's prerogative to share exactly what she wants, if things aren't so rosy you don't have to beat yourself up about it. Yes, pregnancy is a gift, but that shouldn't have to mean that a perfect nine months is the only acceptable experience you're allowed to have.

The Big Taboo: Pregnancy Loss and Social Media

Of course, it's not just struggling to fall pregnant that has implications for our social media use. Even more heartbreaking is going through a loss, especially when the bump is "out" on social media. Up to a million miscarriages happen every year in the US and an estimated one in five of all pregnancies don't make it.

However, what was once a silent and dreadful thing, spoken only about in hushed tones, is now slowly being shared across blogs, forums and, yes, social media. Mark Zuckerberg himself has been part of breaking the taboo. When in 2015 he announced on Facebook that he and his wife, Dr Priscilla Chan, were expecting a baby girl, he revealed that they had previously experienced three miscarriages. He explained: "You feel so hopeful when you learn you're going to have a child... You start making plans, and then they are gone. It's a lonely experience. Most people don't discuss miscarriages because you worry your problems will distance you or reflect upon you – as if you're defective or did something to cause this. So you struggle on your own... When we started talking to our friends, we realized how frequently this happened – that many people we knew had similar issues and that nearly all had healthy children after all. We hope that sharing our experience will give more people the same hope we felt and will help people feel comfortable sharing their stories as well."

While the courage to share is spreading, there are limitations too. Clinical psychologist Dr Jessica Zucker specializes in women's reproductive and maternal health and is also the woman behind the #IHadaMiscarriage hashtag and @IHadaMiscarriage Instagram account – a space for women to tell their stories of loss. As she explains, in many ways, social media can be seen to offer a community of support: "When you share a loss on social media, most often you will find an outpouring of love and you may find everyone's comments are hugely supportive. But the question is: do they follow up a week later, a month later, a year later? Typically, people are so inept about talking about pregnancy loss just generally, and especially stillbirth, which is obviously much rarer. And while there is this initial declaration on social media of wanting to be there, in terms of actual substantive support, women often find themselves feeling very alone. A loss is not something you just get over, it's a process. Social media often appears to provide support, and yet, are these real friendships? It can give a sense of connection, but there's just not the same level of responsibility to each other."

That support can, however, be a comfort at the bleakest of times. Pippa Vosper, a British influencer and boutique owner, lost her son

Axel when she was five months pregnant last year, and she describes the sense of community she found as "a blanket of love". Her story illustrates some of the challenges, but also positives that can be found when dealing with tragedy in the connected world. "My husband and I had been trying to conceive for three years and I couldn't wait to post a picture on social media after three months to tell everyone that I was pregnant. I was so excited! All the congratulations and comments came in and you feel like, 'I can do it; I'm not broken.' There was such a sense of relief. When, after five months, we lost our son, I decided the sooner the better to share the news, because a lot of the pain comes from well-meaning friends who continue to ask about the baby. Strangely, posting the news to Instagram was the moment that it became real to me. It was a week after Axel had died and I took the picture and wrote what I felt was right. I'd been at home with my husband and it had been very surreal: your belly is still pregnant looking and your mind plays lots of tricks with you when you're dealing with that level of grief. But when the messages started coming in it felt like confirmation that baby was really gone."

Pippa says the level of community that she found online was "Truly incredible. There are still a few ladies – that I've never met – who continue to check up on me every few weeks, just to see if I'm OK. Of course, you also feel exposed, but knowing there are people out there that care about me has meant so much. At the time, lots of people shared their stories with me, which was very difficult to hear at the beginning, but also very much appreciated, because I thought I was literally the only person I knew who this had happened to. I felt very alone and I was embarrassed. I thought people were going to judge me, that they would think it was because of my spinning classes or because I'd been working in my shop. But knowing that other people had dealt with similar experiences was a definite comfort." As for the long-term impact on her social media attitude, Pippa explains that it's made her much more fearless and honest. "The experience has definitely made me a lot more 'real' on social media. Beforehand, my Instagram had been very party, party, travel, travel. No-one knew who I was. When Axel died, I had no choice but to expose my real self. Telling tens of thousands of people that your baby has died was extremely difficult to do, because it was so very private. But since I'd been public with the pregnancy, I had to be public with the loss and pain too."

Anna Saccone Joly, an Irish-American YouTuber with an audience of over a million subscribers, lost a baby in a missed miscarriage in 2016. She also says that sharing the experience, which she did in both a personal and a family vlog with her husband, helped her to appreciate how widespread her experience was. "We knew that we were going to have to tell people eventually and it was definitely really difficult. But, at the same time, it was really rewarding because we had so many people reach out to us to say they had been through the same thing," she explains. "When you address something that's generally unspoken and make it OK to talk about it, you realize that you're not alone at all. That's probably the nicest thing about social media. It might feel like a shameful thing when you're going through it, but it's not: it's just very, very common."

By helping to normalize one of the worst things a woman can experience and providing the vehicle to share honest accounts, which can guide expectations, social media has been instrumental in facilitating a true shift in the cultural understanding of miscarriage. When talking about the many positives that these platforms have brought to our lives, this has to be a shining light.

Gaming Pregnancy: The Apps

Another element of the pregnancy journey that's been altered in the digital dimension has been the unprecedented level of documentation that accompanies the gestation period. Technology is changing the experience of pregnancy, specifically through the birth of the pregnancy app, which has popularized the week-by-week collection – and sharing – of data on your impending arrival. Whether it's in the form of belly photographs, which can be stored on not just your phone but also posted to social media in weekly updates for your friends and family to scrutinize, or information about your due date, we are compiling vast pools of records on what it means to be pregnant. These apps' game-like approach also allows you to track your unborn foetus's development in real-time, inch by inch, pound by pound, and usually compare them in size to a piece of fruit week by week. Giving a daily countdown to "B-day" as well as information about symptoms and encouraging words about how close you're getting to the end of the marathon, they offer motivation, reassurance and a feeling of achievement as you tick off the weeks. In addition, they're a rich resource of information about pregnancy, with features like "Is it Safe?", and they allow you to keep a check on your activities as well as providing access to social forums populated by millions of other women from across the globe. A 2015 research paper by Gareth Thomas and Deborah Lupton describes pregnancy apps as covering "threats and thrills", as they both "portray the pregnant body as a site of risk requiring careful self-surveillance using apps to reduce potential harm," and "use ludification [gamification] strategies and encourage the social sharing of pregnancy-related details as part of emphasizing the enjoyable aspects of pregnancy."

Whether you go for a "belly bump" time-lapse video, a more traditional still-shot collection of images via apps like "The Bump", which also has interactive 3D visualizations of what your baby looks like inside you, or the classic BabyCenter "Pregnancy Tracker & Baby Today" app which is downloaded *millions* of times a month, the sheer amount of information at your fingertips on not just your own pregnancy, but countless other women's, is unparalleled. Pregnancy apps are among the most engaged with across the entire app market and can create a powerful sense of wellbeing for expectant mothers. However, at a closer glance, you start to realize how very specific are the assumptions around pregnancy that these apps endorse. Firstly, the information provided is typically heavily gendered – these are apps entirely geared to women, and generally heterosexual women at that, because apparently there's only one person accountable for a baby and that's the mother.

As Thomas and Lupton continue, "pregnant women are portrayed as ideally self-responsible, enthused about their pregnancy and foetus to the point that they are counting the days until the birth and enthusiastic about collecting and sharing details about themselves and their unborn (often via social media)."

There's also a constant drive to consumption, with daily highlights of things you need to buy to make sure your pregnancy progresses without a hitch. But as you provide these apps with your due date, sometimes the sex of your baby and even the knowledge that you are still pregnant, behind the adorable short features and blueberry to pumpkin size guides, many of these companies are selling your data to as many global retailers as possible. According to research carried out by Janet Vertesi, an assistant professor of sociology at Princeton, a pregnant woman's data is worth 15 times the amount of a regular internet punter. And there's seemingly little escape. As soon as you Google "Pregnancy Test", share your conception news on Facebook or download a pregnancy app, you are hounded night and day by brands looking to capitalize on both your new retail needs and insecurities. Vouchers arrive in the post, offers are emailed to your personal account. There is no privacy in pregnancy: you're just too valuable a digital consumer.

Elsewhere in the app world there is a host of actual games, often geared to young girls, which offer new – and sometimes highly worrying – representations of what pregnancy is all about. Take the truly terrifying Barbara Pregnant Shopping app, which introduces the game's Barbie doll-lookalike heroine thus: "I've got wonderful news for you girls: our darling Barbara is expecting a baby! But still Barbara is feeling a bit unconfident. Don't you think she needs something to cheer her up? And every girl knows that there is no better way to raise a girl's spirits than a nice shopping spree! You are Barbara's closest friend, so why don't you take her out for some quality shopping in her favourite mall? Now Barbara is in her fashionable self again and she feels prepared to welcome her baby!" In the Newborn Baby & Mommy Care app we find yet another svelte, blonde Barbie clone and you can "dress the newborn in adorable clothes, accessories and toys!" From Pregnant Mommy's Salon Spa Fun to My New Baby Princess, which enables little girls to "care for a mother during her pregnancy in the pink castle", it seems that all skinny, young, white, blonde women apparently need to be fashionable and well-groomed even as they hit the 40-week mark.

While we may be hearing dissenting voices about the realities of the journey to motherhood from some corners, when it comes to our smartphone apps, pregnant women are reduced to burgeoning bodies and lucrative commercial opportunities, conditioned by patronizing stereotypes and prejudiced one-size-fits-all identities. As long as she keeps off the unpasteurized cheese and gets her manicure down, she'll be well on her way to maternal success. This week I've scanned an article on my pregnancy app about how to get "Glam for the Delivery Room", and read about a woman who made sure she finished icing a cake even though she was in labour. Maybe the Stepford wife hasn't had a 2018 makeover after all.

The Act of Becoming a Mother:
Crowd Birthing and Bounce-Back Bodies

Once upon a time, women gave birth either at home or in hospital in female-only environments, with the father pacing outside with cigars on hand, ready for the "mother and baby doing well" exhale. Fast-forward to the social media age and the tableau looks remarkably different. Detailing your child's birth in ever more cinematic formats has, increasingly, become the norm and, in the blink of an eye, there's been a mainstream acceptance that something which was once one of life's most private, behind-closed-door moments is now appropriate to air to your friends, family and extended public audience. A 2013 survey conducted by a baby photo agency found that, on average, a newborn baby has his or her image uploaded to social media within 57.9 minutes – just shy of an hour – showing just how dramatically the etiquette around birth has evolved.

As parents seek out sharable content to mark the birth of their baby, birth videos have become a booming business. The presence of professional photographers or videographers in the delivery room is no longer a rarity, and parents even work with specialized video editors to put together their birth story film. Anyone expecting will be inundated across social media with studio photographers and birth filmmakers offering deals on "full birth documentary coverage". Taking cues from celebrities and influencers, who have often brought their followers along with them in their pregnancy journeys and want to share the ins and outs of the climax, culturally what counts as TMI has drastically shifted. Images of full-frontal disclosure – we're talking shots of the placenta and babies crowning here – have been popping up across my Instagram and Facebook for months now. Type in "birth stories" to YouTube and you'll find over 3 million clips covering everything from C-sections to water births, the graphic to the art house, the most traumatic to the almost casual. Alongside the video footage are the blogs and social media posts, which are sometimes thousands-of-words-long accounts of individual women's journeys. There's even the real-time Twitter and Facebook birth status updates, which, though rarer, aren't entirely shocking any more. In some ways, this is all totally understandable. Childbirth is one of the most dramatic things that happens to women in their lifetimes and we're all fascinated by it, because, you know, it's an insane miracle. For social media users seeking connection and validation, the birth story offers a huge opportunity to engage with their audience and share something that other people can't help themselves to watch or read.

However, no matter what your personal opinions on the birth story phenomenon, there's little doubt that these labour vlogs, blogs and images are piling even more pressure on to the already heightened atmosphere of modern delivery. In a 2015 study of two thousand UK mums by video blogging site Channel Mum, 60 per cent felt that, as birth becomes more social, it's also becoming more competitive. Few births are predictable and a good proportion don't go exactly the way we might have hoped. A recent survey found that half of all new mothers experience regret, shame, guilt or anger after birth, mostly due to unexpected complications and lack of support. More than 70 per cent say they felt pressured to do things a certain way.

The opposing camps of medicalized vs natural childbirthers have created a social media stand-off comparable to modern political polarization, with each slinging judgements and criticisms at each other. If you post about an emergency C-section or, heaven forbid, an *elective* C-section, you can expect someone to pipe up with a judgey comment about how you've let your baby down by not pushing. While it's true that, even in our recent history, women were deprived of a lot of agency around childbirth, and over-medicalization – often for professional profit – is still a reality in lots of developed counties, the new tyranny of natural birthing is influencing women to believe that, unless they shun interventions and rely on nature to run its course, they've somehow failed their baby. In *TIME* magazine's 2017 cover story entitled "The Goddess Myth", most of the women surveyed said a natural birth was extremely or very important, yet 43 per cent ended up needing drugs or an epidural, and 22 per cent had unplanned C-sections. Is it any wonder they might feel as if they'd failed?

The pressure of living up to a birth story that you can be proud to share is certainly adding yet another layer of stress to a beautiful, but, yes, often traumatic experience. If you've been vocal pre-birth about your "normal" birth plans, of course you're going to feel inadequate if you "succumb" to the drugs. If you've talked about the cons of C-sections for your baby's gut microbiome, you might not be so thrilled to share that you were wheeled into surgery. Until every woman can hold her head up high and say her baby came into the world just as he or she should have, oversharing will come with pitfalls and pressures – many of which will contribute to how a woman views herself postnatally.

Of course, she's not the only one appraising herself after she leaves the labour ward, because the cultural fascination with pregnancy is now about to enter into the "how long until she snaps back" chapter. The scrutiny of the postpartum body is perhaps the most malicious of all issues surrounding motherhood in the digital age, and while celebrities have long dealt with the spotlight when it comes to regaining their pre-pregnancy figure, now, due to social media, we're all under the microscope. In a recent survey, 52 per cent of women said that getting their figure back was their biggest post-birth concern ahead of their relationship and career. And for some inexplicable reason, there seems to be a public ownership of how and at what speed that weight-loss should progress. The thing is that you're damned if you do and you're damned if you don't. If a woman appears to drop her baby weight too quickly, returning within weeks, if not days, to close to her pre-pregnancy shape, she'll be crucified by an audience who make assumptions about eating disorders and diets that she might have embarked on. If she's still carrying an extra 25lb (11.3kg) six months later, she'll feel conversely that she's come up short in comparison to the images posted by other women on social media. Just take a cursory glance at the #PostPartumFitness – it's enough to make any woman staring down at her jelly belly feel that she's not good enough.

As Dr Jessica Zucker explains, "You don't even have to be following these women to see the super-fast return to perfect bodies. Your [Instagram] Explore page, or adverts for this or that weight-loss method, will do that for you. There are a bunch of images out there of women doing side-by-side photos of, say, 39 weeks vs 9 days postpartum. I have both personal and professional feelings about those kinds of message. I can't help wondering why they are sharing this and why they have decided to share it in that way. Do they think it's health promoting, are they looking for praise or is it to make other mothers envious?"

If you google "The postpartum body" one of the hits that comes up is a problem/solution guide to offer tips on getting back into shape. Sadly, the language is full of all the judgements which seem par for the course in this realm. Take this tip, for example: "Many moms-to-be don't stick to a regular upper body workout during pregnancy, leading to flabbiness and weakness." Just what every new mum needs to hear. We know that postnatal depression (PND) isn't a rarity – in the US it's estimated that 15 per cent of all women experience symptoms – and these body politics are definitely part of the PND picture. A 2017 study showed that exposure to images of "snapped-back" new mums fostered a host of negative feelings in women, including body self-consciousness, depression, frustration and hopelessness that they're unable to lose weight as rapidly after childbirth as celebrities. Social platforms were perceived "as having a unique influence because [these messages were] viewed as coming from 'real people', including friends and family."

Troublingly there is also almost no conversation about the dangers of returning to exercise too quickly and most online advice suggests that after six weeks a woman can/should be back on the gym circuit. Whereas the truth is, new mothers can cause serious and sometimes irrevocable damage to their bodies if they hit it too hard too soon. Whether you've given birth naturally or not, the pelvic floor is the only muscle any new mum should be focusing on. Running, any weight work, sit-ups and most core work can further damage the pelvic floor leading to incontinence and prolapse. Seriously sexy stuff, I'm sure you'll agree. If your abs have split in pregnancy – known as diastitus recti, and something which is hugely common – any type of core work before you've slowly knitted the muscles back together can have long-lasting physiological and aesthetic consequences. Equally, if you've had a C-section you need to give the 7 layers of tissue that have been cut through time to heal. For 3 months, that's going to be aggressive, but it will continue to 6–12 months. There's a reason why women who give birth by C-section are counselled to wait a year before trying to conceive again – it's a major operation. Snapping back in this context doesn't just seem like a huge pressure, it's actually massively foolish and certainly not something to be applauded. The idea of a celeb with abs of steel, pounding a treadmill three months post-partum doesn't seem so aspirational when you consider that she might have lost control of her pelvic floor. Obviously that is not everyone's story, but if you speak to any physiotherapist or personal trainer specializing in post-birth fitness, they will tell you: take your time, or else.

Anna Saccone Joly believes that the pressure women are under immediately after giving birth has been intensified by the new media revolution, and she is passionate about covering the postpartum body in a realistic way. "Social media has definitely made me feel a lack of confidence about my body, even now I'm into my fourth pregnancy," she explains. "I think you have to be really careful, especially if you have been through a history of eating disorders or disordered eating. So many women go through pregnancy and post-pregnancy having problems with their body image or maybe food to some extent. It's just not spoken about. It's like you're meant to go through those months and not notice that your body is changing; it's meant to not affect you. But you're still the same person, and the same things and thoughts are going to still go through your mind. Body image in post-pregnancy is so important and you can definitely get lost on social media looking at people that don't look remotely like you, with body types that are not remotely like yours. And when they seem to just bounce back, you can't help but compare yourself. But that is not anything to do with you or your body. Post-birth is such a fragile, precious time. If anything, people need to be rallying around you and trying to build you up, not putting posts on social media making you feel bad about not losing baby weight. That is the least of your concerns at that time. You need to stay focused on really, really looking after yourself mentally as well as physically. The body is amazing and it will do what it needs to do naturally, but you need to give it time."

Whenever there is this level of unrealistic pressure, there will always be dissenters who have the courage to speak out against it – that is one of social media's most positive attributes, and it's certainly the case with the postpartum body. Real, undoctored images of stretchmarked tummies, C-section scars and protruding "pooches" are increasingly being shared by new mothers as an antidote to the "snap-back" narrative. Instead of racing to your body starting line, the #TakeBackPostpartum message is to embrace the way that your skin and figure looks, no matter what the impact of childbirth. While we all love babies, no-one seems to want to look at what it can take to make them. From Demi Moore onwards, we've become accustomed to seeing pregnant women on magazine covers – sometimes completely naked. The question is: why wouldn't we celebrate the post-birth body in the same way? Why is it so shameful that it has to be hidden until it more or less resumes its former shape?

All post-pregnancy bodies should be praised, whether they naturally spring back, prefer to take their sweet time or maybe only go forwards into a new shape. While it's a great thing that mums can now be seen as sexy, it's unrealistic for the vast majority to look like a "yummy mummy" instantly. The real truth is that there are far worse things that can happen while giving birth than stretchmarks, and the focus on the superficial side of reconstructing your body after it's been another human being's house for nine months is so limited it's almost laughable. It's time to tell the crowd to go home and heal at our own pace.

Mama Mafia:
The Pros and Cons of Online Support

Remember the natural vs medicalized childbirth stand-off? That, my friends, is just a penny in a pocketful of change. Before I go on, it's worth taking a moment to highlight how incredibly supportive some women find the community spirit that they find online among other mothers. If you're geographically isolated or struggling to leave the house, the comfort of knowing that there is a sisterhood going through the same experience at the click of a laptop button can provide a support system where one is lacking. These communities, especially on Facebook, have seen a huge uptake among mothers with children at all stages, from newborn to teenage. In the US, 81 per cent of mothers use Facebook to connect with friends, family and motherhood communities. Parents in general are particularly active on the platform: 75 per cent log on daily, including 51 per cent who do so several times a day, and 74 per cent say they receive support from social media. As a tool for parenting and resource for information, these platforms have become indispensable for many mothers, and that's only to be lauded. Nothing is more reassuring than having a lifeline you can reach out to at 3am in the morning to get advice on what's going on with your screaming baby.

And yet. What social media gives, it takes away. While communities can support, they can also almost immediately descend into catfights. Without going into the *rights and wrongs* about the way you've chosen to raise your child, because woe betide you fancy a glass of wine while breastfeeding, move your baby into his own room before six months, hold them back a year from school or – inhale deeply – decide not to vaccinate, it's worth discussing the dawn of the digital school gate. Outside traditional social media platforms, specific forums for discussion of topics related to motherhood have developed to supplement the groups you'll find on Facebook and the like. Generally launched with the best intentions, many of these spaces have become battlegrounds between keyboard warriors, places where misinformation, prejudice and searing judgements abound. The depth of that scrutiny has been so internalized that 68 per cent of mums using social media admit they feel their parenting decisions have been judged at least sometimes by other mums. A healthy debate is one thing, but these forums can also get mean – often verging on hateful.

One woman who has experienced the darker side of mothers-only forums is Laura Fantacci. "I've definitely felt the judgement of other women in a pretty full-on way. I basically decided to close my blog, *Wearing it Today,* because I just couldn't handle the criticism any more. It had got to a point where I felt I was constantly doing or saying something wrong and I was just sick and tired of all the negativity – I just didn't want it in my life any more. A friend had sent me a Mumsnet [British-based forum for mothers] thread about me – which started innocently enough and then very quickly got vile. So vile I couldn't finish reading it. I just had to block it out of my mind and not think about it at all for a few days. Whenever I have to google my own name the thread comes up and it literally repels me. For me, it was just too much to bear."

Especially for first-time mothers, insecurity and a lack of confidence in parenting abilities can surface in many different ways. For example, a 2018 study found that the mothers who post the most on social media are actually the ones who are most likely to be seeking validation or are depressed. Much of the vitriol of the "mummy wars", where battle lines have been drawn across parenting philosophies, styles, sleep-training regimes and educational attitudes are down to misunderstandings and assumptions – as well as those niggling doubts that perhaps the way you've chosen to raise your child isn't actually the "right" one. Catherine Monk, a psychologist and professor at Columbia University Medical Center, explains in *TIME* magazine, "There's a crescendo of voices saying, 'If you don't do X or Y, you're doing it wrong,'" The result is "a kind of over-preciousness about motherhood. It's obsessive, and it's amplified by the internet and social media."

"With my first baby the judgements and comments that people posted really affected me," Anna Saccone Joly recalls. "I remember receiving messages saying that I was so lazy because I wasn't getting out of bed, or that I was using pregnancy as an excuse not to do anything. Then when the baby was born it got even worse because everyone has an opinion about how you're doing everything wrong. It's definitely easy to get sucked into reading the comments and the forums, because the truth is that you *don't* know what you're doing. But with all these criticisms and judgements, you have to remember that you don't know where they're coming from or who is writing them. You just have to take everything with a grain of salt."

When and if you return to work is another area of deep disagreement, with the guilt that many mothers feel about leaving their child or, conversely, staying at home compounded by the social judgements. In the US 88 per cent of workers don't receive paid family leave and in the UK 70 per cent of all women work, but there's still a sense that it's a *choice* whether or not to return to the jobs market. That if only women were happy to sacrifice their Jimmy Choo habit or flagrantly expensive city lifestyles, they could make the decision to be a "proper" mother and stay home to raise their family... Why have children if you're just going to let someone else take care of them? Etcetera, etcetera. The decision to go back to work six or eight weeks after birth isn't something that most mums relish, but it's a reality for many women that, however much they scrimp and save, or move out to the suburbs, they still need to work. And, hell, maybe they want to too.

On the flip side, by choosing to stay at home many women are made to feel like they are happy to live off their partner as a kept woman, rather than the truth of the matter: they are performing an economic service. If it costs between £12–18/hr for another woman to mind your child, your time is obviously equally valuable. Childcare is a job. And not just any job. It's relentless, intense, sometimes mind-numbingly boring. It requires confidence, experience and a cool head. There is no lunch break, there are no union rules. And often you do it entirely alone. So, when you're made to feel that you're setting feminism back, or that you're throwing your career down the pan, it takes a better woman than me to hold her sleep-deprived tongue. From a financial perspective it often makes sense to go back to work asap if you have one child. But two or three in full-time childcare? The maths just stops working in your favour.

With the shift to freelance lifestyles, there's also been an under-reported impact on maternity leave too. As more of us than ever work for ourselves and work from home, the traditional post-birth leave, whether covered by your employer or not, is evolving. Take Korean fashion designer Rejina Pyo, who runs her own label from her home in London. "I went back to work almost immediately after I gave birth to my son, because there was no-one else to run things and I had responsibilities to my factories and retailers," she explains. "I also had a new collection to design. As I hadn't put my email 'out of office' on, work was always present – I was back on email the day after I delivered, though it took about two and a half weeks to get back on my feet again. As the days pass, you become a new person. Because you don't have the luxury of time, you work out how you can fit things in differently and approach your workload in a different way – having a young child is an incredible procrastination killer. Of course, I envy women who have a clearly defined maternity leave that allows them to disconnect from their email for months and months. Of course, I would have liked to spend my time with my baby just holding him while I was feeding instead of multitasking. Of course, it made me feel guilty that I still had to go to a meeting or answer an email. But when I left the hospital, the midwife said to me, 'Firstly you give birth to a baby, then you give birth to your placenta and then you give birth to guilt,' and over the past months I've realized that all women carry that feeling of guilt and inadequacy inside them to some extent, no matter what they do." Stay at home, go back to work, send your baby to a nursery, get a part-time nanny...whatever you choose to do you're going to lose. Which, in a strange way, is liberating. When it comes to work and motherhood, there is no way to gain society's acceptance, so ultimately you should just do you.

x x x

Social media has provided a 24/7 community for mothers and dramatically impacted the sense of isolation that many women once felt. It's been a vehicle for changing cultural attitudes and has begun to break down taboos around miscarriage and the postpartum body. But it's also polarized attitudes on what kind of mother you are, leading to an increased feeling of judgement and anxieties around parenting decisions. Highly charged spaces, social media groups and forums can often undermine confidence in the difficult compromises that every woman has to make as she raises her child and possibly returns to her career. Hanging in a see-saw balance, both the very good and very bad of social media can be seen through its relationship with modern motherhood – but only we can filter the experience to capitalize on the positives while leaving the judgements and venom behind. Ultimately, only you know how you want to raise your child and that is absolutely no-one else's business.

Takeaways

1. Get real about the fantasy

If something looks too good to be true, it's because it is. Pinterest perfect motherhood is something which doesn't exist, simply because all babies scream, puke, smear their food over their faces and dirty their nappies, and if you're involved in caring for your kids at all, you'll be dealing with these great levellers day in, day out. If you really wanted to, you could tidy a space in your kitchen, add some muffin mix to a pan and put your child in a cute outfit. It would probably take about 20 minutes of your day to curate this kind of content, snap it and share it. For the next 23 hours and 40 minutes, you could be stuck to your sofa in sweatpants with baby sick in your hair and no-one outside your four walls would know. You could be feeding your baby McDonald's and no-one would know. The thing is that *anyone* can edit the reality, so there's exactly zero point using those images against which to judge yourself or what you're doing.

But perhaps it's worth stopping and considering if these "perfect" mamas are making you feel inadequate because they seem to be better at taking care of their baby or if you are just envious that they're rich and have a nice island in their kitchen? All children cry, all children wake up in the night and need feeding, all children are a challenge. So, if it doesn't look like that on social media, then you know it can only be fantasy – never forget that. Unfollow at will.

2. Take your emotional temperature

Consuming social media at any point when your emotions – and potentially hormones – are running wild is something we all need to keep a check on. When you're in a balanced frame of mind, seeing shots of your friend's families or an influencer's cute birth story is totally manageable. When you've just got your period after months of peeing on sticks and perfunctory ovulation sex, it's less so. Dr Jessica Zucker explains, "If a woman comes to me and keeps saying that everybody else around her seems to be pregnant, I always ask how much social media she is consuming. I tell her to really check in with herself: is this triggering? Is it helpful? Is it depressing, or making you angrier? Is it inciting more feelings of shame? Taking holidays from scrolling is key on social media, particularly for people who are so overwhelmed emotionally that they can't get a sense of perspective. Yes, there are plenty of pregnant women and mothers on social media, yet we don't know how hard it was for them to get pregnant. It's so easy to think, 'she's glowing', or 'she obviously got pregnant on her first try'. We can very quickly persuade ourselves that she never struggled. Women on Instagram that you don't know aren't any different from a stranger on the street. She may have had a stillbirth. She may have spent $100,000 on fertility treatment to get her child. She may have had an egg donor. *We don't know anything.* When we see these images on social media, it tends to stir feelings that everybody else's life is perfect and ours is fraught and distraught. That can create an abject sense of loneliness when you might think that social media would instead foster a sense of connection. I really hope that people take breaks and listen to themselves when it comes to struggling with that."

3. Give yourself some grace

While you may be lucky enough to slip back into your skinnies after a few weeks, statistically it's unlikely. Equally even if you do fit into your old clothes, you'll doubtless be looking down at a belly, ass and thighs which aren't quite the same firmness or texture as they were before. This isn't some weird aberration, or a genetic quirk your mum hasn't told you about. This is just normal. Atrophied muscles, bad backs, weak pelvic floors and a significantly weakened core are just to be expected, as is loose skin, visible coloured stretchmarks and, if you had a C-section, an obvious scar. If you don't have a chef to cook your meals or a personal trainer to build you back up, again that's OK. Only celebrities and the mega-rich do. Instead, buy a couple of pairs of new jeans to bridge the gap between the elastic band maternity styles you've dreamt of burning and your pre-pregnancy denim collection. You don't have to go mad with building a whole new wardrobe, but don't punish yourself trying to squeeze back into your old size in the first weeks and months. Also, you can thank the Lord that the one-piece is back en vogue, although if you want to wear a bikini or crop top, no matter what your new belly looks like, you go, mama.

4. Social media mums aren't the parenting police

In the vast, nebulous world of parenting, the most notable thing is utter lack of objectivity – in that nearly everything we know about motherhood is an evolving moveable feast of conjecture, fashion and opinion. There are very few set-in-stone standards, like don't drink and take drugs when you're pregnant, and in general, child-rearing advice is in a constant state of flux with no rules that fit all. All you have to do is ask your mum, who was probably told to put her baby to sleep on its tummy, to turf the wee mite into its own room after two months and that she could sleep however she liked when pregnant (whereas research now dictates that babies are put to sleep on their backs and in your room for six months minimum and that pregnant women should only sleep on their side – preferably the left). Of course, anything that improves a baby's chances of good health is amazing – but we have to keep a sense of perspective and know that what we may be so sure of today may be judged in a completely different light in the space of just a few years.

Which brings us to the social media "mummy wars". If you find yourself pitched in a parenting battle online, it's worth keeping in mind that however convinced you are of your chosen philosophy's rightness and however certain you are in your own certainty, you could potentially be wrong. In the 1920s, parenting experts counselled to never hug or kiss your children, and in the 1950s pregnant women were encouraged to smoke. So, you know, there's a precedence for at least a margin of error. Think about it: Amazon returns over a hundred thousand results under the search term "parenting books", which means there are apparently more than a hundred thousand ways to raise your child. It's understandable that we might feel overwhelmed by this lack of clarity, and it's hardly a surprise that a recent study found that women who read the most baby manuals have the most symptoms of depression. But the scary truth is that there isn't a *right way* to be a mother, there's just what we believe. So, the next time you read in a forum that sleep training is "abusive" or see a Facebook post claiming attachment parenting is "anti-feminist", just keep in mind that as long as you feed, clothe and love your child, the rest really is just your choice, just as it is any other mother's. Advice is all well and good, but it's time to leave the judgements behind.

Chapter 6:
Why Social Media is Ruining
Your **Career & Money**

Social media is a world of leisure and pleasure.

Every day we scroll through a fantasyland where life is a mix of holidays, spa trips and home-made acai bowls. It's a place where £2,000 ($2,600) handbags seem inexplicably within reach – even if they cost more than your monthly take-home pay. A rolling conveyor belt of not just goods but also experiences continuously passes before your eyes until you start to believe that *this* is what the meaning of life looks like. Status these days isn't just about the car you drive or the watch you wear. What you do says as much about your success in life as your financial portfolio. Shots of yourself, front row at a Beyoncé concert; reportage of your bucket-list trip to see the Northern Lights; plate pics at a ritzy restaurant – these are the new symbols of success.

Although Australian real-estate mogul Tim Gurner got an international drubbing in 2017 for suggesting that millennials should spend less on avocado toast and save their dollars for a house deposit, there's an element of truth to the fact that living for the 'gram costs cold hard cash – which we're spending on impressing instead of investing in things that other people can't see. A 2017 Direct Line survey of 18–34 year olds revealed that a third of millennials had bragged about their expensive branded goods on social media and 20 per cent said there is no point owning nice things if other people don't know about them. When a presence on social media seems to be a prerequisite for a modern social life, consumerism for content's sake begins to look less like frivolous spending and more like a basic necessity, which everyone "deserves".

It's true that there have always been ladies who lunch and gentlemen of leisure, but on social media *everyone* lives a jet-set life. However, just like a game or a simulation, not everything is quite as it seems. Let's call a spade a spade: something doesn't add up. Unless everyone we know has won the lottery recently, how could they all possibly be paying for it? We know that the average salary does not support a billionaire lifestyle and that people generally have to go to work from nine to five. So how come most mentions of the way we earn our keep are vague and concentrated on office promotions or holiday parties? Where are the 10pm nights on a deadline or meetings which make drying paint look dynamic? Where are the nightmare bosses, computer system failures or terrible canteen food? I don't know about you, but work has sometimes felt like it was my *entire* life. So why don't we see any evidence of it? Reducing our careers to sidenotes, inflating our finances beyond our wildest dreams and airbrushing out anything which requires actual grit, sacrifice, pain or determination, social media is a fairy tale in which the mundane doesn't figure. And that can make us feel alone in the sometimes-soul-crushing experiences that most of us have to deal with in order to pay our own way in life.

The inspiration for launching my site and the reason it's called Work Work Work are down to this very issue. In 2016, I went on a group holiday with a collection of professionally impressive women. Among us were two business owners, a global PR director for one of the biggest fashion businesses in the world, a senior VP at one of the world's biggest television production companies and a well-known celebrity makeup artist and beauty blogger. The holiday – dreamy in so many ways – was often punctuated by calls from our respective offices and no-one was entirely "off". But the only pictures any of us shared from the trip were the cocktails, designer bikinis and sunset views. Sitting back on my sunlounger in paradise, multitasking between a tricky office email and filtering a picture of my lunch for Instagram, I realised how complicit I was in the mass glamorization of our lives; it started to make me feel really culpable. I was suddenly painfully aware that what I was doing – what a lot of us are doing – was telling the next generation of working women coming up behind us that life is all a beach, career success is straightforward and money isn't an object. Which is complete and utter *bullshit*. Every single one of the women on my trip had worked for well over a decade to get to a position where they could afford the cocktails, designer bikinis and sunset views. We had all paid our dues, and then some, and none of us had been born with a silver spoon or handed our success on a plate.

Fashion agent Gabriela Moussaieff represents some of the world's highest-paid set designers and makeup artists, and her work life takes her around the globe on what, she agrees, could look like one long luxurious holiday. While she might be posting shots from her hotel suite, she explains that the reality of life in the fashion fast lane is an optical illusion: "It's easy to forget that, when I'm travelling, I basically have double the amount of work to do. I'm constantly catching up on what I'm missing in the office in between back-to-back meetings, plus I'm working full-on on two different time zones, so there's not really any time to sleep. It is punishing. That glamorous, jet-set life you see on social media? That's just one second that I stopped to take a picture – the rest of the time I'm struggling to keep my head above water."

I'm in no way saying that women shouldn't be proud and share their achievements. But by only presenting half of the story – the rewards without the strife – something which social media explicitly and implicitly encourages, we are all misrepresenting the expectations for both our peers and younger women looking at our lives. There's no doubt that these images shape how others believe life should, or at least could, look like. Is it any wonder that millennials have been labelled the most entitled generation of all time? If all they're seeing is a jolly good time, why wouldn't they think that success comes for free? How can we be surprised that 40 per cent of them believe they should get a promotion every two years, regardless of their performance? Of course they're going to think they'll be a CEO by the time they're 25. It's exactly what the motivational memes on social media have taught them to expect.

The far bleaker reality is that everyone sometimes feels like their life is a version of *Groundhog Day* – a relentless stream of toil in the office, toil through their commute and even the odd toil during the evenings, weekends and holidays too. Even if you love your job, everyone has tough times in the workplace. And, while it might all look like roses online, the vast majority of those young women travelling the world with brands on social media also have dodgy work–life moments too. However much you dress it up on Instagram, when it comes to work, there's always a catch – no matter what you do.

Who Got the Money?

Talking about money in pretty much all situations is considered unacceptable, right? While disclosing your salary has become *slightly* more tolerable in the fight against gender and racial discrimination, blurting out how much you spent on this or that is still definitely seen as déclassé. It's still true that most of us would prefer to share graphic details about our sex life than reveal our monthly bank balance, and it can sometimes be hard to even gauge what you should or shouldn't be paying for basic life requirements like rent, because everyone is too evasive to reveal what they're shelling out. How much cash you really have and what you really earn are perhaps the ultimate taboos – and while that's nothing new, there's no doubt that adding social media into the mix has distorted the perception of how many disposable pounds/dollars/euros/yen/pesos/florins/krone/rupee we're all apparently sitting on.

In my opinion, having a frank discussion about money is one of the most important conversations that we should be having in the social media age. I come from a resolutely modest background. However if you look at my social media account you could easily believe that I'm very wealthy as I definitely have a lot of the trappings of privilege. The shots of me on yachts or images featuring my multiple designer handbags could easily lead viewers to that conclusion. Although I do now earn a good salary and have been able to buy an apartment in London, I'm certainly not rolling in it and I definitely didn't always have the financial stability that I do now. Both of my parents grew up in social housing and were working class to the core. Insecurity around money was a huge part of my upbringing and we often struggled. Like many baby boomers, my parents managed to climb a rung and buy their own home, but when they split there was a lot of hustling. We got by – but money always ran out and that was something I was acutely aware of from a young age.

What really changed my perception of the value of money was enrolling in a selective private girls' school when I was 11. Dad had found a job back in Germany, where my brother and I were both born, but even with child maintenance payments and Mum's secretarial salary, we were far from well-off. However, dad's company offered financial aid for education and he stretched his means to cover the shortfall to send me to a school which my parents believed would give me the best chance in life. It was there that I first really realized that we didn't have much in comparison to some other people. At my primary school, everyone had been in the same boat, give or take, but now girls in my class lived in huge detached homes with acres of land; they wore designer shoes and talked about labels like Burberry and Moschino; their parents drove huge cars and they went skiing and to the Caribbean on holiday. It was like looking on Instagram, but for real – everyone else had so much material stuff, whereas I just didn't. And they knew it too. I can still feel the embarrassment of hearing 12-year-old girls talking about the shabby carpets and small rooms of our two-up, two-down semi on the wrong side of the tracks. Being poorer when everyone else is richer is crappy, no matter how you dress it up, but it's particularly hard when you're young and you haven't yet got a perspective on what happiness is really all about.

These days, when you're a teenager living a normal life, viewing the world through the lives of people flaunting their exaggerated financial position, *everyone* feels like I did at secondary school. Social media doesn't just skew expectations and inspire avarice, it also makes you feel like you're relatively on the breadline, and that can deeply undermine your confidence when you're still trying to work out your place in life. It wasn't like we were worse off growing up than the majority of people – no matter what it looks like on social media, the barefaced truth is that financial struggle is a huge part of most people's lives. But it's the context of what you see all around you that defines how you view yourself, and in the social media age nearly all of us are comparatively poverty-stricken.

When everything seems to come so easy to other people all around you, it can be hugely demoralizing and demotivating. The only way I managed to build the life I have today was by working *really, really* hard. I've legitimately had more jobs than I can remember. Paper rounds, stacking shelves, waitressing, cleaning, retail, temping, secretarial work, cringe promo-girl work, extras (as in on films) work. That is how I got my money, and it was draining, unglamorous and often boring. I also *really, really* studied in school, which is how I got a lot of opportunities afterward. How often do we hear on social media about the power of education to transform your life? Far less than we hear about how teeth whitening can apparently do the same.

Those are the realities behind the achievement of your aspirations. A strong work ethic is far more likely to get you the fantasy life than losing weight to look like a wellness blogger. Social media projects a bankrupt values system in which material goods aren't related to work, and that is such a dangerous message. Millennial and Generation Z kids will grow up to be poorer than their parents, but in an environment where everyone seems to have more than ever before. No wonder these generations are the most anxious, disenchanted and depressed of recent times.

A Rude Awakening: The Devil Definitely Wears Prada

However hard I'd slogged before I started my career, nothing prepared me for trying to get a job working in fashion. Back when I started out, there was no legal imperative to pay interns anything and consequently most of my fellow slaves were extremely wealthy and privileged. I interned for *free* for two entire years, 9am–7pm, every single day of the week at various fashion magazines and newspaper supplements. The "expenses" didn't even cover my train fare. I managed financially by getting a place on a master's degree and using the subsidy from my dad's company (which continued to support my education until I was 26) for my rent. So that I had some money to live on, I got a job on the shop floor and did other side gigs to top it up. It was a whirlwind time – interning during the week, simultaneously studying for my master's, plus the retail grind. I also moved out to the countryside so I could afford my rent – which meant a four-hour round commute. Physically and mentally it was entirely unsustainable, but I got through it – like many others before me and since.

When I met university friends I had plenty of glamorous stories to tell them and could post pictures to Facebook of champagne events and celebrity shoots. But what I didn't mention was the reality of what the early days of my career looked like. A lot of it happened exclusively in a cupboard – and I don't mean a chic, architect-designed office: it was a 3-sq-metre (32-sq-foot) broom cupboard with rotting brown flooring and 72 rails shoved mercilessly inside. During the first seven months of interning, all I did was return clothing samples. Literally just packing and writing dockets on little pink sheets. After a while I was given the responsibility to *request* samples as well. Over the two years I did get to work in all sorts of studios and ran still-life shoots on my own, but in general the job was: request clothes, pack clothes, book courier, unpack clothes, return clothes. When I finally got my first "proper" job on a magazine, I thought that there might be a change-up in tasks. Sadly not. I didn't escape the cupboard. For another two years I had to sit at a desk inside a fashion cupboard since part of the "role" was to guard the clothes at all times for insurance purposes. As in, I was a clothing bodyguard – a bit like a scarecrow, but for Manolos. But obviously that wasn't the way I was selling it to anyone who asked, and I proudly advertised my job titles on every social platform.

I've had some incredible bosses and mentors in my career, but I've also had editors who have left screaming voicemails on my phone, who have harangued me at high-decibel level in front of all my co-workers, who have thrown clothes and shoes at me, and who have made me suck back the tears. One editor made me wash and dry her socks in a public bathroom. Another one would often call me before 6am to talk about her marriage issues but then, behind my back, tell everyone else in the office that I should be fired. Often it got weird and a lot of power play and mind control went on. I was scared to go on holiday in case someone logged into my emails and somehow used something I'd said against me to get me sacked. The stress was constant. My underling status was constantly reiterated and opportunities were often in short supply. However hard I worked, the most important thing was that I understood my place in the office hierarchy – at the bottom. The relationships with a couple of my bosses were probably abusive. I don't think these issues are exclusive to fashion offices – every industry has people who think that they need to crush you to make you earn your spurs. There's a word for them: bullies. However, there do seem to be an oversupply of this personality type in the fashion business in particular – thus the Devil sports Prada. Unsurprisingly I didn't communicate any of this via social media.

When you come from a background in which traditional, blue-collar jobs are the norm, you don't really have anyone to help you work out what is and what isn't OK. The jobs my family had experience in were either factory-based or clerical. Understandably my family *really* didn't understand my career choices. With all that money invested into my education, why the hell was I working for free? For two years? Why was I putting up with a boss who called me at all hours and seemed to despise me?

Then there was the financial side. I got my first paid job in London at 24, which came with a salary of £15,500 ($20,500). After tax, I had just under £1,000 ($1,300) to live on a month. My rent was cheap in the countryside (£350/$460 per month), but the train in was expensive (over £200/$260). After bills, debts and everything else, I had about £80 ($100) to play with a week. Whenever people who work in fashion talk about "investment buys" and how a £300 ($400) dress is accessible (hands up, I have definitely done this), I always try to remember back to my mid-twenties and how much of a fucking struggle it was. It's so important to remember that the reality behind a job title is often just as much of a fantasy as a Facetuned waistline. In your twenties it may seem that everyone around you is doing so well, but how much do you really know about the tasks they do day in and day out? Those trainee-lawyer friends, record-company execs or junior publishers – how do their colleagues treat them? Social media lets us exaggerate the positive sides of our jobs until they are almost unrecognizable from what we actually experience between nine and five.

My next job increased my salary to £19,000 ($25,000) but then I didn't get a raise for the next three years. By this point I was on a national magazine, working 60-hour weeks. While it was dodgy re paying rent, it was also when the free clothes thing started. The glamorous lives of women working in fashion and social media that you see on Instagram and Facebook are all created around this booty. The holidays, the flights, the shoes, the bags, the makeup, you name it – they probably got it for free, or at least at a hefty discount. The perks for editors, YouTube influencers and fashion PRs can be fantastic. At the beginning, I just got a posh breakfast here and there and a dress from River Island. Over the course of my career it's become designer bags, business-class flights and hotel suites in Tokyo, São Paolo and New York. But the key thing is that this lifestyle isn't paid for via *my own bank account*. Most women working in fashion would never be able to pay for all these amazing goods and experiences themselves.

Slowly over my twenties my salaries crept up – not because I got raises but because I changed jobs fairly regularly and negotiated as hard as I could. By 27 I was earning £30,000 ($40,000) and when I left my last staffer role on a magazine, aged 31, I was up to £36,000 ($48,000), which is close to the average London salary. On that amount, I lived a more secure life, but I was by this point in my thirties, single again and really wanting to buy a home for myself. The crunch point (excuse the pun) came when I had to call my dad to ask to borrow some money to get a filling for a cavity. Not being able to afford to go to the dentist when you're living a five-star lifestyle just suddenly seemed too pathetic – the numbers of my life just didn't make sense. I ultimately decided to leave a job that I really did love, pretty much exclusively because of money. Living on accessories is fine when you're young, but to be a fully independent woman who isn't waiting for Prince Charming to sweep her into an open-plan warehouse apartment means making financially responsible decisions. And living a life for the perks had become entirely irresponsible.

I decided to set up my own business – a minefield I stumbled my way through, making mistakes at every corner. But within a year I was earning more than double my magazine salary. After that year, I moved on to an in-house editorial role in fashion tech (which I think was probably my last "job") with a salary of £80,000 ($100,000), and 18 months of hardcore saving later, I bought a flat. While my dad helped and my boyfriend chipped in (we have a joint mortgage), the majority of the deposit was mine and the mortgage was based mainly on my earnings. Now I'm back working for myself again, life isn't straightforward; I feel a huge amount of angst about money, which a secure salary would mitigate. The first few months of waiting for invoices to be paid are particularly brutal. Some months are amazing and I feel on top of the world. Other months I earn *way* less than I did when I had a day job. Falling pregnant has been a challenge too – I worry about maintaining clients and get scared the projects will dry up as I navigate a new life with a newborn. But that's the trade-off – I'd prefer to earn less, be my own boss and have control over my time.

While it might not look like it, most people on social media are living lives just like yours. I'm certain that if Instagram had existed when I'd started out I'd have decided that everyone in fashion was so rich and privileged that it would have been unthinkable for me to even begin to try to break into such a glamorous industry. It would have just seemed like too far a jump from the reality of my life. When you work in an office, you see women wearing nice clothes and handbags. But you can recognize their clothes and handbags. When you look on Instagram, people who work in sexy industries seem to have new clothes and handbags every single day. Or even *twice* a day. Their homes are stacked with designer pieces which are on sale on 1stdibs for £6,756 ($8,946). When you google the hotel they geo-located, Booking.com lets you know rooms *start* at £600 ($800) a night. They are not just wealthy; they are seemingly gazillionaires.

I try to keep things as real as possible on my platforms. If I buy a pair of shoes, I'll wear them in circa 50 Instagrams before they get a rest, and I've posted about how much I love old clothes. I would never, ever work with a brand and not disclose a financial transaction. Not everything in my life or on Instagram is a free dinner, but I'm fortunate enough that a lot of it is, and that so exponentially misrepresents the true picture of my financial situation. Until I bought my flat, I was still sharing a rickety two-bed with my brother and boyfriend well into my thirties and I had no savings, as in not a penny, before I was 31. I feel incredibly thankful that I've been able to buy my current place, but the truth is that it's a 52-sq-metre (560-sq-foot) shoebox on the first floor with no outside space and scant storage. I've made it look really nice (hopefully in real life as much as on social media) and I do share pictures of my décor as interiors, as it's a huge passion. But again, creating a beautiful space takes money, which when you don't have tons of it, means time. It took over a year to buy our dining chairs, because we could only afford them one by one. Without abundant wealth, you can't just click your fingers and have a Pinterest-ready home, stacked with timeless design classics and eccentric, unique trinkets.

So why go into such exhaustive detail about my finances? Basically, because, like me, so many of the people that you follow on social media are in a far more modest position than they may seem to be. What we *all* need to do is kick our assumptions to the kerb, because again, the more we build up expectations, the harder it is for us all to deal with the fact that a lot of this stuff is going to be out of our financial reach, potentially forever.

Spend, Spend, Spend

One of the gravest problems these expectations create is an inability to moderate our materialistic desires. There's zero doubt: social media can drive really dangerous and irresponsible financial behaviour. Why not put that Zara haul on the credit card when everyone else seems to have a new Chloé bag every week? Don't you deserve to book that all-inclusive holiday to Ibiza, even though you know the monthly payments are going to cripple you with debt? #YOLO after all, and since x, y and z seem to manage, you should be able to too, right?

Well, probably not. Consumer debt in the US rose to $12.7 trillion in 2017 and, on the other side of the Atlantic, unsecured personal debt is predicted to hit £15,000 per household in the UK in 2018. A recent study suggests that, while debts are increasing, what we're spending money on is changing: it's experiences rather than things that we're now racking up on our plastic. And the reason the debts are mounting? "A short-term focus on not missing out on that opportunity" – aka FOMO. Take travel, for example. A 2017 report showed that 49 per cent of millennials will go into debt to pay for a trip and, according to a survey by financial planning company LearnVest, Americans take an average of six months to recover financially from a vacation. It's not that I can't understand the motivation: going on holiday is lovely, everyone else seems to be doing it and it also offers great Instagram fodder. But are seven days really worth bankrupting yourself for? For a lot of people, the answer is, very obviously: yes.

Remember when you went to the mall because that was the only place you could buy things? Since the internet explosion, retailers have a whole new arsenal of ways to lure us into spending our cash. Aside from the many, many online stores and countless traps like banner ads and content marketing, we also have social media apps as "inspiration" channels, advertising endless services, products and experiences. There's a reason that social media is big business: peer-to-peer endorsement is incredibly effective at persuading you to part with your money. Almost 40 per cent of adults with social media accounts say that seeing other people's purchases and vacations on social media have prompted them to look into similar purchases or vacations, and more than 11 per cent spent money after seeing someone else's post, according to a recent poll by the American Institute of Certified Public Accountants.

Nene Granville, a fashion and lifestyle PR, explains the mentality: "I'd just been made redundant and I was working on my next steps to launching my own business. Money was obviously a worry. But then I saw this lamp on my Insta-feed and just had this feeling that I had to buy it right away or I'd miss the opportunity. After I'd made the purchase, I realized how crazy it was – you definitely have to catch yourself in those moments. We all need to realize there is more to life than what you think you need to buy on Instagram."

In summary: social media is making us spend money we don't have, buy things we don't need, to impress people we don't know. However, so much of it – at least from the fashion/influencer perspective – isn't real, and I hope my story helps to convey that.

I wasn't raised with money; I didn't have enough for most of my twenties and I made a career in fashion without a single industry contact. A lot of my friends and colleagues are in the same position and are making ends meet in crazily pricey cities and most usually living in the red. While they might have brand new dresses and shoes to keep them up with the Instagram Joneses, they are struggling just as hard as the rest of us to get on the property ladder, to pay their bills and all those other "real life" things that social media obscures. "Two thousand-dollar bag with no cash in your purse," may be Kanye's most eloquent depiction of contemporary materialism, and it certainly applies here.

Of course, there are thousands of young bloggers making bank and the new social media economy has definitely broadened the ability for women from all backgrounds to earn a more than respectable living from lifestyle media. But plenty of them aren't anywhere near as wealthy as you might think. As Anna Newton, of The Anna Edit blog and YouTube channel, explains: "I don't come from money or have a hugely extravagant lifestyle. Yes, I will buy a nice bag now and again, but I'm a real homebody and love spending my time in watching Netflix. The truth is that a lot about the way I live my life isn't unobtainable. I think it's so important to remember that you can't measure your happiness by going on luxurious holidays and posting about them."

Ultimately the message is to take everything on social media with a pinch of salt and remember that you have no idea if all that Instagram swag is "real" or not. From the scores of connections I've made in the industry, only very few are seriously rolling in it. Some do come from privilege, some earn a ton and whittle it away, but the vast majority are "normal" and certainly don't have salaries that could cover the actual receipts of their digital life. There are fashion designers, PRs, influencers, editors and a host of other chic-looking women with fancy job titles who have all come from resolutely ordinary backgrounds. And, while social media might make it look like they have always had everything, they haven't. They had to work for it.

Wait, what? A Deficit of Attention

Does social media make you better or worse at your job? Apparently it's a contested question, but I think we all know the answer.

Let's create the scenario:

You get into work on Monday morning all fired up and ready to go with a mental to-do list playing through your mind. You nail the "must-respond" emails, and as a "reward" have a quick check on your phone to see if anyone has messaged you. You see your family WhatsApp group has accrued 31 messages, so you decide you'd better catch-up or else you'll be lost in the thread. While you're doing that a push notification comes up from Instagram telling you an old school friend has commented on that gym pic you posted from class this morning. You immediately respond. You also see you've had seven new emails and two texts. Mentally adding them to your to-do list, as they're much more interesting than that work you've got to do, you approach them first – after all, you did nail those emails already this morning. Approximately 22 minutes later, you return to your work, which just doesn't feel quite so satisfying any more, but you exert some discipline and focus. You realize you have 19 windows open on your desktop. Seven minutes later you hear your phone ping and, somehow, it's back in your hand again. You put it down and try to recapture your train of thought; what was it you were writing again? Maybe it's on one of these tabs... No, that's not it, but you can now tell your friend Holly that, yes, she should definitely buy that dress. Ugh, back to work. The cycle continues torturously until lunchtime, when, thank the Lord, you can scroll without the guilt as you walk and text to the closest lunch spot. You reach the end of the day and, while you've managed to tick off most of your original list you've also: watched three YouTube videos; spent 47 minutes on Instagram; looked at 12 pictures you could add to Instagram and googled lots of synonyms to help you write a seriously witty caption; didn't post any of the 12 pictures; replied to six WhatsApp conversations with a total of 54 messages; pretended you were researching a new marketing objective while actually updating your Snapstreaks; checked your Tinder inbox seven times; and also inadvertently bought a pair of Miu Miu-alike shoes from Topshop as you saw they were on sale on Facebook. Oh, and there's a DM from LinkedIn... Maybe it's a new job you need, because this one really seems exhausting? The sun sets, you're the last one in the office and your scattergun brain is frazzled. All you can think of doing is tumbling on to your sofa and ordering takeaway...while sitting all evening long watching Netflix with your laptop open and your phone twitching in your palm. Sound familiar?

The description above is a reality shared by far too many of us. Four out of five employees access their private accounts during work time and spend up to 2.35 hours a day on social media, depleting their productivity by an estimated 13 per cent. In a recent blog post, the Bank of England reported that it takes office workers an average of 25 minutes to get back on task after an interruption, while workers who are habitually interrupted by email become likelier to "self-interrupt" with little procrastination breaks. The more we indulge in goldfish brain activity, the more we need these interruptions to function – indeed 34 per cent of people say they use social media at work to take a "mental break". These micro pauses, which come complete with a dopamine hit, are reported to be rewiring the way our brains actually work.

Pre-internet, I can remember being able to work solidly with no respite for two or even three hours at a time. I was a smoker back then, so I'd schedule myself some nicotine time every couple of hours. But aside from that, I was laser-focused on the task at hand and very efficient. Now I'm lucky if I can manage 15 minutes without needing to divert, or more euphemistically "rest", my brain. I am much less productive and it means my work day bleeds over into my free time. It's not so much "work hard, play hard", it's more a blended day of constant work and play (internet/social media) in which I'm incessantly being pulled between what I should be doing (writing this book) and what I'd prefer to be doing (watching Kylie Jenner's pregnancy announcement).

What we know is that our brains prefer novelty over the mundane same-same, which is why distractions are so damn attractive. We also know that multitasking can make us feel superficially more fulfilled with the way we work – even though, in terms of productivity, we actually achieve less. Psychologists now refer to two types of attention: spotlight and floodlight. When we are focused on a single task, we use our spotlight brain to centre all of our efforts on its completion. But when we split our concentration between several tasks, we employ a floodlight approach, where we work on more than one thing at a time. The bad news is that our brains are terrible at this. Indeed, researchers at the Institute of Psychiatry at the University of London concluded that multitasking with electronic media caused a greater decrease in IQ than smoking marijuana or losing a night's sleep. Worse news is the level of multimedia multitasking, as described above, is potentially leading to a reframing of our cognitive paths to favour the less productive, less aware mental juggle.

The brain is a remarkably flexible organ, subject to dramatic shifts in the way it responds to what we feed it. This ability to alter to new experiences is known as neuroplasticity. Many things can change the brain, from learning a musical instrument, taking up a daily crossword to moving to a new city, so it's hardly a surprise that our smartphone use is having an impact. A Microsoft study showed that human attention spans have reduced from 12 to 8 seconds since 2000, and it's worth noting that a goldfish can actually hold a thought for 9 seconds, so I guess we owe them an apology. Heavy multitaskers tend to develop a smaller grey matter area, which is the area of your brain that governs your attention control. If you've become too dependent on your devices and all their many entertainments, chances are you'll find it increasingly hard to be attentive, no matter what the situation.

Other studies have shown evidence that smartphones are changing the way we remember, navigate and even find happiness. Being "present" is something which meditative practices such as mindfulness and yoga teach us is fundamental to our wellbeing, but a 2010 analysis of nearly a quarter of a million responses using the iPhone app trackyourhappiness showed that our minds are wandering elsewhere about 47 per cent of the time, and the more our minds digress, the less happy we are. Whatever we are doing, from shopping to exercising to lovemaking, we're happier when we don't divide our thoughts – even if those contemplations are entirely neutral. Multitasking may seem to be great, but we find our greatest happiness from being present and doing just the one thing at a time.

The fact that we're brain-training ourselves to multitask may, as several academics have suggested, mean we're on the road to a new "superhuman" brain. Others are less convinced, including Mark Bauerlein, a professor of English at Emory University in Atlanta. His 2009 attention-span-testing title, *The Dumbest Generation: How the Digital Age Stupefies Young Americans and Jeopardizes Our Future (Or, Don't Trust Anyone Under 30)*, was pretty clear on his opinions nearly a decade ago. As with a lot of social media research, the jury is officially out. In the workplace, 71 per cent of people say that social media helps them keep in touch with their contacts and 46 per cent use it to find information they need to do their job, which sounds awesome. But how can we know whether or not it's making us smarter, better workers? Perhaps consider a 2015 study of pedestrians in Midtown Manhattan: 42 per cent of those who walked into traffic during a "Don't Walk" signal were wearing headphones, talking on their mobile or looking down at an electronic device. Which doesn't exactly scream "brainiac", does it?

I'm no neuroscientist, but I know my own brain and I know it can now take in huge swathes of information across multiple platforms but has an inability to focus for long periods (I'm talking 20 minutes plus) of time. Whether I'm less intelligent or capable in the workplace now than I was at 18 is up for debate (though those 4 years working in a cupboard can't have helped), but I definitely struggle with tasks which I'd have found very easy before I had a phone to lure me in with its tantalizing array of diversions. We can say swings and roundabouts, but I'd lean personally to saying that social media reduces my ability to think, write and concentrate, which, for a writer, is pretty fundamental. I feel like I'm permanently dealing with information overload and have deep guilt about the amount of time I waste when I could be working. Even though I need the internet for my work, I dream of how much I could get done if the Wi-Fi cut out.

Younger millennials can't even remember a time when their brains weren't like a pinball machine, but the good news is that mindfulness and digital detox have been proven to help us rebuild our attention span and nothing we're doing to our grey matter with the constant multitasking appears to be irreversible – the adaptability works both ways. The brain is an amazing organ, but it needs the right diet of behaviour in order to do what you need it to. Periods of phone-free work and not multitasking across multiple media are essential to retraining our minds to be able to spotlight focus. Think of it as the fruit and vegetables of your day. In this analogy, scanning your attention across multiple platforms is like a diet of hamburgers and eclairs – instantly satisfying, but in the long term not so great for you. (I've just switched my phone to airplane mode – if you want to get any work done today, I'd suggest you do too.)

Work Outside of Work:
Everybody Hurts Sometimes

When it comes to work–life balance, careers and finances obviously fit on the former side of the scales. However, there's plenty of work that goes on outside the office: namely the work that we put into ourselves. While the concept may sound very self-help, becoming a better version of yourself – be it through trying to improve your confidence, motivation or self-acceptance – has become part and parcel of 21st-century womanhood. Personal development is often hidden work, however it's something which social media addresses, though only on the most shallow and superficial terms. The Insta-quotes "Be the Best Version of You!", "Life Improvement Begins with Self-Improvement", or, my favourite, "Dear You, Make Peace with Mirror & Watch Your Reflection Change", are just some examples of the limitless number of saccharine "inspirational" quotes which allude to the efforts that go on behind the filters. But one thing that's been obscured in the social media deceit is the truth that we can't gauge other people's sense of inner contentment through a picture. No matter what your background or life experience, none of us know what it's like to be inside each other's heads. Self-esteem isn't hereditary, and the stark reality is that some of those women you follow who look like they have the world at their feet are more lost than you could ever imagine.

Leandra Medine, founder of ManRepeller.com, expands. "I know that a lot of my experience is wrapped up in the position of privilege I am coming from, both broadly as a white Western woman and more specifically as one who is lucky enough to live in New York and who was raised in a comfortable environment. So often I find myself thinking twice before sharing some version of a lament because I know how tone-deaf that can come across. The thing of it is, though, personal experience is...personal, right? And we all experience the range of emotions – despair, grief, sadness – for various reasons. These reasons might be profoundly different, but the grief of a woman (not myself) dressed entirely in pearls and diamonds and expensive fabrics is no different from that of someone else's? Maybe she is less grateful (it's not for me to say), but she is still feeling a bleak sense of nothingness."

All of us go through times of bland sadness and deep heartbreak, no matter whether we have one hundred or one million followers. Of course, wealth can ameliorate some of the worst effects of life's barrage of challenges, but we all have to work to weather the rough times and a healthy bank balance is certainly no cure-all charm. We are also all complex beings, with both baggage from our past and psychological quirks and ticks created by our specific brain chemistry. You just can't buy contentment, no matter what it might look like when you scroll through your feeds. Working on ourselves is perhaps the biggest task that most of us will face in the pursuit of happiness and no number of trips or designer shopping splurges can make a dent in a process which can be both painful and relentless.

From my experience interviewing, working and travelling with women from all walks, I can, hand on heart, say that the ones who look like they've got it all figured out from the outside are often the ones who are struggling on the "journey" to self-improvement. Influencer Camille Charrière explains why the jet-set life – at least in her particular case – isn't always all it's cracked up to be. "I know how incredibly fortunate I am and that I've got an incredible job, which I'm certainly not complaining about," she says. "But if I'm being really truthful, the lifestyle that goes alongside it can play havoc with my mind. I often lack a solid structure to my life, and it's so easy to get sucked into the Instagram lifestyle. This hotel review here, that party there. A stop-off with a friend, another three-day trip on the other side of the world. Suddenly you've been on ten trips without a reality-check. Your washing is piled high to the ceiling and none of your bills have been paid. No boyfriend, no family time; everything that's important to you is in a total shambles and you're constantly exhausted. But it's so difficult to get off that bus, and practise self-care – far easier to escape all those kinds of thoughts by just jumping to another trip or agreeing to another event. When you're someone that can get really down, it can be a slippery slope. It's taken me until my thirties to be really aware of what I need to do to take care of myself – and it's the kind of boring things like staying in, trying to centre myself and being alone. The kinds of things that you're not going to ever see on social media." Of course, it can be hard to believe that other people are going through relatable issues with personal development when all you see is the best sides of their days showcased, but there are very few fully formed 21 years olds out there with unshakable confidence, self-esteem and direction – no matter what it might seem like from their social profiles. Mostly they're just trying to figure it all out too.

x x x

The advent of the digital age has been the architect of a distinct emergency in self-worth among women. Everything looks so rosy through a social media lens, and when young women enter the workplace they often feel cheated and demoralized that the reality of their burgeoning career doesn't match the image they've been conditioned to expect. The years of graft and grit, which were once seen as inevitable when starting out at work, have been so filtered out of the story that new generations are entirely unprepared for the slog ahead – thus the millennials' reputation for entitlement. Young women can also feel alone with issues of personal development and can easily come to the conclusion that they're the only ones who tussle with self-belief. But the truth is, if we really want to break through those glass ceilings, we've all got to come together to start shattering these illusions and be honest with both each other and ourselves.

Takeaways

1. Stop making presumptions about other people's finances

You are categorically not the only one struggling to make ends meet. As we don't live in a Communist society, inequality is a fact of life. But social media can make everything seem even more unequal than it actually is. Yes, the *Rich Kids of Instagram* are probably spending your annual salary in an evening, but there are also those who attempt to imitate a wealthy lifestyle just for the 'gram. Ask any hotel concierge or boutique owner and they will tell you how many people come in just to take an image in the lobby or dressing room and upload the image to social media as if they were staying at the property or actually buying the things they've tried on. Even IKEA has its share of fantasists, who use the merchandized sets as if they were their own homes for social media shots (especially for Tinder apparently...). Products can be purchased, photographed and returned; just because someone posts a picture from an expensive restaurant doesn't mean they ordered more than a coffee.

Of course, these are all pretty deliberate levels of *Instasham*, and most people will not be going to such lengths to inflate the material aspects of their lives. But the guiding principle of sharing the very best sides of our existence means many people consume in a conspicuous way – "it didn't happen unless it's on Facebook". But again, you have no idea how much it all goes on to plastic or, in the case of influencers, how much of this stuff has been gifted. Just as most people look more attractive on social media, so do their bank balances. Don't let yourself be fooled – you're under no pressure to keep up with anyone's online presence, especially because it's not even their real life.

2. Once-in-a-lifetime experiences don't happen every week

Knowing what "once in a lifetime" actually means to you is the first step to gaining back some control. Make time to consider and write an entirely personalized bucket list of things that you *really* want to do – things that actually *mean* something to you. It could be places that you've dreamed of travelling, physical challenges you've hoped to overcome or simply a quiet retreat somewhere (perhaps one with a no-phone policy!). Then, when other opportunities come up, you'll be in a good place to know whether they are worth the investment or not. And keep in mind that people who seem to flit from one amazing experience to another cannot logically be passionate about all of them. Living for content is just no way to exist – especially if you want a financially secure future.

3. Nothing worth having comes for free

Again, depressing, but sadly true. While you may not see the work in action, every successful person will tell you that their success is built off the back of graft. You're not getting promoted unless you prove yourself. Ultimately anyone can fail if they don't put the legwork in.

While you might roll your eyes at hearing social media stars talk about their workload, it's worth remembering that if it were so easy to build a successful social media business, everyone would have quit their jobs and be running successful YouTube channels by now. Most social media mavens are workaholics, who don't really understand the meaning of downtime, and the competition is *fierce*. As Victoria Magrath, the face behind the *Inthefrow* blog and YouTube channel, explains, "You could look at my social platforms and think I live my life in paradise. And, yes, I can physically be there. But wherever I travel will include hours of time spent inside my hotel room working. I remember one work trip my boyfriend Alex and I did to Mykonos, and it was absolutely beautiful. But we did maybe three or four photoshoots per day and when we weren't shooting we were sat in a shaded area until the sun set, just editing, editing, writing, writing, shooting, shooting. Literally we arrived home and we'd just worked solid. When your business is content, everything is a picture opportunity." There are cons to the pros, just like any other job, and the pictures only tell one part of the story.

Keep in mind that behind every social media post there is some element of work. For every staycation I post about, I've also had days and days sitting at my desk working on copywriting or marketing text – some of which is not sexy or exciting at all. But that's how I pay my bills, and you have to respect the work as much as the rewards. Also, people's lives are much more ordinary than they look on social media – their parents probably don't drive Porsches, they most likely didn't grow up in a mansion. Keep your expectations grounded in reality and make decisions based on your long-term financial priorities rather than short-term FOMO issues. God, it sounds like a slog, doesn't it? That's because it is.

Final note: remember, if you marry only for money, you'll be paying for the rest of your life. Just in case you were considering that option...

4. Be a uni-tasker

Focusing on just one thing at a time may sound like an anathema to the digital generation, but for the sake of experiment, at least give it a try in the workplace, because I will guarantee that you'll get more done and feel happier with yourself.

Step one: put your phone on charge, out of reach (but still in earshot, just in case there is an emergency and someone has to call. I put mine in the bedroom, but an out-of-immediate-reach drawer is a good option too).

Step two: remove any notifications from your desktop or laptop for a defined amount of time per day.

It might look like you're busy and important as you flip between devices, but the reality is that you're not. You're inattentive, less productive, and driving yourself round the bend trying to split your focus in too many directions. We know you can train your brain and that it will respond to the stimuli you give it, so flex the single-thought message and see how quickly you can improve your concentration. Be less floodlight, more spotlight.

I now try to keep 11am–1pm as a distraction-free zone – which enables me to respond to the morning's urgent emails first thing, and then gives me the opportunity to engage with my "phone business" (basically WhatsApp) afterwards, over lunch. Knowing that there's only a finite time I have to be without my phone helps me stick to it, and my productivity has definitely improved over those two hours. Now I'm in the swing, I try to do the same in the afternoon, so at least four hours of my day are focused. Although I'm still on and off my phone for the rest of the day, I feel much happier with my productivity, and it's a real sense of achievement to complete something fully rather than half-doing 97 things at once.

Chapter 7:
Why Social Media is
Ruining Your **Politics**

The straw that broke the camel's back? Or just the inevitable fallout from an industry which grew too big, too fast?

The recent political and privacy scandals concerning social media sites, particularly Facebook, reveal a lot about the human nature of both users and creators. While the exposés about the extent that Facebook manipulated or allowed the manipulation of our personal information continue to trickle into the press at the time of writing (to date we have learned that Cambridge Analytica, a data company employed by Donald Trump's 2016 election team, harvested personal information from around 87 million Facebook accounts without their permission in order to target US voters with political messages based on their psychological profiles; that Facebook knew of the breach back in 2015 but did nothing to stop it; that Facebook scrapes information about users who aren't even logged on to their accounts via a tracking pixel embedded on other internet pages; that the platform has created so called 'shadow profiles' to collect data on people who *don't even have a Facebook account*), the most significant point is the fact that we all so willingly and trustingly gave up so much of our personal information to social media platforms and third parties in the first place. The point that they've been so unscrupulous in their exploitation of those details really is par for the corporate course. But the real question is: why have we all been so careless? The answer says a great deal about the potency of the addictive, almost unthinking, behaviour that social media encourages, and it underlines how oblivious we've all been, casually entrusting the new media platforms with our own – and our friends' – information.

As the old adage goes, if something looks too good to be true, it usually is. Have you ever wondered why most social media sites are free? Sure, back in the day, you could have believed that the founders of Facebook and the like were altruists, aiming to change the landscape of society. Initially all these platforms failed to come close to breaking even. In 2012 Facebook posted $157 million in losses and the very future of the platform seemed untenable as it struggled to work out how to monetize its reach. Understandably, we all felt more relaxed about our privacy settings when we thought we were dealing with student idealists who just wanted to make the world a better place. Obviously, we were more comfortable sharing information about ourselves with these new-era visionaries than with, say, governments. But now we know we were suckers. They weren't utopians at all; they were just like any other businessmen, only dressed up in sweatpants and logo tees.

In nearly every instance I can think of, there's zero chance I'd ever reveal my political leanings on- or offline, no matter who was asking. I'd definitely think, "This must be a scam," or even, "Mind your own business." However, when I first signed up to Facebook, I marked my political affiliation on my "About" page. I also gave information on where I went to school, which university I went to and where I worked. I updated the platform on where I lived and who I was related to; what I liked and disliked; my age, sexual orientation and relationship status. And even if I hadn't explicitly told the platform all of this, we now know that Facebook would have been able to draw data from my posts and likes to psychologically profile me – and go on to help political parties and companies target me on the basis of that information. I, like millions, trusted the platform not to abuse my transparency and thought very little about the dossier of documentation I eagerly shared with them. It's only since working on this book that the true complexion of the social media business model has been laid bare and I've really given it a second thought.

Time and time again these platforms have proven that they're not worth our faith. Social media sites have been unable to address the issues of cyberbullying and unable to fundamentally curb extremism, terrorism, and sexual and racial hate. They've allowed politically motivated lies and fake news to run rampant and facilitated nefarious electoral influence and interference. Their response to concerns about the dangers created by their businesses have always been that free speech, the construction of the internet and the makeup of the human character make it impossible for them to police each and every user. Yet these same sites have invested millions in learning about how we all individually tick – psychologically, politically and economically – in order to sell that data to the highest bidder. Mining our demographics on a granular level has been possible, so it seems inconceivable that more can't be done to root out the menaces. As with any business, if you want to know the true intentions, follow the money – consumer data makes cash; patrolling subversive elements, not so much.

The only explanation for our foolishness is that we were all so distracted by totting up likes, consuming each other's edited existence and desperately curating content to nourish our own digital feeds that we gave the dodgy stuff a free pass. Our own insatiable voyeurism, craving for validation and drive to keep up appearances allowed these businesses to legally (and potentially illegally) reap reward from our identities and alter our perceptions of the world at large. We were all so caught up with where our ex-boyfriends were going on holiday that we nonchalantly allowed these platforms to use us for financial gain, ignoring the silent death knell of privacy as we knew it, spinning ever deeper down into the social media spiral.

All these platforms have done is what they were programmed to do. They've been designed to keep us obsessed for as many seconds, minutes and hours as possible and extract the maximum amount deemed valuable from our lives. Knowledge is powerful and we made them almost omnipotent. The reality is that the habit-forming and seductive makeup of social media platforms caused us to turn a blind eye to our own vulnerabilities, ultimately because we just didn't care enough. Even though we suspected it wasn't really very good for us and that we'd given up far too much of our personal information in exchange, we couldn't pull ourselves away. What's more, we were all happy to pay the price for "free" social media. It's only now, 12 years after Facebook was made public to everyone over the age of 13, that we're finally opening our eyes to the true cost.

Confidence and Cowardice:
Political Polarity Online

In the 2000s being politically engaged as a teenager certainly didn't win you any cool points. Back then I was a fierce debater with very rigid ideas about my political philosophy – which, aside from my teachers, no-one was interested in hearing about. I read voraciously, thought meaningfully and formed many of my adult views, including a belief in progressive social politics and modern liberal economics. I've voted in every election, stayed engaged with manifestos and read both left- and right-leaning papers pretty much every day of my life.

However, I've never really talked about politics on social media and have rarely used my voice or platform for party-political or even broader socio-political and civic issues. Which is strange, even to me. The reasons behind my reticence are many and varied. Firstly, I built my social media presence most significantly on Instagram as an offshoot of my professional work on a fashion magazine and my thoughts on domestic policy didn't feel like a sage or appropriate addition in between the shots of shoes and fashion shows, regardless of whether *all views were my own* or not. It's worth noting that it wasn't so long ago that politics came under the same umbrella as religion and sex – something you didn't mention in the pub and kept to yourself in the office. Having a political opinion even five years ago was something you probably didn't advertise, unless you worked in political circles or wanted people to know that you were *a serious person*. Neutrality and a lack of bias have always been the aims of good journalism, and while, of course, there is no such thing as total objectivity, touting your politics wasn't seen as a boon, let alone something necessary to enrich your personal brand values. Your vote is still between you and the ballot box after all, and as my grandad often reminds me, people died for our right to political privacy.

Obviously, the dial has shifted. While social media has brought political discourse to vast numbers of new participants – always a dream of democracy – it has also fundamentally altered the environment of political debate, making it an often intimidating, polarizing and threatening space. I've always had major anxiety issues with Twitter, which almost from its inception became an ungovernable platform for outrage and aggression. One of the things I always loved about collegiate debating was the Voltairian level of mutual respect afforded to both teams. You could vehemently oppose what someone was saying, but you never lowered your rebuttal to a personal attack. You'd never dream of low blows mentioning a rival's race, background or gender. Nor would you respond to their arguments with rape or death threats, or suggest that you "knew where their children lived". Political discussion and social media have, as we have seen, walked hand in hand with hate. Without even having to mention the sexual harassers, terrorists, neo-Nazis and Russian bots that are rife on platforms like Twitter, the levelling of political theatre has had the unintended consequence of degrading the level of common courtesy. Over half of respondents to a 2016 Pew Research study said they found social media uniquely disrespectful, and 84 per cent said that social media is a space where people say things when discussing politics that they'd never say in person.

Social media has also created a climate in which there's little room for rumination or reflection. Every little thing you say can be pounced on and either wilfully or unwittingly misconstrued. There's little to no opportunity to process your thoughts or listen to reasoned argument – you're now apparently meant to know your opinion instinctively and arrive at your final view of any world event in an instant. And woe betide you make an honest mistake or slip up in your language as you punch out your 280 characters on-the-go. The fallout can be savage.

While there's obviously a place for reasoned critique, what social media has created is a polarized, correct vs incorrect eco-system. However, which of us are without fault? In order to stay the right side of the crowd and protect ourselves from trial by public jury, self-censorship and bowdlerization (removing any potentially offensive material) appear to be the only games in town – unless you fancy facing an army of pious righteousness.

Pandora Sykes, a fashion and social commentary journalist and pop-culture podcast host who regularly uses social media to discuss hot-button issues, agrees that the digital space can be highly charged. "We're living in the age of taking offence, and there's not much that you can say on a public platform without getting a comeback from somewhere. Everyone has become very binary – there isn't much scope for nuance or grey areas. The digital world is so polarized that it's almost impossible to find a centrist identity, which is really scary, because the vast majority of people fall into the middle of opinion. There's also this level of sanctimony which says you *must* be engaged with everything, and that scares off a lot of people who would like to learn and need to learn but don't feel like they have the confidence or knowledge to even enter these conversations. We're at this really tricky juncture, where any time you try and express a sense of conflict you have in trying to figure something out, there's a public takedown."

And that takedown can be blistering, forever associating your name in the digital realm with whatever you were deemed to have said or done wrong. In terms of digital reputation, it really does seem best to keep your thoughts to yourself. Pandora offers an example of the kind of issues that can incite the digital masses: "Take the recent discussion around transgender access to female-only spaces – say, opening Hampstead Ladies' Pond to trans women. If anyone expresses any sense of reservation online, they are point-blank referred to as a TERF [Trans-Exclusionary Radical Feminist]. There is no room for manoeuvre or discussion; no chance to debate anything really at all. As a white, cisgender woman, I would avoid talking about the subject publicly, because I'd be so terrified of being told I'm trans-exclusionary, when actually all I'd ever want to do is discuss the process of how we protect women, but *of course* opening up that definition to include all those who identify as women too. The truth is things are complicated. Shifts in attitude and policy don't happen overnight. But today there is an expectation that it should and that anyone who doesn't instantly agree is standing in the way. Everything has become so immediate online that there is very little understanding that change in real life takes time."

Social media platforms, like the internet, were developed to be open and free systems above all else. The inability to regulate them is, we are constantly told, hard-wired into their original code. Free speech has always taken precedence over our safety, and from their very beginnings, nearly all of the platforms decided to ignore the ticking time bomb of digital hate. From a legal perspective, the only areas of corporate accountability are focused on hosting child pornography and copyright infringement, and the laws established in the social media salad days are woefully limited. These sites don't have to fear being sued for nearly anything their consumers use their services for – even if they were to, say, share footage of mass murder or rape. As far as criminal law against an *individual* is concerned, a social media comment must contain a credible threat of violence, breach of court order or constitute stalking or harassment in order to be deemed unlawful and subject to prosecution. Which leaves a *vast* latitude for the worst of human behaviour to thrive, multiply and disseminate without any liability. Permanently attuned to potential offence, some social media users seem poised at all times to pounce and unleash vitriol. Personally, the pros of sharing my political and civic commentary rarely outweigh the threat of the roused rabble. I have to be really passionate about something to talk openly about it, and generally it will be related to my personal experiences rather than a matter of principle.

There have been rare instances when I've spoken out about the politics of the day. Brexit, as an event, marked a huge watershed for me in terms of my political identity. As I was born in Munich and every other member of my immediate family lives on the continent, I've always seen myself as European first, British second. Even though I went to university in Scotland, I've travelled very little around the UK, have no connection with the countryside and have far, far more knowledge and experience of life in other European cities like Copenhagen, Amsterdam and Paris than anywhere in Britain outside London. As a child of the EU with mixed heritage and a seriously limited sense of patriotic fervour, I was stunned at how out of step my vision of the world was in comparison to my fellow countrymen and women. I'm the only person in my family who doesn't have a claim on European nationality and, as my boyfriend is Irish, even my son will be an EU citizen. To have your identity – and more than likely freedom of movement – stripped from you without your consent is always going to be a bitter pill to swallow, and the nature of the Brexit campaign and social media's involvement in the spread of misinformation (which, like in the US election, has been alleged to include Russian influence) only made the result harder to take. When I posted about my dismay on Instagram, I got a lot of positive response but was also called out as a "snowflake" – the hysterically non-offensive catch-all, which apparently describes someone who thinks they are unique and is unable to handle the grit of real life.

While you'll often be encouraged to use any platform you might be present on to promote causes, that presupposes we all have the capacity to deal with largely unpredictable reactions. Of course, the response can be hugely supportive, help you build a voice and enact change, but the opposite can also be the case. Not everyone wants to spend their days sifting through troll-like comments, so it's understandable that so many prefer political engagement-lite options, such as "clicktivism" (simply clicking a button to support a petition or cause) or sharing an innocuous picture. "Often when people are too intimidated to enter into the debate, they opt for a removal of words instead," says Pandora Sykes. "So, they just put up a picture of Paris or Grenfell Tower with a broken heart emoji to show they're engaged or empathetic. The dangerous thing about that is, instead of going online to read and listen, people have realized they can just put a picture out there, get some likes and feel like they've done their bit. But what's often needed is a damn good conversation, which you rarely find on visual platforms."

Sometimes I definitely feel cowardly when I don't participate in debates about things I care about, and I'd love to be in a position where I didn't worry that sharing my opinion would open the door to aggression and grief. In the current environment, you either need really tough skin and an un-rattleable sense of confidence and conviction to share your opinion, or else you need to be entirely ignorant of the potential consequences. My relative political silence on social media has also bled into my real life. I feel much less comfortable talking about charged issues among friends, as my digital self-censorship has changed the way I express my opinions and made me much more careful about what I say in all contexts. In some ways that's a good thing – being aware of sensitivities and how my privilege spins my outlook is a positive development. But as I lean out of the conversation, many more are leaning in, and the new, more polarized and uncompromising environment has totally shifted the rules of engagement.

A Divided Front: The F-word in the Millennial Age

One area of the public sphere for which social media sites have come under sustained fire is their apparently retrograde attitudes to the female body. While anyone can access pornographic imagery in a nanosecond across any and every social media site, when it comes to female nudity – especially breasts in non-sexual contexts – the new platforms have applied a holier-than-thou attitude. The charges of gender discrimination date back to 2013, when Facebook removed footage of filmmaker Lina Esco running through the streets of New York topless as part of her #FreeTheNipple campaign. Aiming to decriminalize public nudity and establish equality between the male and female chest, the project received a huge amount of attention from celebrities and the general public when the social media platform argued that the films contravened its guidelines. Soon Facebook and Instagram were removing images of women breastfeeding. In 2015, Liverpool-based mother of two Kaya Wright posted a selfie nursing her son in a closed breastfeeding-support Facebook group. After she received a message from moderators saying they were reviewing the images, she spread her story and the site was soon inundated with other women posting similar selfies in solidarity. While Facebook clarified that nursing images were fine "in principle", they reiterated that the nipple must not be visible. The hypocrisy is stunning – all sorts of sexually charged images of girls in bikinis revealing their derrieres and hoicked-up cleavages are fine, but a woman feeding her child in the most non-sexual setting possible is somehow unacceptable.

LA-based fashion editor and publisher of *Voyage d'Etudes* magazine Paula Goldstein has had plenty of experience with the Instagram body police. "There's a lot of nudity on my social media profile, simply because I'm a naked person," she explains. "I love clothes and style, but I don't obsess over them at all. I feel very happy in my own skin and my own body, and I think that's also what drove me towards the West Coast – a level of feminine nudity is much more accepted here. My friends do hang out naked and it's not a strange sexual expression or about showing off or anything like that. I've always seen my own nudity as a human expression, and I think most people that know me wouldn't say I'm overly sexual. Of course, I'm not stupid: I know provocation on social media attracts some weird attention and creepy men. And that bothers some people, but it doesn't really bother me. What I do have an issue with is how these sites choose to censor the female body. My 'nudity' is definitely not pictures of me in perfect bikinis on perfect beaches, like you can see on countless other accounts. There's a rawness to my nakedness – with nothing filtered nor polished. And I think that's why it jars with some people. It's a strange thing – a sliver of skin can somehow be more provocative on social media than a G-string bikini. Photographer Petra Collins got banned from Instagram for wearing swimwear which showed her pubic hair – apparently that was considered over-sexualized. But girls who are shaved and wear bikinis are allowed all over the platform. You have to ask: who is making these rules?"

Expressing a feminist point of view on social media can be problematic, and opinions vary deeply on how the female body fits into the picture. "There's definitely an argument that being sexual – especially when it's influenced so heavily by the male gaze – means you can't be feminist, but I actually think that most young women go through a period when they are trying to understand who they are sexually," Paula continues. "Sometimes that involves a form of expression which might make you feel uncomfortable when you come out the other side. But what it means to be empowered is that you have the freedom to go through that journey and work out what it means to *you* personally to be a sexual individual. And I definitely went through that online."

In the post-#MeToo environment, and in the midst of the burgeoning "fourth-wave feminism" movement, the plot has thickened exponentially. What is and what isn't feminist, or "feminist enough", is now subject to judgement online – a realm which has become the increasingly contentious front line of gender politics. "We're now in a situation where lifetime feminist Germaine Greer is being banned from student unions because of her apparent insufficient commitment to the feminist cause," notes Pandora Sykes. "Her contribution to feminist thought cannot be denied. She may not be a millennial feminist or a 'fourth-wave' feminist. But to dismiss her and other women like Margaret Atwood, who was jumped on for daring to criticize the nature of the #MeToo campaign, is completely nonsensical. As a feminist, not everything you do has to be a feminist act. For example, the Instagram account @MotherofDaughters [operated by author, midwife and mum of four Clemmie Hooper] recently did a sponsored post about Venus razorblades and two of her little girls were watching her as she shaved her legs. She'd written in her caption that she hadn't talked to her daughters about hair-removal options yet, but they enjoyed watching her shave her legs – something like that. Comments rolled in saying, 'Call yourself a feminist? How can you be teaching your girls to shave their legs?' As if you can't do both. I'm a feminist and I shave my legs. And my armpits. So what? It's ridiculous to suggest you can't be a feminist and wear a tight black dress, or an outfit that shows your cleavage. As with so many issues which get dissected to the nth degree on social media, it feels like we career from one extreme to the other, in a way which ends up being exhausting and unproductive in terms of actually facilitating dialogue and enacting change."

I was raised to believe fiercely in equality between the sexes – be that financial, social or in terms of opportunity. However, I often find myself disagreeing with the ways in which the f-word has been re-defined in the millennial age. For example, I deeply believe, like Canadian author Margaret Atwood, that a man deserves a fair trial when accused of sexual assault, rather than public lynching through social media. I'm highly sceptical of Hollywood's hijack of the #MeToo movement, and while the principles of the #TimesUp campaign are obviously laudable, IMHO wearing an LBD on the red carpet doesn't really cut it as an agent for change. While I agree that Germaine Greer's use of the verb "whingeing" to describe women recalling their abuse is unfortunate, ultimately I also believe that consent is consent – and by conflating rape with incidents where women have had a choice whether or not to engage in sexual conduct is counter-productive and can trivialize the seriousness of women's experiences of sexual violence. These and other – pretty moderate and essentially non-radical – views I will continue to keep to myself on social media because, like many other women of judicious opinion, I feel the space has become too hostile for me to express myself in.

While it's amazing that feminists are no longer cast as man-hating, strident bitches, the new media platforms have encouraged a sense of one-upmanship and competition in terms of how complete your feminist credentials *really* are. The result has pushed the conversation to the margins, alienating even those of us who have always championed gender equality. Exactly as Germaine Greer predicted, women have found themselves pitted against other women. Instead of uniting in a single attempt to fight rape and a culture of sexual violence, factions of feminists, each of different strands, battle online to take each other down in pithy Twitter one-liners. And just as Margaret Atwood recently argued in the *Globe and Mail*, "In times of extremes, extremists win. Their ideology becomes a religion; anyone who doesn't puppet their views is seen as an apostate, a heretic or a traitor, and moderates in the middle are annihilated."

As far as truly enacting change in gender inequality and sexual abuse, division in the ranks will only ever hinder the sisterhood. And rifts, polarity and extremism are exactly what social media breeds. As we all become more outspoken and insults are volleyed to and fro, digital aggression serves only to increase discord and undermine the people power which might have led to decisive action. It might look like things are changing, but it's mostly smoke and mirrors.

The Badge of Honour: Wokeness

Being "woke" (aware of injustice) or active politically in the social media age has serious cachet, upturning decades of civic apathy. Teenagers now wear their politics on their sleeve, announce their stripes in their social bios and are as likely to travel to a rally or march as a music festival. After generations in the doldrums, student protest is cool again. As Kenyan-born lifestyle influencer and animal-rights campaigner Kelly Eastwood explains, today we're living in an era where engagement is the new norm. "Social media has changed everything about the way we live and what we accept as standard. Ten years ago, if you'd been sitting at brunch and the whole table started to take pictures of their food, you'd be appalled – but now it's become a totally acceptable thing to do. The same is true when it comes to voicing your opinions. The more we see other people expressing their political or social beliefs and thoughts on social media, the more we feel comfortable, and even a sense of pressure, to do so ourselves too. It's a case of, 'If their opinion is valuable enough to be shared, so is mine.' Now everyone has a platform and has a right to use it as they see fit; what might have once been an internal or private thought process has become highly public."

For all the criticisms of vapidity and ubiquity among social media users, the power of the digital soapbox – from a political perspective – cannot be ignored. Helping those with a cause to find their people, engage with others and magnify their message, social platforms have proven incredibly formidable when it comes to effecting change in both attitudes and political policy. Anna Whitehouse, the journalist behind the @mother_pukka Instagram account and the Flex Appeal campaign – which aims to eradicate maternity discrimination in the workforce and encourage flexible working for both mothers and fathers – explains how social media transformed her personal crusade. "Everything started for me from a very human place when I just couldn't make work work for me," she begins. "I posted on Instagram to say, 'I've quit my job and these are the reasons why', and the response was overwhelming. That's when I realized that I wasn't alone and that maybe I could use the platform to fix the situation that so many women are dealing with. The word 'influence' has taken on some quite sinister connotations over the past couple of years, and the idea of people quietly swaying our behaviour and making people buy stuff doesn't feel positive at all. But I just thought, why can't I use the platform to influence change – not just for me, but also for my daughters? What I know is that this unicorn, rainbow emoji-fuelled, hyper-positive world we often see on social media isn't reflective of what is going on in the streets. Life isn't all positive. So, my drive was to link the pixels with what's actually going on in real life."

Similarly, Kelly Eastwood explains how she has exhibited some of the not so easily digestible sides of human nature on her social media channels: "All you can do is shine a light on what matters to you... I've always gone to protests and social media has been a great way for me to take my audience along. Even if there are only a few of us actually there in person, thousands of others can be there outside the embassies, campaigning virtually alongside me. I recently protested at the Japanese embassy against dolphin slaughter on the coast of Taiji and the sheer number of messages I received afterwards was awe-inspiring. It happened during London Fashion Week and, in terms of connecting with my audience, the protest posts were by far the most engaged with over the week. It wasn't the catwalks that people cared about, it was an authentic expression of political action. There's no doubt in my mind that social media can be an incredible way to reach people and get more people on board. As an influencer, you have to make a choice. Do you want your influence to stop at where people eat or how people shop? Or do you also want to use that position to influence the decisions that people make? Something more fundamental that will make a difference? I want to influence people's buying mentality and awareness of the cost of their purchases on the environment. If you're telling people what to buy, you can also tell people what they should be mindful of."

However, on social media "tall poppy syndrome" (our cultural tendency to cut people down once they've risen above the parapet) is rife. "While it's never been easier to express your opinion, often people don't want to hear what you have to say," says Kelly. "For example, I'm vocally anti-fur in all walks of my life, including on social media. But when you start that conversation in the digital realm, instead of people saying, 'That's interesting, why?', you frequently get hugely defensive and aggressive messages from people criticizing you for being sanctimonious. If you touch a nerve with your opinion, you have to realize that there will be some kind of fallout. On social media it can become, 'This is my opinion, fuck you,' vs 'This is my opinion, fuck you back.' I'm an adult and I can take it, but look at the kids from the latest high-school shooting in Florida. If you've ever wondered how social media has changed the state of play, seeing grown-ass politicians tweeting horrendous things about children gives you a good clue. However, from my experience, young people do seem to be developing that hard shell at a very fast pace because they are exposed to the intensity and severity of that kind of language every day and from a much younger age. To them it's what's to be expected, but I don't know if that's a good thing for the way we communicate with each other or for society at large."

Even something which might seem less contentious, like flexible working arrangements for women, has been met with defiance. When Anna Whitehouse launched her campaign, not all the response was positive. "We've definitely experienced some resistance over the course of the project, and usually it comes from a place of cynicism. I have to be constantly transparent about the fact that we don't make a penny from the work we do for the campaign. There's also a lot of 'Does she think she's the first person to come up with the idea of flexible working?', which obviously I don't. But before Instagram I'd have literally just been shouting to the contacts on my phone; now I can shout to anyone and everyone who will listen, and that is incredibly useful when you want to spread a message."

For better or worse, the rules of digital political engagement are shifting and we all have to plot our position on a new battlefield. Of course, that position could be conscientious objection. "I don't think you necessarily need to have something political to say on social media – there will always be a market for fluffy cats, incredible shoes and someone who can edit in a way that *Vogue* magazine can," argues Anna. "I still think there is a huge space for that brief respite from the intensity of the everyday world and I don't believe that everyone needs to be shouting a message."

One thing is for sure, we're collectively becoming more discerning and savvy to the ways in which people are using their influence. Many social media users are craving deeper connections which go beyond the #ootd (outfit of the day). As Kelly Eastwood says, "Although Instagram may be a place to get away from the real world to have a switch-off scroll, it's also a place where you can engage with people on a much more important level." However, when businesses – and individuals – are using political causes as engagement bait, getting behind a movement for a mere moment or to increase their following, there's no doubt that the potency of people power becomes diluted. There's no point saying something for the sake of saying something; wokeness as a posture does nothing to enact change. We've all seen how social media outcries have been followed with inaction and inertia – to really alter our realities, whether politically, socially or culturally, opinion needs to be galvanized into action, and that's something that can't be achieved through social media alone.

The Echo Chamber

While the digital slanging matches continue apace, elsewhere an equally worrying feature of social media works in the exact opposite direction – to insulate you entirely from what people outside your social circle think and believe. One of the most notable aspects of consuming algorithmic-based media is the fact that you are only served content that the platform "knows" you will like. News, features, events and commercial products which surface on your feeds are curated to suit your tastes and socio-political flavour; new suggested connections are nearly guaranteed to share your belief system and point of view. It's a space where, day to day, you could imagine that all reasonable people agree with you, or at least understand where you're coming from. Which is why it can be quite a surprise to find your perspective on the planet isn't actually shared by the majority of people.

Platforms like Facebook have further contributed to the polarity of opinion and partisan animosity through news bias – for example, feeding liberal news articles to people who have either identified as left-leaning or clicked enough likes on left-leaning pages. Considering that two-thirds (67 per cent) of Americans get a portion of their news from social media, this can have a powerful influence. As we can go weeks without hearing the "other side" of the argument, when these views do break through – as a heated offshoot in a comments stream, for example – it can be profoundly shocking. It can also become almost instinctual to conclude that the other side must just be ill-educated and ill-informed. After weeks, months and years of being fed a diet of media that reflects your internal compass, instead of being well-practised at considering the other side of the coin, it's all too easy to dismiss detractors as idiots – after all, have they not read the news? The reality is that they have – it's just different news to the version tailored for you.

For the first time since 1992, majorities in both parties voting in the US 2016 election expressed not just unfavourable but *very* unfavourable views of the other party. In a 2016 Pew Research study, 70 per cent of Democrats surveyed by Pew Research said that Republicans were "closed minded", while 47 per cent of Republican believed Democrats to be "immoral", and social media has been cited as an agent for this development. Basically, the new platforms have increased our inability to empathize and the level of contempt which we have for those who disagree with us. What's more, over a third of social media users say they are "worn out" by the amount of political content they encounter and more than half describe their online interactions with people they disagree with politically as stressful and frustrating. It doesn't sound fun, does it?

While partiality is hardly a new thing, and people have read or watched media supporting their political persuasion since time immemorial, the holistic, always-on nature of social media has sent it into hyperdrive, simply because it exposes us not just to one publication's view on world events, but also all of our friends' collective perspectives too. When everyone you know thinks the same way, it's extremely easy to convince yourself of your own righteousness. Early on in my career I was taught about the importance of subjectivity. The "truth", if it is ever out there, can only be found by consuming both what you do and *don't* like. Social media sites have been consistently spoiling us, feeding us with content that pleases us in an attempt to curate an environment that is uniquely attuned to our personal preferences. When that is shattered by reality it can feel like a betrayal. Whether it was the US election or the Brexit vote, we have slowly realized that we are all existing in different bubbles and, politically, social media is driving us further and further apart.

Change is afoot at the biggest social media companies, prompted not by worries regarding how they are impacting our bodies, health, or identity but by how they are affecting our votes. The Russian influence in 2016's US election through a drive to manipulate voters' beliefs caused an international uproar. When compounded by the impact of the data scandals, Facebook saw more than $60 million wiped off its value; the number of US respondents who viewed the company unfavourably jumped from 28 per cent in October 2017 to 43 per cent in March 2018; and advertisers including Mozilla and Sonos cancelled their ads while Tesla pulled their page completely. The alleged election interference scandal was a huge catalyst for change – so much so that there are shifts in legislation on both sides of the Atlantic. And in response to the mounting #DeleteFacebook campaign, a slew of new policies has been implemented on the platform to protect our privacy – third-party apps are now restricted from accessing certain kinds of information, including our religious or political views, and there's a new feature to be added to everyone's newsfeed to instantly show users what information apps have collected on them.

But will it truly make any difference? Notably Mark Zuckerberg has declared that Facebook hasn't registered a noticeable change in user behaviour since the personal data scandal ("I don't think there has been any meaningful impact we've observed"), and it's hard to believe that with so many people using the site to maintain their business, family and social connections that a mass exodus will actually happen. Anyhow, most people had an inkling that their data was being mined: we've all been followed around the internet by ads originating from a Facebook status update and, while the sheer extent of the privacy breaches are alarming, it's not a total shock that there was a catch – all those ad profits had to be coming from somewhere. Of course, aside from the convenience of keeping up with our networks, if we deleted Facebook en masse, we'd also all have to give up snooping on each other's lives and those little dopamine hits of validation too. Which, dispiritingly, seems unlikely.

✗ ✗ ✗

From a political perspective, social media has made it easier for us to engage, but at the cost of the erosion of empathy. It's made the differences between us greater and undermined our ability to debate, discuss and deliberate. There are no "safe" spaces to be political on social media, and while it may be fashionable to be active, it's often deeply unpleasant, frustrating and intimidating. It may even have changed the way you see and experience the world, influencing your beliefs, attitudes and even your vote. If we are all going to continue to use social media (as it seems that no outrage is too great to keep us from logging on), there must be ways that we can protect ourselves from data grabs and animosity while using the platforms to enact change, convey our opinions in a respectful manner and listen to those whose point of view differs from our own. These goals should all be at the top of Zuckerberg and friends' to-do list, because if they're truly looking to create a social media utopia, it has to respect and support its users rather than trade them off to the highest bidder.

Takeaways

1. Be aware that your data is a commodity

There is now no excuse – we all know that our own and our friends' data is a valuable commodity and subject to manipulation. We understand that social media sites sell our personal details and that businesses and political bodies can use that information to decide who to target in their campaigns. Whether they want you to buy something or believe something, they all have something to sell. The adverts you see, the news that you're fed, all of it is based on what you share about yourself. So, what can you do? The first step is to take an hour to thoroughly understand all the privacy settings for every platform that you use. Of course, privacy policies are dry and lengthy, and while they are available on every platform, who has the time to do more than scan pages of text? However, what you can do instead is simply assume the worst and go through the privacy settings for each, reducing the reach of your posts and information to either just yourself or you and your friends. Close the circle slightly and your information will not be so widely accessible. Yes, it's an extra step and, yes, the platforms will still have some of your information available for sale, but you will have done your very best to protect yourself in the digital space – something which in today's context seems eminently sensible.

2. Consider the format
Not all platforms are created equal and different social media environments call for different ways of conversing with your audience.

"I think you have to think about the format in which you're engaging in a political conversation," explains Pandora Sykes. "I got into Instagram Stories because I read *a lot* of newspaper and magazine features and it's one of the things that people always comment about on our podcast. I wanted to share what I was reading, but in a way that if you were interested you could look at it, but if you weren't you could just ignore it. So that's why I decided to put it on Instagram Stories rather than my permanent IG [Instagram] account, where it might be flanked by pictures of my friends or images of me working with fashion brands. Not that there would be anything intrinsically wrong with that, but it just feels right that it has its own outlet. I guess it's a little bit less in your face – no-one wants political opinion pushed down their throat."

Twitter is a more natural space to share a short comment on a news story; bringing the same URL into a family discussion on a Facebook stream is far less appropriate. Facebook will always be a great place for events, whether you're organizing them or publicizing them. Due to its high level of inter-generational use, it's also a great place to keep in touch with family and distant friends. However, that is also one of the reasons that political discussions become so problematic: when things get heated, it's not just someone from a random Midwestern town that you're debating with – it's your Uncle Bob. Political discussions on Facebook are like all your worst family Christmases rolled into one, with the arguments both indelible and open for all your "friends" to see.

Think about what you want to achieve from your political post – is it simply to show solidarity, or to educate others on a cause which hasn't had much airtime? Do you want to shine a light on a great piece of journalism or is it really that someone has said something that's riled you and you feel the need to retaliate? Aggression, both direct and passive, rarely results in a positive outcome when you're trying to communicate your thoughts, especially to a hostile audience. When you've decided what you want to achieve, consider where it is best to share meaningfully and tailor your message to the platform.

3. Listen more than you tweet

Seeking out opinions which diverge from your own can be a chore, and it can certainly be both alarming and depressing to hear beliefs which differ fundamentally from what you passionately feel is right and just. But by cutting opposing voices from the conversation, your echo chamber will remain hermetically sealed and your understanding of reality will continue to be worryingly skewed. Debate has always been central to a healthy political system, and that doesn't mean a digital altercation. Practise listening and asking questions – making sure that they're neither patronizing nor sanctimonious. Engaging doesn't mean just expressing yourself, it means participating. Work on how you speak to other people on social media and employ a code of values which you can be proud of; as a rule of thumb, if you wouldn't say something in real life, don't say it online either. If other people are disrespectful or abusive – block them. However, if they just have a different opinion to you and convey it in a civil way, make time to respond – remain engaged in the world around you.

4. Do your research

"Before you make any grand statement on social media, you have to be very aware of what you are saying and what you truly believe in. In such a fast-paced environment, it's easy to make snap assessments, but it's definitely worth taking your time when it comes to conveying your opinions," explains Kelly Eastwood.

Thoroughly researching an issue you care about involves hearing thoughts from all angles and only then coming to your conclusion. If you only pay cursory attention to a story or make a decision based on soundbites and headlines, you're likely to come a cropper. To avoid egg on your face and supporting something you actually don't entirely understand or believe in, do your homework.

5. Focus on tangible change

Opinion has become amorphous on social media, but to actually enact change you need laser focus. "The ability to amplify your voice across social media offers individuals an unprecedented opportunity," Anna Whitehouse explains. "You can make a difference, but there has to be a simple drive to what you're trying to change and there needs to be real emotion behind it. Mine is so clear: I don't want my girls to have an oak door slammed in their face the minute they have children. I don't want to build them up to work hard in school and university and to tell them, 'You can do what you want,' only to have employers say, 'Actually you can't because you've had a baby.'"

As soon as you've settled on your goal, the next step is to anchor your efforts on a single, definable objective. "What's really important is to find something tangible to focus your campaign on," Anna continues. "The call to action for the Flex Appeal is to get companies to sign up to the Equality and Human Rights Commission Working Forward pledge. Simple. Businesses and governmental bodies continue to struggle to connect with people on a one-to-one level. The EHRC had all the stats, all the research, all the information to why companies should be working flexibly, but they couldn't get their message across on a personal level. Whereas I had a voice on social media, which could make a more intimate connection. Since I've been pushing the campaign (alongside the EHRC, of course) 380 big companies have signed up to the pledge, including businesses like BP, BT, John Lewis and Virgin Money. If you're asking about the positives of social media, it's pretty bonkers that nearly four hundred companies have endorsed change on a contractual level basically because I set up an Instagram account. There's no doubt that social media can create powerful voices, it's just understanding how to harness your reach to spread your message."

6. You don't have to have an opinion on everything

Another point to consider is that not every issue requires your voice. In the era of political social media activity, it can be only too easy to believe that your opinion on the daily news is necessary – especially if you want to continue the conversation across your account. But just because something happened, it doesn't need your assessment. Ask yourself, is the issue actually something I'm really interested in? Is it something I'm going to post about on social media again? Is it something that I'm donating money to or going to rallies and talks about?

As Pandora asks, "Are you invested? If so, post confidently and unashamedly. But definitely consider why you are posting. You don't have to put something out there for the sake of it because, actually, that's more insulting than not, and we mustn't presume to be experts on everything. It doesn't make you unintelligent if you don't comment. In fact it's the very opposite."

Epilogue:
How Social Media is Changing Your Future

Like a moving target, the sheer pace of social media's evolution means that you can never quite put your finger on how it has already reshaped and will next alter your life.

Remember when social media sites were only static images on a grid? Before Snapchat and Stories made every second of your life uploadable, complete with half-decent filters and funny GIFs? Or when there was no such thing as a Tinder Super Like, tweets were limited to 140 characters and "click to shop" was all but a dream?

For anyone trying to rationalize or downsize their social media use, the constant pace of change proves another obstacle: if you don't keep up, there's always that feeling that you're going to be left behind. However, as ever, knowledge is power, and looking just a few junctions ahead on the map can both prepare you for the next phase in the social media story as well as help you question exactly how you want to integrate these new developments into your already heavily laden social media schedule. Having an idea where the world of social media may be taking us will help you futureproof your relationship with your favourite platforms as well as enable you to be conscious of the way you interact and engage with its new developments. Equally, there's a value in considering exactly how important it is to stay "up-to-date". Not entirely understanding an update or being familiar with a new filter feature won't harm your happiness, but feeling an obsessive pressure to use every new digital toy thrown your way very well might.

It's worth remembering that, unless you're a social media professional and are being paid to keep up with digital novelties, interactions with in-app innovations aren't mandatory. As they are made expressly to increase eyeballs and suck you further and further into the world inside your screen, you're well within your rights to ignore them completely. The future of social media may seem dizzying, but the underlying premise will stay the same. It might appear that the platforms themselves are the product that these businesses are selling, but that's not the case. *YOU* are the product. Social media sites sell audiences to advertisers, something which will become more and more evident as trust and transparency – or at least paying lip service to transparency – become the next buzzwords.

Influence, But Not As We Know It

Becoming an "influencer" once meant amassing thousands or hundreds of thousands of followers, building a personal brand and contacts at designer labels, then living your best life for all to see. But the super-blogger era is about to face some stiff competition – simply because "influence" as a currency is evolving. We've established that not everything we see on social media is "real", or at least how it is experienced offline, and confirmed that there's a level of curation and simulation involved to varying degrees (depending on one's Photoshop skills). So, it's perhaps little surprise that the next social media step involves influencers that are *entirely* unreal.

The computer-generated influencer, or avatar, lives a fantasy aspirational life. She wears Balenciaga trainers, attends Prada catwalk shows and takes selfies with celebrities...but she's just a figment of a digital designer's imagination. The gamification of social media is about to move up a notch as accounts like @LilMiquela, a Spanish-Brazilian American computer-generated model and music artist based in California, merge elements of fan and science fiction with social media marketing and advertising. With over a million followers – many of whom don't care that she's basically Lara Croft for the Instagram generation – what Lil Miquela wears and where she goes in her Insta-It-girl lifestyle can be just as influential as if she were flesh and blood. With a Spotify single release last year and new narratives for followers to engage with, Miquela is the highest profile of a new wave of tastemakers for whom IRL simply doesn't exist. Of course, you can see the appeal for brands – no potential for off-message rants or chance of a meltdown on Stories. The pseudo influencer is nearly human, but not human enough to undermine a marketing directive.

Elsewhere, the power of the micro-influencer is slowly being harnessed. Even if you have five hundred followers, what you recommend can be valuable to brands, especially if they had a way of incentivizing you to promote their products at scale. Step in a host of new platforms which allow nearly *anyone* to profit from their ability to affect other people's buying decisions. Don't think you've got enough followers to be an influencer? It's time to get savvy. Rina Hansen, co-founder of micro-influencer platform Brandheroes, explains: "Currently our platform has over five thousand micro-influencers working in more than forty countries, each with between five hundred and ten thousand followers. Heavyweight brands, especially in the beauty market, are starting to seriously invest in smaller influencers because they know how effective they can be. Whereas macro-influencers [30k-plus followers] have an average engagement rate of 1.8 per cent, micro-influencers can have over 8 per cent engagement. And when you think you can get around a hundred micro-influencers for the price of one macro-influencer, you can see the appeal. I'd also say micro-influencer content is seen as more relatable and authentic and really more like a digitized version of word of mouth. Our vision is that in the future there will be a true democracy on social media, because we believe that every person is their own media platform, whether they have five hundred or three hundred thousand followers. Everyone should be rewarded for sharing the brands and the services that they love."

So, how does it all work? You might have heard about cryptocurrencies like Bitcoin and the blockchain technology which powers them. The premise is simple: an international, independent banking system which exchanges "coins" for services and goods. This digital banking system has plenty of applications for social media, offering nearly *anyone* the opportunity, no matter how small their audience, to get paid as a micro-influencer. As Rina explains, "with our platform, as soon as content is approved by a brand then uploaded with the correct hashtags, the influencer gets paid in a points system. These points, which we call Brandcoins, are then redeemable against products in our webshop. We realized almost immediately that with so many global influencers we needed a global currency, and the architecture of the platform has been built like a cryptocurrency."

The technology is in place and the brands are already on board, so it's only a matter of time before micro-influence goes mega. When your audience is mini in size, it's also likely that you'll know most of your followers personally, so the question is: are you ready to start profiting from influencing your friends and family? And, perhaps even more profound, is the question of what it means for our collective mental state and relationships when we are *all* curating worlds to appeal to brands and influence our personal networks to buy things. The dawn of the mass monetization of both our lives and our address books is here; will you be joining in?

As for the established influencers, especially those who have already been blogging and 'gramming for a decade or more, things are also changing. Shini Park, a polymathic content creator who started her blog in 2008, explains, "The innocence there once was in blogging and social media – the true desire to share creativity just because? That's basically over. It's pretty much a business through and through." Sandra Hagelstam, the Finnish bombshell behind @5InchandUp goes on to explain that these days "just" blogging isn't enough: "today there's a sense that it's not enough *just* to be an influencer. As we all become known as characters, people are looking for more than just self-promotion. I get it – I'm 30 now and I don't want to be known only for my outfits forever, which is why I decided to diversify into acting, something I've always wanted to do. Two years ago, I started studying and my first film is coming out this summer. Having a strong following is really useful for any other career path you want to explore and I've seen a lot of influencers have started to move into music, consulting or writing." Shini agrees: "Influencers who have been blogging for a long time are starting to see their social accounts as a showcase for their other talents. It's like a portal into your portfolio career." And where the old-school influencers lead, the rest of us shall follow: forget about taking the perfect picture of poached eggs; now you need to be filming a music video for YouTube, brushing up on your life-drawing skills and penning a book to stay interesting.

So, what are the implications? If you can create an avatar to project the social media lifestyle you'd like to be leading, does it matter any more if you gain a few pounds, have a bad hair day or breakout? Might we be released from the pressure of being the face of our own personal brand and no longer chained to the limitations of the genetic lottery? If I made a computer-generated version of myself, I'm not sure I'd replicate the snaggletooth, open pores or knee fat, and perhaps I'd care less about them in real life if I knew I didn't have to worry about what they looked like in a picture. Or perhaps instead I'd prefer to go blonde. And tall. And *really* leggy. Think of the savings in air miles if you didn't actually have to go to Paris/Santorini/Marrakech, but could just super-impose yourself into hotels for social glory. I can definitely see the appeal of being able to live my "real life" away from the pressure to publish, but would people still be as eager to invest in experiences if they could manufacture them digitally? If something doesn't happen unless you Instagram it, where will we be when you can Instagram things that don't even happen? Not just a swipe of Facetune, but an entire Second Life virtual version of yourself; your complete existence fabricated?

Elsewhere, when it comes to micro-influence, if everyone can be a player in the social media economy and we all have the power to make money from each other, does the social world become fully transactional? No longer a place to connect, but to collect? As new media platforms become ever more commercialized and co-opted by advertisers, it's understandable that people will seek spaces to recreate the original atmosphere and environment that social media used to stand for – but that doesn't mean they'll shut their accounts. On the contrary, if social continues to become monetized and professionalized, it will retain its user base, but entirely lose the intimacy and authenticity it once represented. No wonder the people that first made social cool are so keen to showcase other career opportunities.

The Move to Dark Social

If social becomes a purely buy-and-sell space, where might we all go to express ourselves socially? The trend towards off-social communication isn't some newfangled concept – since 2015 there have been more messages sent via private services like Messenger and WhatsApp than on public platforms like Facebook and Twitter, and it's been years since anyone considered public walls a place for private discussions. These days it seems inconceivable that you'd post your Saturday night plans for all to see or have tête-à-tête chats across public feeds. Of course, the recent privacy scandals have served to underline this shift: fewer and fewer of us see the new media platforms as primarily a place to chat with close friends; instead they've become spaces for personal branding, recommendation and content sharing. In 2016, Facebook noted a 21 per cent drop in original, personal updates as users around the globe have increasingly learnt to commune through memes, articles and video clips. By reposting content viewed elsewhere, the platforms have become more like information loops, with viral news and entertainment trumping shared personal content. If the trend isn't reversed, soon Facebook will become faceless – a glorified news filter with annoying ads on the side. Though, as the biggest social network in the world also owns WhatsApp and Messenger, it's unlikely to be running short of personal information to sell any time soon.

The idea of social media interaction happening outside the social environment has led to what tech insiders are calling the rise of "dark social", or social sharing which can't be tracked by analytics. But don't think these "off social" spaces are closed to advertisers and social media professionals: they will be coming for your messages sooner than you can type "CUL8TR". By using chatbots, artificial intelligence and voice assistants, brands are looking to offer personalized shopping experiences on messaging apps. Paid social advertising spend was up to $41 billion in 2017, but an estimated 75 per cent of sharing occurred off social – meaning there's a huge amount of communication for brands yet to exploit. Before you know it, your messages may also come with a sidebar of exclusive instore offers and that link your friend sent you to those Topshop shoes might soon be followed up by a message from an instore customer service team. Seriously creepy stuff.

One solution to the endless incursion into our communication platforms is a fee-based model in which users exchange data anonymity and ad blocking for a subscription. Apple co-founder Steve Wozniak told *USA Today* that he'd quit Facebook in early 2018 due to concerns regarding the use of his personal data, but that he would consider rejoining – even for a fee – if he could opt out of data-based advertising, and there are plenty more of us out there who would be prepared to pay for anonymity. In order to recoup lost profits from tougher restrictions and regain the trust of users turned off by the data grab, it's only a matter of time before the concept of free social media begins to erode.

So, what would a subscription-based social media service look like, and what would it mean for your digital diet? Imagine if you could screen all the advertising noise and keep all of your personal information personal. How much would that be worth to you? A hundred a year? Or perhaps more? You'd still be able to communicate with your friends and upload your personal branding updates, but shield yourself from the incessant efforts to make you buy things. One such service is the platform Vero, which launched quietly in 2015 and has been dubbed "the anti-Facebook". The platform's manifesto states, "People naturally seek connection... As time passed an imbalance began to form between the interests of the [social] platforms and the best interests of the users. And a false sense of connection left us lonelier than ever... So we decided to create something more authentic. We created a social network that lets you be yourself... We made our business model subscription-based. Making our users our customers, not advertisers. The greatest social network is the one that already exists between people. Vero's mission is to make it available online." Operating under the tagline "true social", Vero (meaning truth) allows you to choose the audience for your posts from "close friend" to "follower" to reduce the pressure you feel when posting and publishes updates chronologically rather than via an algorithm (something which has attracted the creative community). Vero's CEO Ayman Hariri explained to US technology site The Verge that on other social media sites "you're performing for the crowd. Research shows that people are becoming more and more negatively affected by having to do that all the time. We wanted to create an online social network...that allows you to just be yourself."

With over three million downloads and counting, and having enjoyed a brief stint at the top of Apple's App chart in early 2018, Vero has shown that the appetite for a lower stakes, ad-free, more *humane* social is clearly there. But will a subscription service inevitably lead to a two-tier, class-based experience? One where those that have the money to protect themselves enjoy an ad-free environment, while others are forced to endure incessant prompts from spurious companies trying to sell us weight-loss shakes? With all the debate and dismantling of regulations around net neutrality (the principle that internet service providers treat all data equally and no-one has access to a preferential service – so providers cannot slow, block or charge money for specific websites), a hierarchy of access to the web appears just around the corner. Without a doubt, the egalitarian ideals of the digital world are under serious threat.

Social Media Concierge

We've discussed what a time-sap social media can be on your life. Who couldn't think of a better use for those two hours plus on average of scrolling every day? Step in the new industry of social media management. Whether you employ a living, breathing individual to clear your DM inbox, respond to comments and post encouraging messages to your followers (and yes, this is actually a job in 2018), *or* look forward to the new developments in robotics and AI to help you run your on-platform life, the chance to reclaim some of your precious time is now within reach. It's just a question of how happy you are to pass over your digital personality to someone, or indeed something, else.

Whether you'd prefer to hire someone to capture a special day – to live-tweet your wedding for example, because these days a photographer just isn't enough – or to maintain your social accounts updates from a professional perspective, there are plenty of services available to you. W Hotels offers a $3,000 (£2,300) package for your *big day*, ensuring that your hashtag is on point, and your guests are "encouraged" to participate digitally. And CEOs are adding social maintenance to the list of roles required of their PAs. For the rest of us, there's software just around the corner. Google's experimental lab Area 120 is currently working on a new system simply called Reply, an AI-based autoreply system that will work across platforms such as WhatsApp, Messenger, Skype, Twitter DMs and Slack. In an email to testers, the lab says, "You probably get a lot of chat messages. And you want to be there for people, but also for people in the real world. What if replying were literally one tap away?" The age of assistance will offer us all a digital secretary. By using information in our calendars, tracking our commute through Google maps and using chatbot technology, soon Reply and similar services will be able to offer passable responses to simple messages, freeing us from the weight of the constant stream of communication.

Aside from the convenience, the end of the line of this thinking has pretty dramatic implications for human interaction, because the more we get used to and accept robots standing in for us, the more the power of conversation and connection gets undermined. "We're lonely but we're afraid of intimacy. So, from social networks to social robots, we're designing technologies which will give us the illusion of companionship without the demands of friendship," foresees Sherry Turkle in her TED Talk. While it might seem to be alleviating the pressure cooker of always-on messaging, AI and chatbot technology will ultimately only serve to drive us further apart.

Imagine you need to have a really complicated conversation with a friend or family member and you just can't face the confrontation. Or to take it down a notch, you've got a really *boring* conversation to have with a friend or family member, say a grandparent or an old school friend who goes on and on endlessly. Don't tell me you wouldn't be tempted to palm the conversation off to a passable robot. I have one family member that I often just let speak away from my ear on the phone. Seriously, aside from the occasional "um" and "ah" from me, they're happy to continue on with their soliloquy. I would definitely be tempted to use a robot to deal with them on WhatsApp or Facebook if I could, which sounds dreadful.

But really who has the time to listen? We have to ask ourselves though, what do we lose when we stop practising the art of conversation? And when did we all get so incredibly rude?

Another related development in technology involves providing elderly people with robotic social company. In the UK, 17 per cent of seniors are in contact with their friends, family and neighbours less than once a week and two-fifths of older people say that their television is their main companion. So obviously it makes sense that social robots could provide what society currently can't. But the trend for delegating our interactions to machines can only lead in one direction, and how desperately depressing that the only connection you might be getting is through a *Blade Runner*-esque replicant. As ethics and what is culturally acceptable shifts in line with the technology, it's everyone's job to preserve true human contact both on and offline, or else – like many of the other skills that innovation has rendered obsolete – the very thing that defines us, makes us happy and fulfils us may be degraded and eventually lost.

Augmented Reality Bites

Think social media has become as all-encompassing as it could ever be? Think again, because virtual reality is about to add yet another level to the totality of your experience. The fourth dimension is already here, and now Facebook, Google and Snapchat are all on the cusp of launching mainstream applications – through a variety of affordable virtual reality (VR) headsets. Ever since Facebook purchased virtual-reality company Oculus VR, there's been a social arms race on. If you've not experienced VR, in a nutshell: when you put on a headset you become blind to the real world and immersed in a completely alternative reality, say on a safari or swimming with sharks. *Augmented* reality conversely superimposes computer-generated graphics on to your real-world environment, so instead of looking out your window and seeing a rainy street below, you'll see a sunny pavement – think the technology behind Pokémon GO and Snapchat filters. Both VR and augmented reality have broad applications for the future of social media.

Wearable technology may have hit stumbling blocks along the way (remember Google Glasses?) but the next step is still undoubtedly the device which eliminates the division between us and the screen. In 2017, Facebook launched a beta version of Spaces, a multi-user virtual reality platform that lets Oculus Rift and HTC Vive headsets customize avatars based on their profile pictures and interact with friends in a virtual online environment. The tagline of Facebook's virtual dimension is, "Spend quality time together wherever you are", and it's certainly mind boggling that you could virtually occupy the same space as your friend in Tokyo or Cape Town. Another platform, AltSpaceVR ("be there, together"), allows users to attend concerts, business meetings and house parties virtually. Until now, these platforms have been just about limited to gamers and early adopters, but with the launch of Oculus Go in 2018, a headset priced under £200/$200 (joining Samsung's Gear VR headset priced at around the price of under

£100/$150), the technology is set to go mainstream. Currently about 6 per cent of the British population currently own a VR headset and new, more accessible headsets are already being developed.

In many ways, the VR focus on actual social interaction serves as a rejoinder to the passive personal-brand consumption that we now see on social media platforms. And while avatars remain cartoon-like, there's a sense of naivety to the digital connection. But of course, it's only a matter of time before the technology evolves and 4D Miquelas start to populate virtual spaces, bringing all the swag of social media aspiration with them. Just imagine the stab of envy if you could actually experience to a fully immersive level all the blogger holidays, shopping trips and ritzy dinners. The level of voyeurism if you could actually *be there* for their birth stories and mountaintop engagements… If you think you're obsessed or addicted now, just imagine how much deeper down the rabbit hole you could go.

Tech Humanism: Believe It When You See It

As the studies revealing the harm social media is inflicting on our youth and the scandals around the use of our personal information pour forth quicker than the news cycle can cover them, there's a new, vocal movement of tech insiders, arguing for a more nuanced, considered approach to our social consumption. Snapchat CEO Evan Spiegel has blamed social media for inspiring "mindless scrambles for friends or unworthy distractions"; Jack Dorsey, CEO of Twitter, has highlighted "conversational health" as a priority; and Mark Zuckerberg has repeatedly mentioned the phrase "time well spent" alongside concerns for Facebook users' wellbeing. Structurally, social platforms are being altered in an attempt to lessen the worst of the media's negative effects – a development being labelled *humane tech*. "Compassionate design" may be trending in Silicon Valley circles, but you'd be forgiven for raising a serious eyebrow in scepticism. Until lawmakers embark on a concerted attempt to police social sites on a global scale, operating profits will continue to guide any attempts at self-governance. While Facebook and friends may publicly address the concerns highlighted in this book, how could we possibly trust those so deeply enmeshed in the system – both culturally and financially – to supervise the necessary corrections? It's akin to asking Big Tobacco to ditch the nicotine.

Now my eyes are open it's much harder to pull the wool back over them. However, that's not to say that there aren't individuals working to create healthier social products, and there's little doubt that we're going to see all sorts of new functions and warnings for our mental health along the way. But I, for one, will be taking matters into my own hands.

When you stop to think about how far social media has come in such a short lapse of time: of avatars and chatbots, of lives voluntarily lived in an all-seeing Panoptican, of addiction to aspiration, and expectations so completely moulded, it begs the questions, where will it all end?

Can we even begin to understand how social media will stretch out and contort itself in order to fit further into our daily lives? Will generations ahead look back at our pre-digital social existence and feel the same way as we do about the advent of electricity? Will old-fashioned conversation be somehow a lower form of civilized communication? Technology has already stopped being an add-on to our lives – so intrinsic and fundamental as it now is to our existence. The fact that social media is a human code created entirely by other humans who understand our instincts, primal desires and emotional responses, marks another stage in the evolution of our society, and one that's not likely to reverse any time soon. As with all progress, there will be laments for the good old days, but ultimately the thing of most importance is that we collectively use our agency to consume *consciously*, no matter how alluring the new technology might be. Forget about the new Atkins, Paleo or 5:2 – in the digital age it's your social media diet that really matters, and in this case, you really are what you eat.

Indeed, the biggest change for the future may come from disenchanted users desperately seeking a reprieve. As we all start to talk more openly about the way social media makes us feel, as we begin to realize that we are not alone in our addictive, often masochistic, behaviour, as the shine slowly wears off the fantasy, the bubble will struggle to stay intact. And maybe, just maybe, we'll be able to leave our destructive habits behind and enjoy social media for what it is: the best 1 per cent of our lives, with the real stuff, the other 99 per cent, hidden for only our real friends to discover.

Endnotes

All websites accessed 17 July 2018.

Introduction

7   **2.77 billion of us** http://www.statista.com/statistics/278414/number-of-worldwide-social-network-users/

7   **95 per cent of Americans** http://www.pewinternet.org/fact-sheet/mobile/

9   **"brain hacking"** Tristan Harris coined the term: https://www.youtube.com/watch?feature=share&v=JgkvTRz_Alo&app=desktop

9   **women use social media** http://www.pewinternet.org/fact-sheet/social-media/

10 **just one hour a day** McDool, Emily, Powell, Philip, Roberts, Jennifer and Taylor, Karl, "Social Media Use and Children's Wellbeing", IZA Discussion Paper No. 10412, December 2016, p.22.

11 **children admitted to hospital** Data obtained under the Freedom of Information Act by the National Society for the Prevention of Cruelty to Children (NSPCC) found that 18,778 children aged 11 to 18 were admitted to hospital for self-harm in 2015/16 in England and Wales. This is up on the 16,416 in 2013/14 and represents a 14 per cent rise. Peter Wanless, chief executive of the NSPCC: "It is clear from the thousands of calls Childline receives that we have a nation of deeply unhappy children. We know this unhappiness is partly due to the constant pressure they feel, particularly from social media, to have the perfect life or attain a certain image which is often unrealistic."

11 **"pressure to be the perfect mum"** "Data from London-based mothers' meet-up app Mush found the image-based social network was making many women feel more isolated. More than 80 per cent of respondents said Instagram and Facebook 'added pressure to be the perfect mum'"; cited in the *Evening Standard*, https://www.standard.co.uk/lifestyle/london-life/perfect-lives-of-instamums-are-making-london-mothers-feel-inadaquate-a3468426.html

11 **"social media representations of ideal families"** http://www.abc.net.au/news/2017-11-14/how-social-media-is-fuelling-anxiety,-perinatal-depression/9143318

11 **frequently compared themselves** Coyne, Sarah, McDaniel, Brandon and Stockdale, Laura A, "'Do you dare to compare?': Associations between maternal social comparisons on social networking sites and parenting, mental health, and romantic relationship outcomes", *Computers in Human Behavior*, vol. 70, issue C, May 2017, pp.335–340.

11 **"detract from face-to-face relationships"** https://hbr.org/2017/04/a-new-more-rigorous-study-confirms-the-more-you-use-facebook-the-worse-you-feel

12 **"passively consuming information"** https://newsroom.fb.com/news/2017/12/hard-questions-is-spending-time-on-social-media-bad-for-us/

12 **eight social media accounts** GlobalWebIndex, "GWI Social Summary, Q3 2016"; http://insight.globalwebindex.net/hubfs/GWI-Social-Q3-2016-Summary.pdf

13 **the typical mobile phone user** https://blog.dscout.com/mobile-touches

13 **unlocks their phone** ABC News report confirmed by Apple; https://abcnews.go.com/Technology/guess-average-iphone-user-unlocks-device-day/story?id=38510812

13 **seven years of our lives** More than 50 per cent of millennials use their phones for up to three hours a day. If we multiply three hours a day by 365 days then by 60 years (worldwide life expectancy of 70 minus the first 10 years) then you get 65,700 hours, which equates to approximately seven years; The Smartphone and IoT Consumer Trends 2017 study, published by B2X in cooperation with Professor Dr Anton Meyer and Professor Dr Thomas Hess from the Institutes of Marketing and New Media at the Ludwig-Maximilians University of Munich; https://resources.b2x.com/registration-study-smartphone-and-iot-consumer-trends

13 **using their phones on the toilet** From a 2013 poll of 2,000 people conducted by Sony & O2; cited in the *Telegraph*, https://www.telegraph.co.uk/technology/mobile-phones/9914594/Quarter-of-men-admit-to-sitting-down-on-the-loo-so-they-can-keep-using-mobile-phone.html

14 **lose their sense of *smell*** https://www.scribd.com/doc/56263899/McCann-Worldgroup-Truth-About-Youth

14 **by or in their bed** Accel and Qualtrics, "The Millennial Study", October 2016; https://www.qualtrics.com/millennials/

14 **within 15 minutes of waking** "Mobile Consumer 2015: The UK Cut: Game of Phones", Deloitte, 2015; http://www.deloitte.co.uk/mobileuk2015/assets/pdf/Deloitte-Mobile-Consumer-2015.pdf

14 **the longer your screen time** Levenson, Jessica C, Shensa, Ariel, Sidani, Jaime E, Colditz, Jason B, Primack, Brian A, "Social Media Use Before Bed and Sleep Disturbance Among Young Adults in the United States: A Nationally Representative Study", *Sleep*, vol. 40, issue 9, 1 September 2017.

14 **"empathy gap"** Turkle, Sherry, *Reclaiming Conversation: The Power of Talk in a Digital Age* (Penguin, 2015).

15 **at their last social encounter** http://www.pewinternet.org/2015/08/26/americans-views-on-mobile-etiquette/

15 **inhibits conversation** Przybyliski, Andrew and Weinstein, Netta, "Can you connect with me now? How the presence of mobile communication technology influences face-to-face conversation quality", *Journal of Social and Personal Relationships*, vol 30, issue 3, 2013, pp. 237–246.

21 **compare their appearance** Fardouly, J, Pinkus, R T and Vartanian, L R, "The impact of appearance comparisons made through social media, traditional media, and in person in women's everyday lives", *Body Image*, vol. 20, March 2017, pp.31–39.

23 **social comparison theory** Festinger, Leon, "A Theory of Social Comparison Processes", *Human Relations*, vol. 7, issue 2, May 1954, pp.117–140.

23 **improvement in self-appraisal** Wills, T A, "Downward comparison principles in social psychology", *Psychological Bulletin*, vol. 90, issue 2, September 1981, pp.245–271.

24 **biggest worry online** https://www.girlguiding.org.uk/what-we-do/our-stories-and-news/news/over-a-third-of-girls-say-the-pressure-to-live-the-perfect-life-online-is-affecting-their-wellbeing/

24 **feelings of jealousy** From a poll of around 1,500 social media users by the charity Scope; cited in the *Telegraph*, https://www.telegraph.co.uk/technology/social-media/10990297/Social-media-users-feel-ugly-inadequate-and-jealous.html

26 **"social-validation feedback loop"** https://www.axios.com/sean-parker-unloads-on-facebook-god-only-knows-what-its-doing-to-our-childrens-brains-1513306792-f855e7b4-4e99-4d60-8d51-2775559c2671.html

27 **"affect their thoughts"** https://www.bangkokpost.com/news/local/394102/youngsters-warned-over-elfie-addiction

27 **examine the brains of teenagers** Sherman, L E, Payton, A A, Hernandez, L M, Greenfield, P M and Dapretto, M, "The Power of the 'Like' in Adolescence, Effects of Peer Influence on Neural and Behavioral Responses to Social Media", *Psychological Science*, vol. 27, issue 7, July 2016, pp.1027–1035.

27 **viewing likes underneath a picture** *ibid*. and http://newsroom.ucla.edu/releases/the-teenage-brain-on-social-media;

28 **high level of likes** https://www.newstatesman.com/science-tech/social-media/2017/01/both-hugely-uplifting-and-depressing-how-do-social-media-likes

29 **"exploits this craving"** https://www.theglobeandmail.com/technology/your-smartphone-is-making-you-stupid/article37511900/

29 **increase your life satisfaction** The Facebook Experiment, Copenhagen Happiness Institute, 2015; https://docs.wixstatic.com/ugd/928487_680fc12644c8428eb728cde7d61b13e7.pdf

30 **lied or misrepresented themselves** Toma, Catalina L, Hancock, Jeffrey T, Ellison, Nicole B, "Separating Fact from Fiction: An Examination of Deceptive Self-Presentation in Online Dating Profiles", *Personality and Social Psychology Bulletin*, vol. 34, issue 8, May 2018, pp.1023–1036.

31 **screen candidates before hiring** https://www.careerbuilder.com/advice/social-media-survey-2017

32 **"erosion of authenticity online"** https://www.newstatesman.com/science-tech/social-media/2018/03/inside-story-one-instagrammer-s-fake-trip-disneyland

Chapter 1: Why Social Media is Ruining Your **Identity**

38 mobile phone than a toothbrush According to the Mobile Marketing Association Asia, there are 6.8 billion people on the planet and 5.1 billion of them own a mobile phone, but only 4.2 billion own a toothbrush; https://60secondmarketer.com/blog/2011/10/18/more-mobile-phones-than-toothbrushes/)

39 the self-promotion–envy spiral Krasnova, Hanna, Wenninger, Helena, Widjaja, Thomas and Buxmann, Peter, "Envy on Facebook: A Hidden Threat to Users' Life Satisfaction?", *Wirtschaftsinformatik*, 2013, p.12.

39 "Of the seven deadly sins" Epstein, Joseph, *Envy* (The Seven Deadly Sins series), (Oxford University Press, 2003).

39 the power that envy has Mujcic, Redzo and Oswald, Andrew J, "Is envy harmful to a society's psychological health and wellbeing? A longitudinal study of 18,000 adults", *Social Science & Medicine*, vol. 198, February 2018, pp.103–111.

41 most damaging platforms https://www.rsph.org.uk/about-us/news/instagram-ranked-worst-for-young-people-s-mental-health.html

41 "dual coding theory" Paivio, Allan, *Imagery and Verbal Processes* (Holt, Rinehart and Winston, 1971) and Paivio, Allan, "Mental Imagery in Associative Learning and Memory", *Psychological Review*, vol. 76, issue 3, May 1969, pp.241–263.

41 that image-based advertisements Childers, Terry L and Houston, Michael J, "Conditions for a Picture-Superiority Effect on Consumer Memory", *Journal of Consumer Research*, vol. 11, issue 2, September 1984, pp.643–654.

42 "Instagrammability" of a destination A survey by home insurance company Schofields Insurance asked over 1,000 UK adults aged between 18 and 33 what was most important when choosing a holiday destination; cited in the *Independent*, https://www.independent.co.uk/travel/instagrammability-holiday-factor-millenials-holiday-destination-choosing-travel-social-media-photos-a7648706.html#r3z-addoor

43 "memeification of human experience" https://www.theguardian.com/commentisfree/2018/jan/17/instagrammers-travel-sri-lanka-tourists-peachy-backsides-social-media-obsessed

44 caption didn't match what they felt From the *Women's Health*-National Alliance on Mental Illness, 2017; https://www.womenshealthmag.com/health/a19973575/true-emotion-behind-smiling-instagram-pictures/

46 "breadcrumbs of the same persona" https://www.theguardian.com/media-network/2015/sep/24/online-offline-personality-digital-identity

48 impostor syndrome Sakulku, Jaruwan, Alexander, James, "The Impostor Phenomenon", *The International Journal of Behavioral Science*, vol. 6, issue 1, 2011, 75–97.

48 inadequate about their own lives A poll of around 1,500 social media users by the charity Scope; cited in the *Telegraph*, https://www.telegraph.co.uk/technology/social-media/10990297/Social-media-users-feel-ugly-inadequate-and-jealous.html

50 "familiar strangers" Milgram, Stanley, "The Familiar Stranger: An Aspect of Urban Anonymity", *The Division 8 Newsletter, Division of Personality and Social Psychology*. Washington: American Psychological Association.

50 "strange familiarity" Senft, Theresa, "Micro Celebrity and the Branded Self" in *A Companion to New Media Dynamics*, Eds Hartley, John, Burgess, Jean and Bruns, Axel (Wiley-Blackwell, January 2013), pp.346–354.

52 "works in progress" Gilbert, Dan. "The Psychology of Your Future Self" TED. June 2014. Lecture.

Chapter 2: Why Social Media is Ruining Your **Body Image**

60   **uploaded approximately 24 billion selfies** https://blog.google/products/photos/google-photos-one-year-200-million/

60   **preparing for selfies** From the Dove Self Esteem Project 2015; https://www.dove.com/uk/stories/campaigns/nolikesneeded-campaign.html

60   **turn their phone camera on themselves** From a Now Sourcing and Frames Direct survey, 2016; cited in *Teen Vogue*, https://www.teenvogue.com/story/millennials-instagram-selfies-study

62   **act of snapping a selfie** Shin, Youngsoo, Kim, Minji, Im, Chaerin, and Chong, Sang Chui, "Selfie and self: The effect of selfies on self-esteem and social sensitivity", *Personality and Individual Differences*, vol. 111, June 2017, pp.139–145.

62   **"a craving for reassurance"** https://www.telegraph.co.uk/women/life/we-take-1-million-selfies-every-day---but-what-are-they-doing-to/

62   **crop, filter or doctor** https://www.beautyheaven.com.au/makeup/concealer/beauty-tips-for-selfies-14200; http://www.dailymail.co.uk/news/article-2948410/More-half-women-admit-editing-social-media-photos-posting-despite-two-thirds-thinking-s-wrong-magazines-it.html

63   **nine out of ten teenage girls** https://www.telegraph.co.uk/news/health/news/11875084/Nine-out-of-10-teenage-girls-digitally-enhance-their-own-Facebook-pictures-claim.html

65   **negative thoughts about their body** https://www.glamour.com/story/body-image-how-do-you-feel-about-your-body

67   **report eating and body-image concerns** Sidani, Jaime E, Shensa, Ariel, Hoffman, Beth, Hanmer, Janel and Primack, Brian A, "The Association between Social Media Use and Eating Concerns among US Young Adults", *Journal of the Academy of Nutrition and Dietetics*, vol. 116, issue 9, September 2016, pp.1465–1472.

67   *20 minutes* **of scrolling on Facebook** Mabe, Annalise G, Forney, K Jean and Keel, Pamela K, "Do you 'like' my photo? Facebook use maintains eating disorder risk", *International Journal of Eating Disorders*, vol. 47, issue 5, July 2014, pp.516–523.

67   **"eating disorders thrive"** https://eu.usatoday.com/story/news/nation/2014/06/01/social-media-helps-fuel-eating-disorders/9817513/

67   **eating disorders had nearly doubled** https://www.telegraph.co.uk/news/health/news/11647713/Number-of-teenagers-admitted-to-hospital-with-eating-disorders-doubles.html

68   **one in five anorexics** https://www.telegraph.co.uk/women/womens-health/11649411/How-social-media-is-fuelling-the-worrying-rise-in-eating-disorders.html

68   **every 62 minutes someone dies** http://www.anad.org/education-and-awareness/about-eating-disorders/eating-disorders-statistics/

71   **"onslaught of beauty pressures"** https://www.psychologytoday.com/intl/blog/girls-women-and-wellness/201511/why-are-media-beauty-ideals-toxic-our-daughters?amp

73   **images of this new beauty standard** Benton, Catherine and Karazsia, Bryan T, "The effect of thin and muscular images on women's body satisfaction", *Body Image*, vol. 13, March 2015, pp.22–27.

73   **looked at "fitspo" images** Fardouly, Jasmine, Willburger, Brydie K and Vartanian, Lenny R, "Instagram use and young women's body image concerns and self-objectification: Testing mediational pathways", *New Media & Society*, vol. 20, issue 4, April 2018, pp.1380–1395.

73   **clear link between orthorexia nervosa** Turner, Pixie G, and Lefevre, Carmen E, "Instagram use is linked to increased symptoms of orthorexia nervosa", *Eating and Weight Disorders*, vol. 22, issue 2, June 2017, pp.277–284.

73   **"fitspiration image"** Tiggemann, Marika and Zaccardo, Mia, "'Strong is the new skinny': A content analysis of #fitspiration images on Instagram", *Journal of Health Psychology*, vol. 23, issue 8, March 2016, pp.1003–1011.

Chapter 3: Why Social Media is Ruining Your **Health**

84 equated Snapchat to heroin https://www.theguardian.com/technology/2017/oct/05/smartphone-addiction-silicon-valley-dystopia

84 "more addictive than cigarettes" https://www.rsph.org.uk/about-us/news/instagram-ranked-worst-for-young-people-s-mental-health.html

84 manipulating exactly when users receive likes https://www.theglobeandmail.com/technology/your-smartphone-is-making-you-stupid/article37511900/

84 neurological vulnerabilities https://www.theguardian.com/technology/2017/oct/05/smartphone-addiction-silicon-valley-dystopia

85 half of all cases of mental illness Kessler, R C, Berglund, P, Demler, O, Jin, R, Merikangas, K R and Walters, E E, "Lifetime Prevalence and Age-of-Onset Distributions of DSM-IV Disorders in the National Comorbidity Survey Replication", *Archives of General Psychiatry*, vol. 62, issue 6, June 2005, pp.593–602.

85 1 in 4 girls https://www.theguardian.com/society/2017/sep/20/one-in-four-girls-have-depression-by-the-time-they-hit-14-study-reveals

85 44 million adults https://www.nimh.nih.gov/health/statistics/mental-illness.shtml

85 "The more you use Facebook" https://hbr.org/2017/04/a-new-more-rigorous-study-confirms-the-more-you-use-facebook-the-worse-you-feel

86 worldwide sufferers http://www.who.int/news-room/fact-sheets/detail/depression

89 One in three women Australia: Cox, P/Australia's National Research Organisation for Women's Safety (ANROWS), "Violence against women: Additional analysis of the Australian Bureau of Statistics' Personal Safety Survey 2012", *Horizons Research Report*, Issue 1, October 2015, p.2; Worldwide: https://edition.cnn.com/2013/06/20/health/global-violence-women/index.html. US: National Coalition Against Domestic Violence, https://www.speakcdn.com/assets/2497/domestic_violence2.pdf

89 a hundred calls an hour HMIC, "Increasingly everyone's business: A progress report on the police response to domestic abuse", December 2015, p.28; https://www.justiceinspectorates.gov.uk/hmicfrs/wp-content/uploads/increasingly-everyones-business-domestic-abuse-progress-report.pdf

89 40 per cent of women https://www.thelocal.it/20170328/over-8-million-women-suffer-psychological-abuse-in-italy

92 internal Facebook document https://www.theguardian.com/technology/2017/may/01/facebook-advertising-data-insecure-teens

92 "what buttons you can push" https://www.theguardian.com/technology/2017/oct/05/smartphone-addiction-silicon-valley-dystopia

93 newsfeed experiment https://www.nytimes.com/2014/06/30/technology/facebook-tinkers-with-users-emotions-in-news-feed-experiment-stirring-outcry.html

93 released a statement *ibid.*

95 17.5 per cent of female college students American College Health Association, National College Health Assessment Spring 2014 Reference Group Executive Summary; http://www.acha-ncha.org/docs/ACHA-NCHA-II_ReferenceGroup_ExecutiveSummary_Spring2014.pdf

95 "multidimensional perfectionism" Curran, Thomas and Hill, Andrew P, "Perfectionism is increasing over time: A meta-analysis of birth cohort differences from 1989 to 2016", *Psychological Bulletin*, December 2017, advance online publication.

98 rise of self-poisoning https://www.theguardian.com/society/2016/may/16/teenagers-girls-self-poisoning-uk-alcohol-mental-health-self-harm

98 increase in hospital admissions https://www.theguardian.com/society/2017/oct/18/self-harm-girls-aged-13-to-16-rose-68pc-three-years

98 cutting themselves https://www.theguardian.com/society/2017/sep/23/stress-anxiety-fuel-mental-health-crisis-girls-young-women

98 difficulties with boys "https://www.theguardian.com/society/2017/sep/23/stress-anxiety-fuel-mental-health-crisis-girls-young-women

98 US suicide rates https://nypost.com/2017/11/14/rise-in-teen-suicide-connected-to-social-media-popularity-study/

98 forty-year high https://www.huffingtonpost.co.uk/entry/suicide-rates-teen-girls_us_59848b64e4b0cb15b1be13f4

98 taking their own lives Twenge, Jean M, Joiner, Thomas E, Rogers, Megan L and Martin, Gabrielle N, "Increases in Depressive Symptoms, Suicide-Related Outcomes, and Suicide Rates Among U.S. Adolescents After 2010 and Links to Increased New Media Screen Time", *Clinical Psychological Science*, vol. 6, issue 1, November 2017, pp.3–17.

98 "overusing" social media *ibid.*

99 25 per cent of teenage girls https://www.theguardian.com/society/2017/sep/20/one-in-four-girls-have-depression-by-the-time-they-hit-14-study-reveals

99 touching our phones http://uk.businessinsider.com/dscout-research-people-touch-cell-phones-2617-times-a-day-2016-7

100 sit with and entertain ourselves Wilson, Timothy D, Reinhard, David A, Westgate, Erin C, Gilbert, Daniel T, Ellerbeck, Nicole, Hahn, Cheryl, Brown, Casey L, Shaked, Adi, "Just think: The challenges of the disengaged mind", *Science*, vol. 345, issue 6192, July 2014, pp.75–77.

101 "Solitude is where you find yourself" Turkle, Sherry, "Connected, but alone?" TED. February 2012. Lecture.

101 6.8 hours of sleep a night https://news.gallup.com/poll/166553/less-recommended-amount-sleep.aspx

102 explicit images of themselves shared Lenhart, Amanda, Ybarra, Michele and Price-Feeney, Myeshia, "Nonconsensual Image Sharing: One in 25 Americans Has Been a Victim of 'Revenge Porn'", Data & Society Research Institute and the Center for Innovative Public Health Research data memo, December 2016; https://datasociety.net/pubs/oh/Nonconsensual_Image_Sharing_2016.pdf

102 47 per cent of Americans *ibid.*

102 up to 50 per cent of school-age girls https://www.theguardian.com/uk-news/2017/aug/14/half-uk-girls-bullied-social-media-survey

103 up to 40 per cent don't tell their parents https://www.theguardian.com/society/2015/sep/22/cyberbullying-teenagers-worse-than-drug-abuse-says-report

103 study of 2,215 students https://jamanetwork.com/journals/jamapsychiatry/fullarticle/210833

103 88 per cent increase in calls https://www.theguardian.com/society/2016/nov/14/nspcc-records-88-rise-in-children-seeking-help-for-online-abuse

104 three-quarters of women under thirty https://www.theguardian.com/lifeandstyle/2016/mar/08/online-harassment-of-women-at-risk-of-becoming-established-norm-study

105 deemed to be inadequate https://www.theguardian.com/uk-news/2017/jul/05/stalking-and-harassment-crimes-routinely-badly-handled-uk-report-says

105 digitally stalked https://datasociety.net/blog/2016/11/21/online-harassment/

105 Half of all millennials http://www.dailymail.co.uk/femail/article-3225666/HALF-millennials-admit-sent-naked-pictures-text-quarter-say-rely-online-dating-sites-love.html

105 shared intimate images https://www.childnet.com/blog/press-release-uk-youth-targeted-with-sexual-harassment-on-the-internet

105 contemplated suicide Figures from the End Revenge Porn campaign; http://www.wired.co.uk/article/revenge-porn-facebook-social-media

106 no action being taken http://www.bbc.co.uk/news/uk-37278264

107 impersonated by a criminal https://www.theguardian.com/money/2017/aug/23/identity-fraud-figures-cifas-theft

107 burglars use social media https://www.adt.co.uk/protecting-you/adts-top-tips-for-online-security

107 cyberstalking is now more common https://www.telegraph.co.uk/news/uknews/crime/8439833/Computer-stalking-outstrips-face-to-face-harassment.html

109 people with epilepsy Conrad, Peter, Bandini, Julia and Vasquez, Alexandria, "Illness and the Internet: From Private to Public Experience", *Health*, vol. 20, issue 1, January 2016 pp.22–32.

Chapter 4: Why Social Media is Ruining Your **Relationships**

120 "ambient intimacy" https://www.nytimes.com/2008/09/07/magazine/07awareness-t.html

120 finite number of relationships Dunbar, Robin I M, "The social brain hypothesis", *Evolutionary Anthropology*, vol. 6, issue 5, December 1998, pp.178–190.

121 "A lot of times I feel lonely," https://www.theatlantic.com/magazine/archive/2017/09/has-the-smartphone-destroyed-a-generation/534198/

121 confide their personal troubles and triumphs to https://spectator.org/59230_loneliness-american-society/

121 as damaging to our health as smoking Holt-Lunstad, Julianne, Smith, Timothy B, Baker, Mark, Harris, Tyler and Stephenson, David, "Loneliness and Social Isolation as Risk Factors for Mortality: A Meta-Analytic Review", *Perspectives on Psychological Science*, vol. 10, issue 2, March 2015, pp.227–237.

124 prefer conversing digitally https://www.news.com.au/finance/business/weve-raised-generation-hopeless-millennials-who-lack-basic-life-and-workplace-skills-and-its-a-big-issue/news-story/f3256c05c19c356002103eb50e50cee1

124 get together with their friends https://www.theatlantic.com/magazine/archive/2017/09/has-the-smartphone-destroyed-a-generation/534198/

126 "real life stage fright" https://www.news.com.au/finance/business/weve-raised-generation-hopeless-millennials-who-lack-basic-life-and-workplace-skills-and-its-a-big-issue/news-story/f3256c05c19c356002103eb50e50cee1

127 verbal and non-verbal messages Mehrabian, Albert, *Silent Messages* (1st ed.), (Wadsworth, 1971).

128 56 per cent of US high-school seniors https://www.theatlantic.com/magazine/archive/2017/09/has-the-smartphone-destroyed-a-generation/534198/

128 the number of sexually active teens https://www.theatlantic.com/magazine/archive/2017/09/has-the-smartphone-destroyed-a-generation/534198/

128 teen birth rate in the UK https://www.theguardian.com/society/2016/jul/18/how-uk-halved-teenage-pregnancy-rate-public-health-strategy

128 UK levels of alcohol consumption https://www.independent.co.uk/news/health/alcohol-drinking-britain-habits-booze-consumption-ons-data-a7716186.html

128 less likely to be taking illicit drugs https://edition.cnn.com/2016/12/13/health/drug-use-teens/index.html

129 show how much they care Lenhart, Amanda, Smith, Aaron and Anderson, Monica, "Teens, Technology and Romantic Relationships", Pew Research Center, October 2015; http://www.pewinternet.org/files/2015/10/PI_2015-10-01_teens-technology-romance_FINAL.pdf

129 make their relationships visible Emery, Lydia F, Muise, Amy, Dix, Emily L, and Le, Benjamin, "Can You Tell That I'm in a Relationship? Attachment and Relationship Visibility on Facebook", *Personality and Social Psychology Bulletin*, vol. 40, issue 11, September 2014, pp.1466–1479.

131 "holds everything in an unchanging past" https://www.psychologytoday.com/intl/blog/mental-mishaps/201406/how-social-networks-can-inflame-jealousy?amp

134 "lower levels of satisfaction" Strübel, Jessica and Petrie, Trent, "Love me Tinder: Body image and psychosocial functioning among men and women", *Body Image*, vol. 21, June 2017, pp.34–38.

134 addicted to the process https://www.bustle.com/p/new-app-ona-wants-to-make-your-dating-life-better-but-its-not-a-dating-app-36054

137 social media makes them feel jealous Lenhart, Amanda, Smith, Aaron and Anderson, Monica, "Teens, Technology and Romantic Relationships", Pew Research Center, October 2015; http://www.pewinternet.org/files/2015/10/PI_2015-10-01_teens-technology-romance_FINAL.pdf

138 a third of all divorce cases https://www.mirror.co.uk/news/technology-science/technology/facebook-now-crops-up-third-5011205

138 80 per cent of US divorce lawyers http://aaml.org/about-the-academy/press/press-releases/e-discovery/big-surge-social-networking-evidence-says-survey-

138 "seen somebody on Tinder" Weiser, Dana A, Niehuis, Sylvia, Flora, Jeanne, Punyanunt-Carter, Narissra M, Arias, Vladimir S, Hannah Baird, R, "Swiping right: Sociosexuality, intentions to engage in infidelity, and infidelity experiences on Tinder", *Personality and Individual Differences*, vol. 133, October 2018, pp.29–33.

Chapter 5: Why Social Media is Ruining **Motherhood**

143 at least 1 child https://www.telegraph.co.uk/news/2017/11/24/proportion-women-never-have-children-has-doubled-generation/; http://www.pewsocialtrends.org/2018/01/18/theyre-waiting-longer-but-u-s-women-today-more-likely-to-have-children-than-a-decade-ago/

144 a third of British mothers According to a 2017 online survey of 1,800 British parents by the BBC Radio 5 live and YouGov; https://www.bbc.co.uk/news/health-42140028

145 The average age of a mum https://www.ons.gov.uk/peoplepopulationandcommunity/birthsdeathsandmarriages/livebirths/bulletins/birthsummarytablesengland andwales/2015

145 US picture is broadly similar https://www.bloomberg.com/news/articles/2017-05-17/women-in-30s-now-having-more-babies-than-younger-moms-in-us

146 "motherhood ideologies" Henderson, Angie, Harmon, Sandra & Newman, Harmony D, "The Price Mothers Pay, Even When They Are Not Buying It: Mental Health Consequences of Idealized Motherhood", *Sex Roles*, vol. 74, issues 11–12, September 2015, pp.512–526.

146 experiencing increased stress and anxiety *ibid.*

147 "The quest to be a 'perfect' mother" https://www.theguardian.com/commentisfree/2016/may/10/perfect-mother-good-parenting-child-behaviour

147 "pressure to be the perfect mum" https://www.standard.co.uk/lifestyle/london-life/perfect-lives-of-instamums-are-making-london-mothers-feel-inadaquate-a3468426.html

148 sperm counts among Western men https://www.theguardian.com/lifeandstyle/2017/jul/25/sperm-counts-among-western-men-have-halved-in-last-40-years-study

149 one in seven couples in the UK https://www.nice.org.uk/guidance/cg156/chapter/context

149 one in eight couples in the US https://news.aetna.com/2016/09/1-8-couples-fertility-issues/

156 a million miscarriages happen http://time.com/3849280/pregnancy-miscarriage/

156 one in five of all pregnancies https://www.independent.co.uk/life-style/health-and-families/features/new-research-could-help-to-predict-which-women-are-at-risk-of-miscarriage-a6910141.html

160 "the pregnant body as a site of risk" Thomas, Gareth M, and Lupton, Deborah, "Threats and thrills: pregnancy apps, risk and consumption", *Health, Risk & Society*, vol. 17, issues 7–8, November 2015, pp.495–509.

161 pregnant woman's data https://thinkprogress.org/meet-the-woman-who-did-everything-in-her-power-to-hide-her-pregnancy-from-big-data-80070cf6edd2/

162 uploaded to social media https://www.telegraph.co.uk/technology/10268615/Babies-appear-on-social-media-within-an-hour-of-birth.html

163 becoming more competitive https://www.daynurseries.co.uk/news/article.cfm/id/1570243/An-audience-at-birth

164 regret, shame, guilt or anger http://time.com/4989068/motherhood-is-hard-to-get-wrong/

164 "The Goddess Myth" http://time.com/4989068/motherhood-is-hard-to-get-wrong/?xid=tcoshare

165 getting their figure back http://www.dailymail.co.uk/femail/article-3586743/New-mums-worried-snapping-shape-relationship.html

166 15 per cent of all women https://www.nimh.nih.gov/health/publications/postpartum-depression-facts/index.shtml

166 "snapped-back" new mums Coyne, Sarah M, Liechty, Toni, Collier, Kevin M, Sharp, Aubrey D, Davis, Emilie J and Kroff, Savannah L, "The Effect of Media on Body Image in Pregnant and Postpartum Women", *Health Communication*, May 2017, vol. 33, issue 7, pp.793–799.

168 active on the platform http://www.pewinternet.org/2015/07/16/parents-and-social-media/

169 parenting decisions have been judged http://www.dailymail.co.uk/femail/article-2676671/70-parents-feel-judged-decisions-make-child-three-quarters-given-advice-without-asking-it.html

170 seeking validation or are depressed
Schoppe-Sullivan, S J, Yavorsky, J E,
Bartholomew, M K, Sullivan, J M, Lee,
M A, Kamp Dush, C M, Glassman, M,
"Doing Gender Online: New Mothers'
Psychological Characteristics, Facebook
Use, and Depressive Symptoms", *Sex Roles*,
vol. 76, issue 5, March 2017, pp.276–289.

170 "over-preciousness about motherhood"
http://time.com/4989068/motherhood-
is-hard-to-get-wrong/?xid=tcoshare

170 don't receive paid family leave https://
www.nytimes.com/2015/06/22/upshot/a-
federal-policy-on-paid-leave-suddenly-
seems-plausible.html

170 70 per cent of all women work
https://www.ons.gov.uk/
employmentandlabourmarket/
peopleinwork/employmentandemployee
types/bulletins/uklabourmarket/
march2018

176 read the most baby manuals Harries, V
and Brown, A, "The association between
use of infant parenting books that promote
strict routines, and maternal depression,
self-efficacy, and parenting confidence",
Early Child Development and Care,
September 2017.

Chapter 6: Why Social Media is Ruining Your **Career & Money**

177 expensive branded goods https://
www.directlinegroup.com/media/news/
brand/2017/26072017.aspx

188 Consumer debt in the US rose
Federal Reserve Bank of New York,
"Quarterly Report on Household
Debt and Credit", May 2017; https://
www.newyorkfed.org/medialibrary/
interactives/householdcredit/data/pdf/
HHDC_2017Q1.pdf

188 predicted to hit £15,000 https://www.
bbc.com/news/uk-42498343

188 experiences rather than things https://
www.home.barclaycard/media-centre/
press-releases/consumer-spending-grew-
5-point-5-per-cent-in-april.html

188 "A short-term focus" Tully, Stephanie M
and Sharma, Eesha, "Context Dependent
Drivers of Discretionary Debt Decisions:
Explaining Willingness to Borrow for
Experiential Purchases", *Journal of
Consumer Research*, vol. 44, issue 5,
June 2017, pp.960–973.

188 go into debt to pay for a trip https://
nypost.com/2017/06/21/most-americans-
will-go-into-debt-to-pay-for-a-vacation/

188 six months to recover financially https://
www.reuters.com/article/us-money-
travel-vacation-idUSKBN19B1SY

**189 spent money after seeing someone
else's post** https://www.aicpa.org/press/
pressreleases/2016/keeping-up-with-the-
joneses-goes-online.html

192 Four out of five employees Garrett, R
Kelly and Danziger, James N, "Disaffection
or expected outcomes: Understanding
personal Internet use during work", *Journal
of Computer-Mediated Communication*,
vol. 13, issue 4, July 2008, pp.937–958.

192 depleting their productivity http://www.
teamleasegroup.com/blog/social-media-
affecting-workplace-productivity

192 25 minutes to get back on task https://
www.theglobeandmail.com/technology/
your-smartphone-is-making-you-stupid/
article37511900/

192 to take a "mental break" http://www.
pewinternet.org/2016/06/22/social-
media-and-the-workplace/

**192 rewiring the way our brains actually
work** https://www.theguardian.com/
technology/2018/mar/04/has-dopamine-
got-us-hooked-on-tech-facebook-apps-
addiction

193 greater decrease in IQ https://
www.forbes.com/sites/
vanessaloder/2014/06/11/why-multi-
tasking-is-worse-than-marijuana-for-
your-iq/#316ae27d7c11

193 attention spans have reduced https://
www.bbc.co.uk/news/health-38896790

193 our minds digress Killingsworth, Matthew
A and Gilbert, Daniel T, "A Wandering Mind
Is an Unhappy Mind", *Science*, vol. 180, issue
6006, November 2010, p.932.

194 new "superhuman" brain Brogaard, Berit:
"The Superhuman Mind: Free the Genius in
Your Brain" (Hudson Street Press, 2015)

194 keep in touch with their contacts http://
www.pewinternet.org/2016/06/22/social-
media-and-the-workplace/

194 walked into traffic Basch, Corey H,
Ethan, Danna, Zybert, P and Basch, C E,
"Pedestrian Behavior at Five Dangerous
and Busy Manhattan Intersections",
Journal of Community Health, vol. 40,
issue 4, August 2015, pp.789–792.

Chapter 7: Why Social Media is Ruining Your **Politics**

206 uniquely disrespectful Duggan, Maeve and Smith, Aaron, "The Political Environment on Social Media", Pew Research Center, October 2016; http://assets.pewresearch.org/wp-content/uploads/sites/14/2016/10/24160747/PI_2016.10.25_Politics-and-Social-Media_FINAL.pdf

214 "In times of extremes" https://www.theglobeandmail.com/opinion/am-i-a-bad-feminist/article37591823/

218 news from social media Shearer, Elisa and Gottfried, Jeffrey, "News Use Across Social Media Platforms 2017", Pew Research Center, October 2017; http://assets.pewresearch.org/wp-content/uploads/sites/13/2017/09/13163032/PJ_17.08.23_socialMediaUpdate_FINAL.pdf

219 Republicans were "closed minded" Pew Research Center, "Partisanship and Political Animosity in 2016", June 2016, https://assets.pewresearch.org/wp-content/uploads/sites/5/2016/06/06-22-16-Partisanship-and-animosity-release.pdf

219 "worn out" Duggan, Maeve and Smith, Aaron, "The Political Environment on Social Media", Pew Research Center, October 2016; http://assets.pewresearch.org/wp-content/uploads/sites/14/2016/10/24160747/PI_2016.10.25_Politics-and-Social-Media_FINAL.pdf

Epilogue: How Social Media is Changing Your Future

231 messages sent via private services http://uk.businessinsider.com/the-messaging-app-report-2015-11

231 21 per cent drop https://www.bloomberg.com/news/articles/2016-04-07/facebook-said-to-face-decline-in-people-posting-personal-content

232 opt out of data-based advertising https://eu.usatoday.com/story/tech/2018/04/08/apple-co-founder-steve-wozniak-says-hes-leaving-facebook/497392002/

233 "allows you to just be yourself" https://www.theverge.com/2018/3/2/17067610/vero-social-media-ayman-hariri-downloads

234 "We're lonely but we're afraid of intimacy" Turkle, Sherry, "Connected, but alone?" TED. February 2012. Lecture.

235 17 per cent of seniors https://www.campaigntoendloneliness.org/loneliness-research/

235 television is their main companion *ibid.*

237 own a VR headset https://yougov.co.uk/news/2017/05/19/vr-headsets-more-popular-tablets-and-wearables-wer/

237 vocal movement of tech insiders https://www.theguardian.com/news/2018/may/03/why-silicon-valley-cant-fix-itself-tech-humanism

Contributors

Kelly Agnew @kellyagnew

Lauren Alexander @laurenalexander

Pip Black @moveyourframe

Camille Charrière @camillecharrière

Charly Cox @charlycox1

Kelly Eastwood @thelondonchatter

Laura Fantacci @laura.fantacci

Kat Farmer @doesmybumlook40

Paula Goldstein @paulasanexplorer

Nene Granville @industrymenu

Lizzy Hadfield @shotfromthestreet

Sandra Hagelstam @5inchandup

Freddie Harrel @freddieharrel

Lindsey Holland @ropesofholland

Victoria Magrath @inthefrow

Lauren Mahon @girlstolelondon

Claire Marshall @heyclaire

Leandra Medine @leandramcohen

Sara Melotti @saramelotti_

Gabriela Moussaieff
   @gabrielamoussaieff

Joan Murphy @moveyourframe

Roxie Nafousi @roxienafousi

Anna Newton @theannaedit

Shini Park @parkncube

Lily Pebbles @lilypebbles

Rejina Pyo @rejinapyo

Anna Saccone Joly @annasaccone

Niomi Smart @niomismart

Pandora Sykes @pandorasykes

Callie Thorpe @calliethorpe

Courtney Trop @alwaysjudging

Pippa Vosper @pippavosper

Anna Whitehouse @mother__pukka

Lucy Williams @lucywilliams02

Dr Jessica Zucker @ihadamiscarriage

Index

Acknowledgements

Without the support and candour of the many women who are featured in its pages, this book would be nothing. I'm so grateful to my digital network for trusting me with the not-so-perfect sides of their lives. I hope I've done you proud.

Offline, there's another bunch of exceptional ladies to thank: my literary agent Abigail who first persuaded me to start this project and has put up with months of my hormones. Also, my editors Romilly, Leanne and Louise at Octopus for believing in me and bringing their razor-sharp eyes to every sentence.

And, while it's a woman's world, I also need to thank my brother Sam for his feedback and skilful research, and my other half, Haden, for holding the baby and keeping me going through the dark days of sleep deprivation. I quite literally wouldn't have been able to do it without you.

Finally, the biggest thank you to my mum, Bev, who taught me that life is a patchwork of love and that oversharing is caring.